D0438047

IN THE TIME OF MADNESS

IN THE TIME
OF MADNESS

INDONESIA ON THE EDGE OF CHAOS

Richard Lloyd Parry

Grove Press
New York

Copyright © 2005 by Richard Lloyd Parry

All rights reserved. No part of this book may be reproduced in any form or by
any electronic or mechanical means, including information storage and
retrieval systems, without permission in writing from the publisher, except by
a reviewer, who may quote brief passages in a review. Any members of
educational institutions wishing to photocopy part or all of the work for
classroom use, or publishers who would like to obtain permission to include
the work in an anthology, should send their inquiries to Grove/Atlantic, Inc.,
841 Broadway, New York, NY 10003.

First published in Great Britain in 2005 by Jonathan Cape,
Random House, London

Printed in the United States of America

FIRST AMERICAN EDITION

Library of Congress Cataloging-in-Publication Data

Parry, Richard Lloyd.
    In the time of madness : Indonesia on the edge of chaos / Richard Lloyd
Parry.
        p. cm.
    ISBN 0-8021-1808-9
    1. Indonesia—Description and travel. 2. Parry, Richard Lloyd—
Travel—Indonesia. 3. East Timor—History—Autonomy and independence
movements. I. Title.

DS620.2.P37 2006
959.803'9—dc22   2005050302

Maps designed by Reginald Piggott

Grove Press
an imprint of Grove/Atlantic, Inc.
841 Broadway
New York, NY 10003

06 07 08 09 10   10 9 8 7 6 5 4 3 2 1

Someone will always do what the gods want us to do.
I remember rats swarming all of a sudden
From unknown holes, just before the war.

Goenawan Mohamad

CONTENTS

PROLOGUE

BAD DREAMS IN BALI 1996

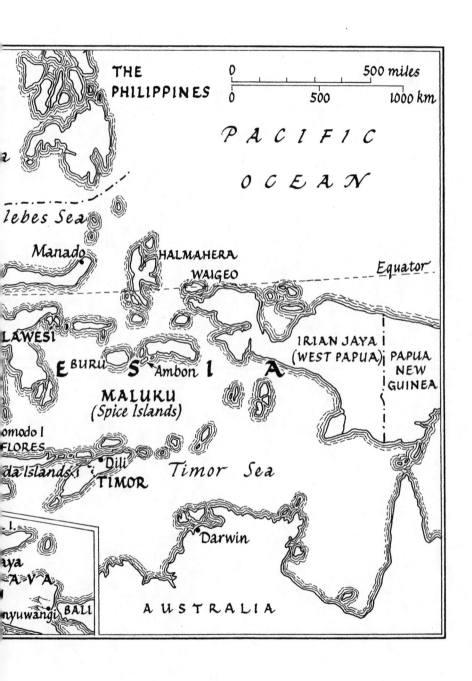

THE
PHILIPPINES

0   500 miles

0   500   1000 km

PACIFIC

OCEAN

lebes Sea

Manado

HALMAHERA
WAIGEO

Equator

LAWESI

E BURU S Ambon l A

IRIAN JAYA
(WEST PAPUA)

PAPUA
NEW
GUINEA

MALUKU
(Spice Islands)

omodo I
FLORES
da Islands Dili
TIMOR

Timor Sea

Darwin

I.

aya

A-V A

nyuwangi BALI

A U S T R A L I A

Towards the end of my first time in Indonesia I stayed in a house on the edge of the jungle and dreamed the worst nightmares I have known since I was a child. The house was a bungalow of wood and thatch with a road on one side and on the other a wooden couch where I slept under the sky. A thicket of palms and flowering trees descended to a river at the bottom of a steep valley. At night, the sound of cars and motorbikes fell away and the noises of the forest rose up around my bed: the electrical sound of the insects, the flutter of birds' wings, the rush of water.

I spent the evenings alone in the tourist cafés and bars down the road. Later, after I had fallen asleep with the jungle in my ears, I dreamed of knives and faces, and gigantic alien creatures which were half-lobster and half-wasp. I dreamed of a mobile telephone that would not stop ringing and of endless conversations with a man named Colonel Mehmet.

The island of Bali, where I was staying, was peaceful. The violence in Jakarta had caused no reverberation here. Or that was the impression which the local people were at pains to give: the smiling woman who gave me the bungalow key, the boy in the sarong who came in the mornings to sweep the floor and change the linen. Every day he brought offerings of petals and rice which he placed on high ledges, to thank the benevolent spirits, and on the ground, to appease the demons. He showed me how to summon him by means of a wooden gong which hung from the eaves of the bungalow. Its hollow body was carved into the shape of a grimacing goblin; the stick was the giant erect penis which the goblin brandished between its claws. But either the offerings were too small or the goblin was not fearsome enough, for the next night the evil dreams came again.

They began with Colonel Mehmet on the mobile phone. 'You not strong enough are!' he bellowed. 'Or not clever enough. *Ja!* And all the time you are such a fine fellow, too!' In my dreams I tried throwing the phone away, burning it, even drowning it in the bath, but always it floated ringing to the surface as the colonel and his men drew nearer.

The trouble in Jakarta had upset me, perhaps more than I realised.

It had begun a month earlier with an unprecedented event: a mass demonstration by members of the opposition democratic party. All day and night, hundreds of people had camped out in the party headquarters, singing songs, telling stories and delivering speeches in support of democracy. All had been careful not to mention the president by name, but everyone knew that the demonstration was a direct challenge to him, the strongest and most intense criticism he had faced in thirty years. It was breathtakingly bold; it seemed unthinkable that it could be allowed to go on. But days passed and the demonstrators were left undisturbed.

One evening I had visited them in their headquarters. It was festooned with flags and poster-sized portraits of the opposition leader. The next morning, just after dawn, it was raided by commandos dressed in plain clothes. Lines of police kept spectators at bay as the attackers threw stones at the building; once inside, they produced knives. Hundreds of the demonstrators were arrested and people said that many of them had been stabbed to death and their bodies disposed of in secret. That afternoon there were riots across the city, and tall concrete office buildings burned with black smoke. For the first time in my life, I saw streets of broken glass, armoured cars advancing slowly upon crowds, men and women weeping with anger and trepidation.

It is important never to lose the sense of wonder at such things.

But now I was in Bali, the small, green holiday island east of Java, and I was here to relax. I chose to stay away from the beaches and travelled instead to the island's interior. The jungle soothed me, but it polluted my sleep with bad dreams.

I dreamed of climbing into an immense rusty ship. It was overladen with silent, dark-skinned passengers, and lurched sickeningly in the water as I stepped aboard. I dreamed that I was chasing a magnificent butterfly through the forest. A black beast was watching me with green eyes. Then the mobile phone rang, and I knew that when I answered it I would hear the barking voice of Colonel Mehmet.

During the day I sat reading in front of the bungalow, or walked past the restaurants and into the village. I visited a park where monkeys stared sulkily from trees and later, at a souvenir shop, I purchased one of the ithyphallic gongs. I met a German couple who confessed that they too were having bad dreams in Bali, he of a giant black pig, she of 'ghosts and visitors.' And on my last day I encountered a ghost story of my own.

I had cycled out to a spot on the outskirts of the village where thousands of white herons gathered at dusk. They flew in from across the island, all black legs and thin necks, folding themselves up as they dipped into the tops of the trees. A Balinese man told me that they were the spirits of people who had died in a great massacre thirty years ago. Most had never been buried; no prayers were ever said for them. They wandered the jungles and rice paddies as ghosts, and thousands of them roosted here in the form of white birds.

That night I opened the history book I had bought in Jakarta and began to read about the anti-communist killings of 1965 and 1966, by any standard one of the worst mass murders of the twentieth century.

They had begun after a mysterious coup attempt against the

old president, led by left-wing army officers. Within a few weeks, bands of militia men and soldiers were rounding up communists, real and imagined. There were denunciations and death lists. Whole families, entire villages, were seized. The suspects were driven away to ditches or clearings in the jungle and executed with sickles, machetes and iron bars.

Across the country perhaps half a million people died, one-fifth of them in tiny Bali. 'Many party members were killed by knife or bayonet,' the book said. 'Bodies were often maimed and decapitated and dumped in rivers ... On the island of Bali, Indonesia's only overtly Hindu province, the killings developed just as fervently, with priests calling for fresh sacrifices to satisfy vengeful spirits.'

It was amid this terror and madness that President Sukarno had lost power in 1966 to the 'New Order', the government of General – now President – Suharto. In the three decades since then Suharto had rebuilt the country, extinguished democracy and snuffed out opposition to his rule. And now, in the summer of 1996, the New Order was beginning to unravel.

Nobody realised it at that time. But within eighteen months of the suppression of the democracy demonstrations, violent change would be spreading across Indonesia. Money would become worthless, people would go hungry, and the jungles would burn in uncontrollable fires. Within two years Suharto himself – the longest-serving dictator in Asia – would be forced from power in a popular uprising. Within three years, bloody local wars would flame up across the islands, to reach their climax in the vengeful, programmed destruction of East Timor.

They were to be the last such events of the twentieth century – the overthrow and collapse of a military dictatorship, in the fourth largest nation in the world. I was there in Jakarta when they started, at the beginning of the end of Suharto. Over the next three years, I followed them through until the end.

* * *

I lived in Japan as the correspondent for a British newspaper. I had come to Jakarta, by chance, the week before the riots, for a dull and unimportant meeting of Asian leaders. I knew little about Indonesia, I had found few books on the subject, and my expectations were vague. Elsewhere in the world, I had always travelled with a set of advance impressions, to be confirmed or contradicted by experience; in Indonesia, I arrived without even prejudices. The country had no distinct outlines in my mind. I didn't know where to begin.

The map which I had bought in Tokyo did not help much. Indonesia sprawled across its folds, a swirl of islands shrinking and thinning from west to east: plump Sumatra, compact Java, then the scattered trail of the Lesser Sunda Islands and the Moluccas. I recognised, as a geographical oddity, the crazed shape of Sulawesi: an island of peninsulas, flailing like the arms of an acrobat. And then there were the great half islands: Borneo, divided between Indonesia and Malaysia by a jagged frontier; New Guinea, transected by a line almost dead straight. Across this profusion of unruly forms, the Equator cut with scientific severity. From east to west I traced the names along its length: Waigeo, Kayoa, Muarakaman, Longiram, Pontianak, Lubuksikaping.

Stare long enough at an unfamiliar map and it becomes possible to construct a fantasy of it through its place names. But Indonesia's gave so little away. They were diverse to the point of excess; too many different associations were called to mind to create any consistent impression. They ranged from the brutal (Fakfak) to the majestic (Jayapura). Some looked more African than Asian (Kwatisore); others sounded almost European (Flores and Tanimbar). There were occasional suggestions of exploration and colonialism (Hollandia, Dampier Strait), but one place alone – Krakatoa – stood out as unmistakably historic. The names on the map chattered and rumbled. With a little nudging, they formed themselves into lines and verses:

Buru, Fakfak, Manokwari,
Ujung Pandang, Probolinggo,
Nikiniki, Balikpapan,
Halmahera, Berebere.

Gorontalo, Samarinda,
Gumzai, Bangka, Pekalongan,
Watolari, Krakatoa,
Wetar, Kisar, Har, Viqueque!

Everything I learned about Indonesia added to my excitement and confusion. The country was made up of 17,500 islands, ranging from seaweed-covered rocks to the largest on earth. The distance from one end to the other was broader than the span of the Atlantic Ocean or as great as the distance between Britain and Iraq. Its 235 million people were made up of 300 ethnic groups and spoke 365 languages. As an independent republic Indonesia was fifty years old, but it sounded more like an unwieldy empire than a modern nation state. I had travelled a good deal, but never to a country of which I knew so little. All my ignorance of the world, all the experience I had to come, seemed to be stored up in the shapes of those islands, and in their names.

This is a book about violence, and about being afraid. After the crushing of the democracy demonstrators, I returned to Indonesia again and again. I stayed for weeks at a time, usually at moments of crisis and tumult. I was young and avid, with a callous innocence common among young men. Although I prided myself on deploring violence, if it should – tragically – break out, I wanted to witness it for myself. In Borneo, I saw heads severed from their bodies and men eating human flesh. In Jakarta, I saw burned corpses in the street, and shots were fired around and towards me. I encountered death, but remained untouched; these experiences felt like important ones. Secretly, I imagined that they had imparted something to my character, an invisible shell which would stand me in good stead the next time I found myself in violent or unpredictable circumstances. But then I went to East Timor, where I discovered that such experience is never externalised, only absorbed, and that it builds up inside one, like a toxin. In East Timor, I became afraid, and couldn't control my fear. I ran away, and afterwards I was ashamed.

I resist the idea of defining experiences, when an entire life comes to its point. But I am haunted by that period. For a long time I believed that I had lost something good about myself in East Timor: my strength and will; courage. In three years of travelling in Indonesia, I had found myself at the heart of things. I could land anywhere, it seemed, and within a few hours the dramas of the vast country would create themselves around me. Cars and guides would be found, victims and perpetrators would appear, and marvellous and terrible scenes would enact themselves before my eyes. I loved the intoxication of leaving behind the town and travelling into the forest by road, by boat or on foot. And I loved to sleep next to the jungle, and to wake up the next morning in the tang of strange dreams. But after East Timor, there was never such glamour again.

On my last night in Bali, I stayed up late with my book of Indonesian history; as I expected, when I finally fell asleep, Colonel Mehmet was waiting. He seemed to know what I had been reading, and to be angry about it. 'Yes!' he bellowed. 'Very funny this terrible thing is.' But there was a quiver of anxiety in his voice and I could tell that he was losing spirit.

'Go away, Colonel,' I said, because my new knowledge had made me powerful.

'You not always can keep your eyes shut!' he barked, but his voice was becoming weaker. 'It is not good for you to find you cannot make your dream.'

'Goodbye, Colonel Mehmet,' I said.

'To the destructive element . . .' the colonel wailed, but he was already fading and trailing away, '... submit yourself!' I hung up the phone and found myself lying on the outdoor bed with my eyes open, wide awake in the mouth of the jungle.

I left Bali a few hours later. In Jakarta, the broken glass had been cleared up, the opposition headquarters had been hosed down and boarded over, but the soldiers were still on the streets and it was as hot and tense as before. I flew out of Indonesia the next day, as the government began to arrest people accused of orchestrating the riots. Trade unionists and young political activists were being picked up from their homes in Jakarta and Yogyakarta. Twenty-eight people, the newspapers reported, had been seized for political activities in Bali.

SOMETHING CLOSE TO SHAME:
BORNEO 1997–1999

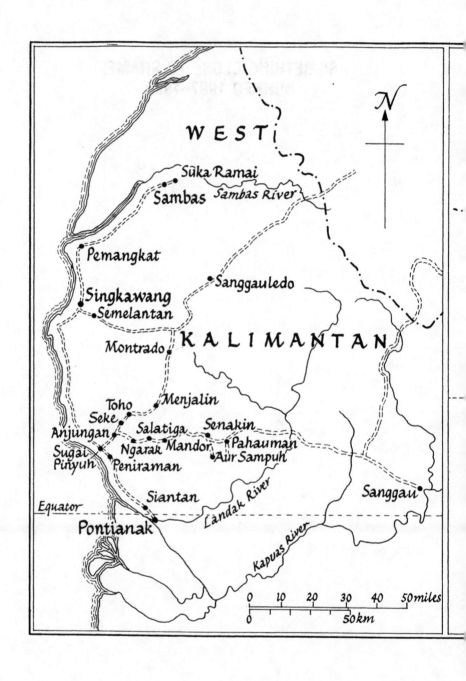

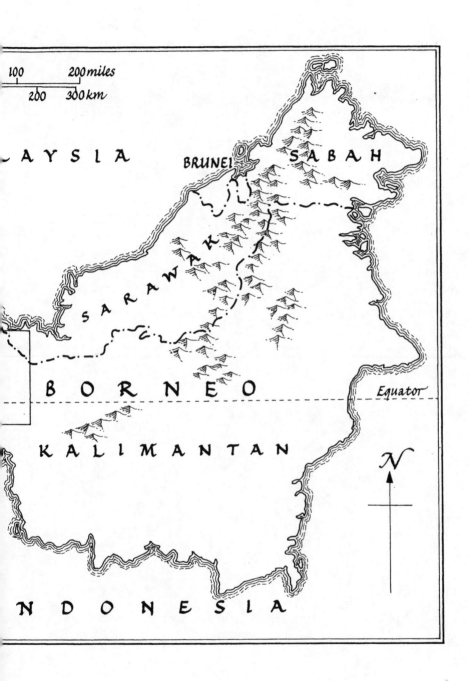

WHAT YOUNG MEN DO

One

A friend of mine in Jakarta, a television reporter for one of the big international networks, came back from Borneo with a photograph of a severed head. To be accurate, what he had was the video of a photograph; the man who had taken the original, a local journalist, had refused to hand the print over, and making a copy was risky because the photo labs were under surveillance. So the cameraman had zoomed in on it, and held the camera steady. A newspaper could never reproduce such an image, and in my friend's film it remained on the screen for only a second or two.

It was lying on the ground, appeared to be male, and was rather decomposed. It was more absurd than atrocious, with a Mr Punch leer and wild holes for eyes. It looked mask-like and carnivalesque, but almost immediately it was gone and the film cut away to burned-out houses, and to soldiers stopping the car and confiscating tapes. The image flashed so quickly across my eye that at first I didn't realise what I had seen. The second time, I thought: so *that's* what a severed head looks like – well, it could be worse.

It was May 1997, ten months since my visit to Bali, and I was back in Indonesia to report on the elections. It was the last few days of the official campaign period and thousands of teenage boys had occupied the streets of Jakarta in long, aimless parades of chanting and flag waving. There were three official parties, and each had its own colour, its own symbol and its own number. Red Bull Number Two (the democratic party) and Green Star

Number One (the Muslim party) were on good terms, but when either encountered Yellow Banyan Tree Number Three, the ruling party, there were jeers and scuffles which usually ended with burned cars, thrown rocks, and water cannon and tear-gas charges by the police. The president referred to the elections as the 'Festival of Democracy', and the atmosphere in the street marches was closer to that of a football crowd than a political rally. There were party T-shirts and bandannas, party pop songs, and the sky above the flyovers was full of kites.

My friend Jonathan made ravishing films of the rallies. The dominant colours – red, yellow or green – gave them a medieval quality, like battle scenes from the films of Kurosawa. In Jakarta, the newspapers kept a count of 'campaign-related deaths' which, by the official reckoning, were always the result of traffic accidents rather than political unrest. But every few days, stories filtered through of more sinister trouble in other cities and other provinces – East Java, Sulawesi, Madura Island. The morning after the tumultuous final day of the election campaign, I flew to one of these cities, Banjarmasin in southern Borneo, where grim news had been reported the day before.

Taxi drivers at the airport were reluctant to go into town. Even on its outskirts I could smell smoke, and a Protestant church at its centre was still burning after twenty-four hours. An entire slum block had been destroyed, and the rioters had set fire to the offices of the ruling party, a dozen shops and cinemas, and the best hotel in town. In the big shopping centre, 132 bodies were found. A police colonel from Jakarta told me that they were looters, trapped by their own fire, though others said that they were victims of the military who had been murdered elsewhere and covertly dumped in the burning building. I saw two of these bodies in the hospital mortuary. They were burned beyond recognition, their skulls cracked by the heat.

As I was preparing to leave Banjarmasin, I glanced at the map of Borneo and noticed a name in the province of West

Kalimantan: Pontianak – the place where Jonathan had filmed the photograph of the severed head. Borneo is vast, and the two cities are hundreds of miles apart. But the Chinese travel agent in the hotel was enthusiastic: Pontianak was a splendid city, he said, with a large Chinese population. He quickly fixed the flights, and gave me the telephone number of a friend who could act as my guide there.

From the plane, West Kalimantan was flat and regular, but cut through with exciting rivers of chocolate brown. There were naked patches in the jungle, and thin lines of smoke rose from invisible fires. Through the porthole I saw metal roofs and boats, and more brown river water. Then the plane banked and I was looking at jungle again, then at an airport in the jungle.

The city below me was Pontianak (the word means 'evil spirit'); it lies on the Equator (dead on it, according to my map). Things learned about the Equator as a child came back to me, such as the way the direction of water going down the plughole reverses when you cross it. I caught myself thinking about ways of testing this – perhaps in different hotels, one north, one south. Then the plane tilted down and began its descent towards the centre of the earth.

Two

My knowledge of Borneo was vague. I seemed to remember that it was the second biggest island in the world. I thought of jungles, of course, and of copperplate encounters between European explorers in canoes and cannibal chieftains. I thought of a poster which I had seen as a child, featuring a wrestler known as the Wild Man of Borneo. I found myself trying to remember if the adventures of Tintin had ever taken him there. At the airport, I bought a glossy guidebook and recalled what I had heard in Jakarta.

In February, rumours had filtered through of fighting between two ethnic groups, the Dayaks and the Madurese.

The Dayaks were the original inhabitants of Borneo, famous during the nineteenth century as the archetypal Victorian 'savages'. For thousands of years, before the arrival of the Dutch and the British, they had dominated the immense island. They were a scattered collection of tribes who lived in communal long-houses, practised a form of animism, and survived by hunting and by slash-and-burn agriculture.

More titillating, to the Victorian mind, was the promiscuity held to be rampant in the longhouses, and the practice of 'male enhancement' – the piercing of the penis with a metal pin. Dayak warriors increased their prestige, and brought good luck to their villages, by collecting the heads of rival tribes in formalised, set piece raids. Certain of the victims' organs, including the heart, brains and blood, were believed to bestow potency on those who consumed them, and the heads were preserved and worshipped in elaborate rituals. 'Beautiful young girls,' my guidebook informed me, 'would snatch up the heads and use the grisly trophies as props in a wild and erotic burlesque.'

The Dayaks' bloodier traditions were outlawed by the Christian colonists; since 1945 they had been full citizens of the Republic of Indonesia. My guidebook contained photographs of old people in beaded headdresses and men in loincloths clutching blowpipes, but they had about them the glazed neat-ness of tourist entertainments. 'These days Dayaks keep their penis pins and tattoos well hidden beneath jeans and T-shirts,' I read. 'Apart from a few villages in the interior, the longhouses have been replaced by simple homes of wood and plaster.'

The Madurese, I had heard several times, were 'the Sicilians of Indonesia'; educated Jakartans smiled wearily and shook their heads when they spoke of them. Madura was a dry, barren island off the east coast of Java, the frequent beneficiary of the govern-ment's programme of subsidised 'transmigration' to the more fertile territories of the outer archipelago. Its inhabitants had a national reputation for coarseness, armed violence and an uncompromising form of Islam. I had heard them blamed for church burnings, attacks on Christians, and several riots during the election campaign. Everywhere they settled, the Madurese had become the neighbours that nobody wanted.

As transmigrants, they were accused of thievery and thuggishness, but their differences with the Dayaks ran deeper than that. The Madurese were proud bearers of curved sickles; Dayak tradition abhorred the public flaunting of blades. The Dayaks hunted and reared pigs; the Madurese were strict Muslims. Violence had been breaking out between the two groups since the first Madurese arrived in West Kalimantan a century before. But nothing had ever been seen like the events of the previous months.

I had a cutting from the *Asia Times* of 20 February 1997. It was headlined FIGHT TO THE DEATH FOR TRIBAL RIGHTS.

It's been two generations since the last reports of head-hunting by the Dayak, one of the most feared tribes in Southeast Asia. Now one of Indonesia's oldest societies is running amok and returning to its brutal traditions.

The Madurese, a migrant ethnic group from the island of Madura, east of Java, are bearing the brunt of the Dayaks' anger, fueled not only by cultural conflicts but by political and economic discontent. Following several clashes between the two groups, Madurese have watched dozens of their settlements northeast of Pontianak, the capital of West Kalimantan, burn to the ground.

The burnings and killings continue. Despite repeated government announcements that the area is safe, the Dayak and Indonesian army roadblocks still stand. There is widespread fear that violence, even in Pontianak, can break out anytime.

'This is a time bomb. It can explode at any minute,' said one Dayak.

A government estimate of a few hundred dead was quoted. 'Local Christian church leaders' were said to put them 'in the thousands'.

21

The author of the article, a woman from Sumatra, was a friend of Jonathan; her visit to West Kalimantan, he told me, had left her badly scared. 'At a roadblock the next day – during a 300km journey my companion and I encountered 32 roadblocks –' she wrote, 'an old Dayak man with a rifle asked: "Are you Madurese? I want to drink some Madurese blood."'

But her article made no explicit reference to the most striking fact about the war in West Kalimantan. For the Dayaks had not merely driven out and killed their Madurese neighbours. They had ritually decapitated them, carried off their heads as trophies and eaten their hearts and livers.

Months later, when the forests were burning and money had become worthless, the killings in Borneo seemed like a portent, the first faint rumbling of a catastrophe that would overtake the entire country. At the time, though, they went virtually unreported. Jonathan had heard vague stories about the violence in February; a few days later, he flew over to Pontianak with a small group of foreign journalists based in Jakarta. They checked into the city's one good hotel, the same one to which I was heading. Its lounge, restaurant and karaoke bar were full of poorly disguised military spies, the men known to everyone as Intels. The next day, they hired a driver and a jeep, and drove north out of Pontianak. There were soldiers on the streets, and checkpoints every few miles with spikes and mines spread across the road. They got through the first few by waving press passes, or by pretending to be tourists.

At a village called Salatiga, they saw the first signs of destruction: dozens of burned, skeletal houses. They pulled over, but after the cameraman started filming, a group of soldiers appeared, angry and nervous. Calls were made to headquarters, and the cameraman's tapes were confiscated (though a few had been hastily concealed in the jeep). Back in Pontianak, they were held for several hours and then released, with orders not to wander outside the city itself.

They spent the evening in the bar of the hotel, watching the Intel men get drunk and sing karaoke.

The next day they talked to people in Pontianak, and realised for the first time how little of the full story had reached Jakarta. There had been massacres, people said, in most of the villages in the interior. First, the Madurese had attacked the Dayaks, then the Dayaks had taken revenge. They assembled from all over Kalimantan, ritually summoned by an artifact known as the 'Red Bowl'. Then they had systematically purged the villages of Madurese settlers, burning their houses and hunting them down.

The Dayaks' magic made them invulnerable to bullets, people said. They could identify the Madurese by their smell. A woman from Salatiga claimed to have looked out of her window and seen a man walking down the road carrying a head impaled on a stick. A journalist on a local magazine had a photograph of a severed head – the photograph which Jonathan would use in his film.

The Dayaks were trying to get through to Pontianak where thousands of Madurese were living as refugees. The army was protecting the Madurese and, it was said, killing Dayaks. According to the official count three hundred people had died. It was obvious that the true figure was far, far higher.

Everyone was scared of something: the Madurese of the Dayaks, the Dayaks of the army, and the army and the local government of the terrible trouble which this was going to cause back in Jakarta. Military reinforcements had been flown in from Java, and the hospitals were under guard.

The Intels followed Jonathan and his friends everywhere they went, and people were afraid to talk to them. After a couple more nights of karaoke, they flew back to Jakarta.

That was three months ago. Since then, there had been no more reports of significant trouble, and these days everyone in Jakarta was preoccupied with the election. An extraordinary thing had taken place, and passed by with no more than a glance from the outside world: an ethnic war of scarcely imaginable savagery, fought according to principles of black magic, a couple of hours' drive from a modern city of banks, hotels and airports.

Three

The morning after arriving in Pontianak, I drove out of the city with my guide, a Chinese man named Budi who always wore black shoes, black trousers and a white shirt.

We crossed Pontianak's two rivers, where the seagoing schooners docked, glistening and curved like great white ice-cream scoops, and where the riverboats began the long chug to the interior. The outskirts of the town were dominated by water, and wide ditches divided the houses from the road and from one another. Bouncing planks were laid across them; some families even kept tiny tublike boats moored by their front doors. We passed the Equator monument, a strange black sculpture of concentric hoops, and drove north along a crisp new road unrolled like a carpet on an underlay of dusty red earth.

Budi could tell at a glance which houses were Dayak and which were Madurese, by the arrangement of the stilts, the direction of the windows, and the presence or absence of batik decorations above the door. His English was as crisp as his clothes; he could put a date or a number to everything. As we drove north, he told me what he knew about the struggle between the Dayaks and the Madurese. He had no hesitation in calling it a war.

It had begun at the very end of the previous year in a town called Sanggauledo, close to the border with Malaysian Sarawak. A stage had been specially built for a live performance of *dangdut*, the bouncy, Indian-influenced pop music adored all over Indonesia. At some point during the course of the evening, two Dayak women had been bothered by a pair of Madurese boys. A fight broke out, the Madurese brandished their sickles, and a young Dayak, the son of the local village head, was stabbed.

Scared and outnumbered, the Madurese took refuge in the local military outpost, where a delegation of Dayaks quickly presented themselves, demanding that the two be handed over. The soldiers refused, so they walked to the nearest Madurese enclave and set it on fire. 'Nine hundred and ninety-eight houses were burned,' Budi said. 'Some of them were completely destroyed.'

Tension between the two races had been building for years; there had been a similar spasm of violence a decade before. But this time, as news of the latest stabbing spread from Sanggauledo, there were revenge attacks on Madurese living in the interior. Within a few days the government in Pontianak got together a group of Dayak and Madurese leaders and drew up a 'treaty' to end the fighting.

Over the years the Madurese had not been the only objects of the Dayaks' fury. During the Second World War, they had been recruited by both sides in the fighting between the Japanese and the Allies. Twenty years later, during the great bloodletting of the mid-1960s, they had turned on the Chinese of Kalimantan. Budi was old enough to remember that time, but he spoke warmly of the Dayaks.

'Inside, I am pro-Dayak,' he said. 'They are good people, very gentle, they don't cause trouble for no one. They want to be left alone. But they are lazy. My brother works with Dayaks in his office, and if you leave them alone they will sit there all day talking and smiling. Their IQ is very low, unfortunately.'

Even from our brief acquaintance I knew that Budi worked from seven o'clock in the morning until midnight every day. I suspected that, through his eyes, the world was a very lazy place.

For an hour the jungle had been close on either side, broken up by the occasional lonely hut and wooden stands selling cigarettes and Coke. Now there were houses on both sides of the road, and suddenly we were in a small town of concrete offices and bright, dusty shop signs. Right in its centre was a fire-gutted house, flanked on both sides by undamaged buildings. Budi was not sure what this meant. 'This town has a reputation for burning down houses,' he said. 'By accident. Maybe they are careless with matches.'

I was looking for the town's priests, friends of an anthropologist in Pontianak, and witnesses, I was told, to much of the worst violence. On the outskirts, we followed a trail of schoolchildren to a tin-roofed church and a school, built of flaking planks on low stilts, which stood back from the road. The schoolmaster was locking up for the afternoon, and he guided us around the corner to the house of Father Anselmus and Father Andreas.

They were young priests, Dayaks in their late twenties, who had studied at a Catholic seminary in Java. But apart from a crucifix nailed to one wall, there was nothing remotely priestly about their bungalow. The main room contained a shelf of novels, a table of ashtrays and discarded fruit peel, and a wide TV connected to a dish on the roof. On the walls were a painting of a volcano, a Dayak shield and scabbard, and a dry marker board, bearing a scrawled list of dates and appointments in Indonesian and the following words of English:

Don't forget to show the champion's final
on Thursday, May 28 (dawn)
Borussia Dortmund vs Juventus!

Next to the board was a five-foot-high cut-out of Father Christmas.

Andreas was bearded and sleepy-eyed, with a dazed grin. He smoked lots of the clove cigarettes called *kretek* which he held between three fingers, as if he didn't quite know what to make of them. Anselmus was taller and more talkative, and gave the impression of being a bit too muscular and handsome for this kind of life.

They were the first Dayaks I had encountered and I expected to be met with wariness and reserve – in the car, Budi and I had rehearsed a reassuring preamble emphasising the seriousness of

my intentions, and the confidentiality with which any information would be treated. It was quite unnecessary with these two,
who reminded me more than anything of certain friends in
London, aimless well-meaning bachelors resigned to the light
duties of dole-claiming, TV-watching and smoking. They
welcomed us immediately; there was always coffee and fruit on
the table, and after a few days it became natural, almost routine,
to drop round at Anselmus and Andreas's house for durian or
rambutan and a conversation about headhunting and cannibalism.

They took up the story where Budi had left off.

The 'peace treaty' had been signed by the Dayak and
Madurese leaders in mid-January, but even before the end of the
month the violence had begun again. On 29 January, news spread
of two Dayak girls, former pupils at Anselmus and Andreas's
school, who had been lying in bed in a suburb of Pontianak,
when two Madurese men broke in. The girls were molested;
their nightdresses were cut with sickles. Anticipating another
round of revenge attacks, a mob of Madurese gathered on the
road that led from Pontianak to the Dayak interior.

By four o'clock in the afternoon, a thousand people armed
with sickles had assembled, old men and children among them.
But no Dayaks appeared. The mob grew impatient and burned
down a Dayak house. Then they began stopping cars and
demanding to see the occupants' papers.

They set up a roadblock in the town of Peniraman, where a
family was driving back from a daughter's university graduation
ceremony. Their jeep was stopped and the five occupants were
dragged out. All but a child and a young woman were cut down
on the spot. Andreas conducted the funeral of a young man
named Alun, whose head had been almost severed by the sickles.
The body of an old man, a village elder named Nyuncat, was
found later in the jungle.

Word of the atrocities passed around the Dayak villages. The more they killed, the more convinced the Madurese became that retaliation was imminent, and the more inclined to pre-empt it with their own violence. On 29 January half a dozen Dayak houses had been burned in the village of Senakin. On the following morning, the Madurese in Paci Karangan were attacked by Dayaks. That afternoon, Madurese threw stones at a Dayak bus in Seke. The next day, Andreas saw Dayaks burning down Madurese houses in Seke, which had already been abandoned.

'In the afternoon in Paci I saw dead bodies on the road without heads and without hearts,' said Andreas. Both the priests had thin smiles on their faces, and the more detail I pressed out of them, the wider the smiles became.

'What had happened to them?' I asked, through Budi.

'Some Dayak people killed them and cut their heads off.' Smile.

'What did they do with the heads?'

'The heads they took away.' Grin. 'The bodies were all empty. Near the bodies were the stomachs and the insides. They were there for a long time. None of the pastors was brave enough to perform the burials for a month.'

'It must have been terrible, seeing the bodies there.'

'This was my first time to see a body without a head and, as a pastor, it was terrible. It was as if everything I have been teaching has had no effect at all.' Anselmus nodded in agreement, and they looked at one another and smiled again. They smiled widely, their straggly moustaches crinkled and lifted, and they laughed out loud in puzzlement and dismay.

It was four o'clock when we left the pastors; the shadows were thickening as we drove on past a military barracks with painted signs bearing divisional crests.

When the trouble had begun at the end of January, the smaller military outposts beyond here had quickly lost control and, having cleared the villages of the interior, the Dayaks had moved towards Pontianak. But the army mustered its forces; troops were brought in from other parts of Indonesia. At a town called Anjungan the Dayaks were stopped by force. There were stories that busloads of them had been massacred by the soldiers.

The gateways of the barracks bore the numbers 17.8.45 – Independence Day – and the gold eagle of the Republic of Indonesia, hunched and stylised like the Roman eagle. It was easy to think of these soldiers as Roman legionaries, gathered up from Java, from Sulawesi or Bali, and forced to do their time in this outpost of the empire, marooned among equatorial Picts and Huns, people with strange ways who wished them no good.

I tensed when a soldier standing on a corner waved us down, and Budi glanced nervously at me as we slowed to a stop. But all he wanted was a lift, and we were going in the wrong direction. My heart was racing as we drove on, but I was childishly disappointed. When my friends from Jakarta had come here there had been roadblocks and landmines, and soldiers stepping out of the jungle. But this evening there were only dogs skulking on the street corners; the stalls by the side of the road, with their jars of cigarettes and chewing gum, were switching on their feeble electric bulbs. We passed a marshy lake. Low hills rose in the distance. Girls could be seen bathing in the river below a bridge. The road narrowed and a tunnel of trees joined arms above our heads, casting stripes of shadow as the sun declined on our left.

Then, at a point difficult to define, we crossed Dayak lines.

The first sign was a burned-out house. Then there was another one, a few yards back from the road, just black beams and twists of corrugated iron. The third ruin had retained three of its pillars, so that it looked almost classical; next to it was a house with half of its front wall intact. Budi slowed and read the words scraped on it with charcoal: MADURESE OFFSPRING OF DOGS.

Four, five, six burned houses so far, in the space of a few hundred yards. Then twelve, thirteen, and probably more behind, shrouded by the dusk and jungle. I counted fifteen in the course of a mile, and then suddenly we were back in a village again. There was a wooden chapel and a shop selling baskets and jerrycans.

People in shorts, most of them young, walked up and down the road, or squatted with cigarettes on the verges. The houses were plaster and a few of them supported big grey satellite dishes. There was a church, but no mosque, and a soccer game was in progress on a patch of rough ground. The black ruins with their violent messages seemed like a hallucination.

Budi did not slow down. Just as suddenly as we had entered the village, we had passed through it, and we were driving through the jungle again.

We drove on as the light ebbed away. The headlights picked out a man's jacket, carefully spreadeagled on the road ahead. 'There must be some accident,' said Budi and, sure enough, round the next curve a minibus lay neatly on its side with its wheels above the roadside ditch. It was hard to tell when the accident had happened. It could have been hours ago. There were about a dozen people around the bus, apparently its passengers, although they looked unhurt and unsurprised. The men were standing with cigarettes in their hands. The women were laughing and talking, seated on a stack of large chests and suitcases which, lashed to the roof, must have contributed to the bus's instability. 'You have to be careful driving here,' said Budi. 'Animals come out of the jungle. Dayak people walk straight out into the road. They are kind people, but they are vague. Sometimes you stop and ask directions. They say, "It's not far," but then you drive a long way and still don't get there. And these people walk it – they walk for kilometres and kilometres but still they say when you ask them, "It's not far."'

Later Budi said, 'You don't see them from the road, but a lot of people live there, inside the jungle. People die here quite often, outside of the statistics. They just die and nobody knows about them.' When we drove back along the same road, four hours later, the bus was still there, along with its passengers, smiling and smoking in the darkness.

Four

It was before six, but it felt very late by the time we reached Menjalin, another plaster-and-satellite-dish village where teenagers sat in open doorways under dim flickering bulbs. They smiled at Budi, and jumped up to offer help when he stopped for directions. In the middle of the village was a large wooden building where a group of figures were arrayed in an unconsciously picturesque composition. A dozen Dayak boys were lying or sitting on the veranda, and at their centre was an old man with spectacles and a white beard, a portly old white man with a tin of rolling tobacco on his knee, gesturing and talking as the boys looked up at him.

His name was Father Kristof, and he was a Dutch Capuchin. He had been in Indonesia for thirty-one years, and in Menjalin for sixteen. There was a Swiss priest in Ngarak, and another Dutchman in Singkawang, but foreigners here were few and he said without regret that he didn't get many visitors. He wore a fake Calvin Klein T-shirt, but the room where he led us was dark and timeless, with a stone floor, a wooden dining table and a shelf of cracked leather spines. He understood English and spoke it with a strong accent, but the effort made him frown and, after nodding at my questions, he would direct the answers at Budi in Indonesian, and correct the translation as it was relayed back to me.

Menjalin had been tense since the new year. When the news came through of the Madurese attacks on the schoolgirls and the motorists, some kind of reaction had been inevitable.

'It was not unexpected,' said Father Kristof, 'but it was very sudden. People from all walks of life, even children, gathered outside. They were unanimous, they decided as a community to fight for their rights. Everyone wanted to go – even my friends, these boys outside, they made bamboo spears, they carried knives. They marched to Seke and Salatiga. They said that they must defend themselves. They say that the Madurese have killed Dayaks so very, very many times but this is enough. All Madurese must leave Kalimantan.'

It was a collective decision, he kept emphasising; there was no leader. It was entirely spontaneous, but all the participants abided strictly by three rules. First, they would not damage any mosques. Second, they would not burn down any state-owned offices. 'Now this is very wise, because if they burn mosques, then they are Christians against Muslims . . .' He fixed me with his eye and shook his head, as if to emphasise what the consequences of this would have been, how close they had come to a holy war. 'If they damage government property, they are against the government, and nobody can defeat the government.' The third rule was no looting. 'They are not rich people, but when they found cars or nice furniture, they burned them.'

Since the trouble at the pop concert, Dayaks all over West Kalimantan had been preparing. When the fighting began in December they had had only sharpened bamboo poles and a few hunting rifles. A month later they had metal heads for the spears, and newly forged *mandau*, the traditional hacking machete. They had rifles, bought illegally from the Indonesian army, smuggled across the border from Malaysia, or made out of metal tubing by local blacksmiths. Father Kristof passed an album of photographs which showed the Menjalin Dayaks preparing for battle. They had feathers tied to their heads with red ribbons, and ribbons on their spears. Their mouths were strangely synchronised: all closed, or simultaneously open in a pursed O. 'You can see from their faces that they are in a trance,' said Father Kristof. 'Individual responsibility is very, very little from person to person.'

I asked about magic, and the stories I had heard of Dayaks who were invulnerable to bullets.

'There is a lot of truth there,' said the pastor. 'If they believe that they are bulletproof, they become bulletproof. This power varies.' The priest himself had seen one man who was shot by a Madurese rifle. The bullet had entered into his ear, he said, and then stopped. 'He reached in' – Father Kristof mimed the action – 'and pulled it out.' In a trance, a man could walk through the jungle for hours, without eating or drinking, and without any fatigue. 'Twenty-five or thirty kilometres they go, to Salatiga and then back again. Sixty kilometres on foot, they run there and back, and they don't even drink water. When the *kamang tariu* are inside the Dayaks they scream and yell. When they return they have almost no voice left. But they can do these things because they are not themselves, because they are in a trance.'

The *kamang tariu* is the spirit which possesses the Dayaks in time of war. When it is present, it provides physical protection and immunity from thirst and fatigue, but it has a powerful appetite of its own. 'The *kamang tariu* drinks blood, it has to be fed blood,' said the pastor. 'There were Dayaks in Pontianak who could not go to the war, but who were possessed. Their friends had to cut the throat of a chicken and give it to them, to feed the spirit.'

I asked what happened when the Dayaks returned from an attack on a village.

'They brought back bags of heads. The heart, they eat directly. The idea is that it should be still fresh. A fresh heart has different power from lungs, and lungs are different from stomachs. Even the blood. From children to old people to babies, no exceptions at all. Four thousand of them, all beheaded with *mandau*. Yes, it is remarkable.'

For two weeks, there was an atmosphere of emergency. Having purged the villages of the interior, the Dayaks were attempting to reach Pontianak to do the same. It was remarkable, given the punishment which they had inflicted on their enemies, but they felt themselves to be the ones in acute peril. 'It was very dangerous,' said Father Kristof. 'There were a lot of Madurese hiding in the bush, and people were afraid that they would come back and take their revenge.' Beyond Anjungan, the small military outposts were separated from one another by hours of road and miles of jungle. Central control had broken down completely.

Eventually, military reinforcements were flown in, and the roads were blocked by tyre spikes and mines. The soldiers went into the jungle and laid boobytraps along the tracks, consisting of hand grenades and tripwires. Soon the Dayaks were being killed. 'I would say that fewer than two hundred Dayak people died, and roughly four thousand Madurese,' said Father Kristof. 'Two thousand is sure. This is the information we have today.'

Having stopped the killing, the government in Pontianak did what it had always done after this kind of trouble: it held a peace ceremony.

The authorities were experienced enough to know that ending the violence was not enough to bring about peace. They knew about the magical aspects of the conflict, and they knew that to control the situation on the ground they had to control the spirits. They knew about the two kinds of spirit, the *kamang*, the protector of the headhunters, and the *sumangat*, the spirit of life. In time of war, the *sumangat* flee the hearts of the people to make way for the *kamang*. So they assembled a group of compliant Dayak elders, who summoned the peaceful spirits back.

'During the government's ceremony they called back all the *sumangat* which are harmony, peace, the spirit of life,' said Father Kristof. 'But the *kamang tariu* has not gone away. They called back the spirit of life, without sending the spirit of war back to the mountain.' This was a theological impossibility, as the old men who performed the ceremony must have known. Only the civil servants in Pontianak believed that the spirits of killing had gone. 'The government ceremony was a nonsense,' said Father Kristof.

Suddenly the lights cut out in the stone-floored room. The noises of the jungle rose up from behind the house: the shimmering cheeps and kackacks of invisible insects, the shiver of the trees. For two seconds we were held in darkness. Then the generator restarted its whirring.

I blinked and said, 'Father, as a priest, how do you see all this?'

'It's difficult to say in two or three words, but to understand you have to go back sixteen years to when I arrived here. Compared to then, all the Dayaks are now Christians. They go to war with a cross. They've all bought rosaries. They are not killers.' And then, in English: 'It's very difficult to explain . . .

'Those involved in the war didn't want any of it. They did it against their will. They didn't intend to do anything wrong. They did it all unconsciously. Even if they killed four thousand people, they are not the killers of the Madurese.

'Dayaks have two sets of rules and teachings – the ones of their ancestors, and the rules and regulations set by the government. But when they are under pressure and need to express what they are all feeling in the face of that pressure, they have no choice. They have to go by the ancestral book.'

I asked where the Bible fitted into this.

'It's difficult to say. Maybe those involved in the situation, deep in a trance based on the teachings of their ancestors, poorly educated . . .' He shook his head, and began another train of thought. 'The educated ones didn't get involved – they refused that kind of belief . . .'

I asked: 'Is it a sin to cut the heads off Madurese?'

'I cannot see into people's souls,' said the priest. 'I can only see their actions and here I can see that they act together, not on their own, that they act because they believe it is a good thing. I say in church it is wrong to murder, you must save the life of every person living on earth and they understand that, but when it is war . . . there are other things.'

'Did you try to persuade them not to go?'

'Oh, yah, but it was not possible. They laughed at it.' There was a long pause, and the jungle seemed to have grown louder. Now I could hear the tympanic noises of the insects even above the generator.

Finally, Father Kristof said, 'When we love people . . .' then stopped, then started again. 'If a son commits murder and goes to prison, the mother always loves him. She says, "My son is a good boy still." I don't say that what has happened here is good. You have to try to understand the position of the Dayak people now. They are ignored by the government. They have no political role. No one in the key positions, no people of influence in the army. They are under pressure and they have no economic power. All they have is land, land that has been theirs for thousands of years. Now the government appropriates the land for transmigration. The timber companies come, other commercial concerns. The Dayaks become upset, alienated from society. That's what makes them stand up for their rights. They are . . .' – he struggled for the right word, back in English again now – '. . . natural people. They are in conflict with a tribe that has totally different traditions.

'It is one thing, one thing inspired it all: powerlessness. They are ignored by the government, but pressured and punished at the same time. The only way out was to do what they did.'

'These heads, Father, which they brought back from Salatiga. Where are they now?'

'They are in the villages. They bring them back into their homes, and usually perform some kind of charms or prayers. In the old days, they kept the head in a special place in the longhouse but now they keep it in a hidden place, a secret place where they pray.'

'Would they show them to you?'

'They would if I asked.'

'Would they show me?'

He did not smile, but tilted his head and looked at me. 'No. Not in this situation. It's impossible for many reasons. Because of ... protocol, and because they believe the magic power will be lost.'

Later, as we were leaving, Father Kristof led us to the back of the house and a crude wooden shed on the very edge of the jungle. Inside were tables and upright boards bearing dozens of black-and-white photographs, pre-war shots of Dayaks and Dutch fathers, praying together, standing stiffly at a harvest celebration alongside bales of rice and the carcasses of hogs. One picture dated from 1935. In it a father, portly and bearded like Kristof, sat on a wooden chair beneath a string of nine enemy heads. The expression on his face gave nothing away. The tattoos were still visible on the cheeks of the decapitated warriors.

Five

'When you are accustomed to using scientific means of investigation, your mind shies away from these things,' a Dayak anthropologist said to me in Pontianak. 'But I believe there is a supernatural world. I have to believe it, because I have heard about it from soldiers, policemen, Dayak elders, Chinese, Malays. It is hard to disbelieve these people, but it is also hard to believe them.'

Everyone I met in West Kalimantan had tales of Dayak magic.

I heard early on about the *panglima*, the 'generals', or war magicians, who led the Dayaks in time of emergency. I was told how a *panglima* had summoned bees to attack the Indonesian soldiers, and how he could fly, or transform himself into the form of a dog, and behead his enemies with the stroke of a leaf from a certain tree. How a pair of army officers in the north died vomiting blood after a curse was placed upon them, and how the psychiatric wards were filled with soldiers unhinged by what they had seen. 'I've talked to soldiers who have served in East Timor, and Aceh,' said Father Andreas. 'They are tough men. They have killed and been shot at before, but they say that they have never been more scared than they were by the Dayak people.'

In Sanggau, a river city deep in the interior, a small group of Dayaks was crying for the blood of six Madurese who were under guard in a small military outpost. The soldiers kept them at bay, until the *panglima* arrived at the head of an army of thousands of warriors. The soldiers were not fools; a few of them were Dayaks themselves. They handed over the doomed Madurese and surrendered.

But the *panglima* was alone; there was no Dayak army. The warriors at his side were the *kamang*, the spirits of war and killing, made visible in the minds of the soldiers by the general's incantation.

At the house of the young priests, Father Anselmus showed me the collection of magical objects given to him by his parishioners.

There was a cracked plastic bottle containing a few inches of oily black liquid. 'Poison,' he said with a grin. 'They put it on the edge of the *mandau*, or the blowpipe arrows. Even if you just have a cut or a scratch and it gets on your skin, you'll be dead in five minutes.' The plastic bottle was printed with the words *Metro Face Tonic*.

There was a bag of dried roots and tubers for use against the same poison, and a black stone which soothed stings and bites. There was a matchbox filled with pieces of a dried leaf, a couple of shreds of which ensured protection from the blows of the *mandau*. 'The leaf is very rare,' said Anselmus. 'They find where it is growing in their dreams. When someone has eaten *this*, the only thing which can kill them is *this*.' He presented a spear sharply whittled out of a pale, unbending wood. 'Since this war began, there's been a lot of interest in black magic.'

Andreas nodded his head and smiled. 'A man once came to me and said, "Father, why do you pray so hard for things which never come true? When we pray to the evil spirits, our wishes are fulfilled.'"

A taxi driver told the story of a Dayak who, alone of his companions, had made it to the town without being shot, captured or killed by boobytraps in the jungle. Finally, he fell into the hands of a group of Madurese who pinned him down, and stabbed him repeatedly. But the blows had no effect. They kicked his head until his nose hung loose and his lips were shredded, but he still looked them in the eye. It was only when they held him face down in a basin of water that he stopped moving.

It was not easy to find people who had witnessed such things first-hand.

One man, a Dayak schoolmaster in a village which saw one of the worst battles, described to me the most widely known manifestation of Dayak magic, the invulnerability to bullets. 'In my town, there were only three soldiers,' he said, 'and when the Dayaks first arrived they fired into the air. But they were completely outnumbered by the Dayaks, and soon they began shooting straight into them. There was one Dayak, he was thirty yards away. The soldier aimed the gun, it went bang-bang! – but it didn't hurt him. They were firing to kill, but none of the Dayaks got shot. I'd heard about it, but until then I never believed it. When they are in that state, when they are filled with the spirits, nothing can harm them.'

I went to see a man named Miden, a *timanggong* or tribal elder, in a hamlet called Aur Sampuh. He was a small alert man, the picture of respectability in an ironed shirt and cream trousers, and his neat, cool house was a centre of village activity. On the wall were two carved Dayak shields, and a calendar in the yellow colours of the Indonesian ruling party.

Snake tattoos ran down Miden's arms, from the top of his shoulders to the back of his hand. He began by explaining the animistic principles of Dayak religion. Spirits reside in everything, and it is the duty of Dayaks to acknowledge and propitiate these spirits at each stage of the farming cycle. 'When we cut down a tree we have to show the tree's spirit that we only do it to make our living. When we plant the rice, we sing a song. When the rice grows to a certain height there is a ceremony; there is another ceremony to thank the gods at harvest time.'

As a *timanggong*, Miden performed marriages, christenings and funerals. There were rituals to purify the paddies and keep away birds. 'But I am a farmer as well as a priest – I also use pesticides.' I asked him how he had become a Dayak priest. 'When I was a child I followed the *timanggong* in the village, and I learned much.' As well as keeping their own religion, the Dayaks in this village were all Christians, most of them Catholics.

I asked about the trouble in January and February. He said that there had been none in Aur Sampuh, because there were no Madurese here, and therefore no grievance. It was a frustrating conversation, and I felt as if there were two sides to Miden: the *timanggong* with his ritual knowledge, and the local politician with the ruling party's calendar on his wall. Whenever the former was about to say something interesting, the latter always butted in with vague, conciliatory politeness.

He spoke with authority of the Dayak war rituals, but always in the abstract, as something from which he had been entirely removed. The fighting had stranded him in his village – for two months he had been unable to leave Aur Sampuh, he said, in a way that made it sound like an isolated island rather than a small village less than an hour from some of the worst killing.

'What is the Red Bowl?' I asked.

'The Red Bowl is used to call people. It's a symbol of communication used during times of emergency. When a messenger carries it from one tribe to the next it means, "Come and help us."'

Each tribe had its bowl which was red with blood and decorated with chicken feathers. If a *timanggong* received the Red

Bowl then he was obliged to send at least seven warriors to help his brothers. It passed from village to village – during the Japanese occupation, and in 1967 when the government was fighting the Chinese 'communists', every village received the Red Bowl. 'Compared to then, this was not a big war,' Miden said emphatically. 'I am very glad that this village did not see the Red Bowl.'

One of the mysteries of the killings in January and February was how quickly the Dayaks mobilised, and the coordination they displayed across a large area with poor roads and few telephones. If the war parties did have ringleaders, they had not been publicly identified, and Miden insisted that the ceremonies were conducted spontaneously, and that he himself would never have anything to do with the summoning of the war spirits.

'If a *timanggong* knows that they are going to hold this ritual, he will forbid it.' There was, he supposed, someone who 'co-ordinated' the ceremony. He did not know who it was.

I asked him about the nature of the mysterious 'generals', the *panglima*. My impression had been that nobody knew who they were, that they lived in the mountains as hermits, halfway to being spirits themselves, and that they appeared mysteriously in the villages at just the right moment. Miden confirmed that the *panglima* could be killed, and that they could sniff out Madurese and tell them apart from Malays and Javanese. But a *panglima* was a man, and he could be any man; until the summoning began no one could tell whom the spirits of killing would choose. 'The *panglima* could be a different person every time,' he said. 'He is whoever is the strongest of the Dayaks.'

In other words, there were no ringleaders, no decision-making process, and no responsibility. The Dayaks had been provoked, and had gathered together to hold a ceremony. With that decision they had surrendered their free will to the spirits.

Later, I read an article on this subject by Stephanus Djuweng, a Dayak who was director of the Institute of Dayakology Research and Development in Pontianak. It took as its starting point the architecture of the traditional Dayak longhouse, of which a handful survive in use. The old long-houses contained family apartments called *bilek*, which gave on to a communal area called the *soah*. 'Each *bilek* is owned by an individual,' he wrote, 'whereas each *soah* is a collective part of the longhouse. This type of architectural pattern symbolizes the balance between individual and collective rights.'

It is an attractive analogy, particularly useful, as Djuweng pointed out, for a country like Indonesia, a sprawling archipel-agic empire of hundreds of different races and languages. 'The Dayak are normal human beings. They will protect themselves if any of their ancestral lands or property rights are violated, or if community members are treated beyond the limits of toler-ance,' Djuweng said. But earlier in the same article he had put it rather differently. 'What honey bees,' he asked, 'would not defend themselves when their honey, nests and community members are threatened?'

Six

Every day for a week, Budi and I drove up and down the road that led to the interior, past burned-out houses with the jungle grass rising up through the ashes. It was three months since they had been destroyed, but most of the ruins were undisturbed, and you could still discern the outline of individual rooms beneath the twists of corrugated iron – a tin bathtub here, there a nest of forks and spoons, fused together in what must have been a kitchen.

The people we spoke to on the way knew exactly what had happened and were happy to talk about it.

In Pahauman, the man who sold us bottles of Coca-Cola decribed the altars which people built along the road in front of their houses. They had decorated them with severed heads. 'Less than ten,' he said, when I asked him how many heads he had seen. 'There was nobody I knew well.'

His wife said that there had been hundreds of Madurese living here before, and that she had never had any trouble with them. 'Some of them escaped to Pontianak, I suppose, but not very many probably,' she said. What did she feel about what had happened, we asked. 'Oh, it's terrible,' she said, rather cheerfully. 'I was afraid.'

In Salatiga, a man wearing a T-shirt with the logo of the government teachers' union approached us giggling. 'I speek Indonesia!' he spluttered. 'I do not speek Inggris!' He was a local Malay with a dark complexion, and with great hilarity he related the story of how the Dayak warriors had entered his house and held a knife to his throat. '"You're Madurese, you're Madurese!" they say' – with the palm of his hand he mimed the *mandau* blade at his neck – 'I say, "No, no, I'm Malay, I'm Malay!" So they ask someone in the village who knows me, and they say' – pause for dramatic effect – '"It's OK! He's *not* Madurese!" Ha ha ha ha ha!'

On the third day, Father Anselmus agreed to accompany us on the road to the interior. He would introduce us to 'key people', he said, who knew a lot about what had happened. Before we left, Andreas – who had clearly been thinking things over – talked about what he had seen during the first round of killings over the new year.

His family home was north of Pontianak, and he had been near Sanggauledo when the first trouble began there. On 31 December, he saw the Dayaks arriving from the interior and burning the Madurese houses. On New Year's Day, he was in the town square when a crowd of a thousand Dayaks returned from one of their expeditions. 'They were wailing like Indians in a Western, "Whoo-woo-woo-woo." One of them was carrying a head, and another guy came up to me holding something that looked like a piece of tongue. He said, "This is a heart," and raised it to his mouth and started eating it in front of my face.'

Andreas mimicked the action of someone ripping a lump out of a piece of meat. 'It was dark red, but there wasn't a lot of blood on it. It wasn't fresh.' His droopy grin was wider than ever.

The first of Anselmus's key people was a prominent Dayak from Salatiga, which used to have one of the largest Madurese populations. We went to see him at his gold mine, on a huge naked expanse of white sand which suddenly bared itself out of the jungle at the end of a dusty track. It was like a cartoonist's rendering of the archetypal desert: undulating sand dunes dotted with the skulls of animals. The mine consisted of a large open pit into which water trickled through blue rubber tubes. Five boys in headscarves splashed around up to their necks, breaking up the sandy sides of the pond to enrich the mud, which was sucked out by pump through a Heath Robinson construction of bamboo pipes. At the end of the pipes, it trickled over a zigzagging arrangement of wooden steps which were covered with thick sacking. It was in this sacking, if he was lucky, that Sabdi, our miner, would find grains of gold.

He had found none for a week. We sat under an improvised tent, where young men in flip-flops fiddled with oily pieces of dismantled machinery. Sabdi lived on the main road of Salatiga. The houses opposite had been owned by Madurese. On 30 January, they had responded to the rumours about the trouble in Pontianak by taking up their guns and harassing Dayak motorists. Sabdi took his family to stay with friends in the next town, and then returned to Salatiga. On 1 February, five Dayak houses were burned early in the morning. 'I saw clearly what happened,' he said.

Within a few hours, Dayaks started arriving from out of town. The Madurese were soon outnumbered, and began making their escape into the jungle, but about fifty of them stayed behind and found themselves facing a thousand Dayaks. 'Three of them got shot,' said Sabdi. 'Sinem, Haji Marsuli, and another man I didn't know well. The Dayaks took the bodies and cut their heads off with *mandau*. Then they cut open their backs and pulled out the hearts, and they ate the hearts and drank the blood.'

The rest of the Madurese fled. Their houses were burned down and some of the occupants burned to death inside them. The Dayaks followed the fugitives into the jungle. 'Within a week they had killed everyone hiding in the forest,' said Sabdi. 'A couple of days later, I saw about twenty bodies of Madurese on the roadside. They didn't have heads or hearts.' About five of them were children.

Of all the Dayaks I met, Sabdi appeared to be the most troubled by what he had seen, the least susceptible to the glassy grin which spread so reliably over the faces of those who talked about severed heads and decapitated children. 'Yes, I'm glad that the Madurese have gone,' he said, 'because as long as they were here they never stopped fighting. When I saw the bodies, to be honest I felt nothing, as long as they were people I didn't know. But Sinem was my neighbour and my very good friend. I felt sad to see him shot, to see his heart cut out from behind.'

This strange and confused answer comforted me at the time. But when we driving back, Anselmus smiled at me, and asked me what I had made of Sabdi. I said that he was intelligent and precise, a good witness, and Anselmus smiled again. He had run into Sabdi himself, he explained, just after the incident that had been described to us. After the rout of the Madurese, Sabdi had left Salatiga to rejoin his family in the next town where Anselmus also happened to be. The priest had met him as he arrived, and Sabdi's mouth and face had been wet with fresh blood. 'He ate somebody's heart,' smiled Anselmus. 'Maybe he had to do it, so that they would let him leave Salatiga. But it looked to me as if he was in a trance too. He did not know what he had been doing.'

No one we spoke to ever owned up to any personal part in the killings.

*   *   *

Every morning I drove with Budi past the black monument marking the centre of the earth. The day was spent in the northern hemisphere, talking to people in the Dayak villages; in the evening I returned across the Equator to my hotel in the south.

One day in Salatiga a man said, 'Would you like to see the Madurese in the jungle?'

We were sitting in a little restaurant, a concrete room covered with a rusty iron roof, eating big bowls of pork noodle soup. The soup was steaming hot and made us sweat. The man we were talking to was another Dayak leader. He seasoned his soup elaborately with several different kinds of ferocious spice. He sent for his teenage son who arrived on a scooter and climbed into the jeep with Budi and me.

We pulled up in front of a group of a dozen burned-out houses on the edge of the village. In front of them was a bus stop with graffiti which said *Thank you for going back to Madura Island.* We walked towards the jungle, past a mosque. It was deserted, and there was a litter of leaves and broken coconuts in the covered courtyard, but otherwise it was unspoiled. The forest rose up like a wall at the edge of the clearing and, on the far side of the wall, the keening of the insects became suddenly deafening. It was like being inside a huge, violently electrical machine.

We were walking along a thin track, encroached on by ferns and jungle grasses. Every few yards was a rubber tree with a bright gash of white sap running down the trunk into a cup of leaves. Our young guide stopped every now and then to check on one. Behind him walked Budi and then me.

I found myself thinking about tripwires and hand grenades.

Apparently at random, we turned off the track into the thicket. The boy hacked a path for us with his blade. How did he know that this was the place to make the turning? We were five minutes from the road, but I no longer knew which direction it was, and when Budi spoke to him, the boy just smiled vacantly at us and kept hacking. I began making calculations, such as: would a boobytrap be laid so as to kill the person who triggered it, the person at the front? Or would the hand grenade be a few yards behind the tripwire, say where I was now stepping? And would Budi and I be able to overpower this boy if he turned on us? He was eighteen inches shorter than me and skinny, but he had a *mandau*. The vegetation was a yard above my head. I could taste the pork soup in my mouth.

Someone called out from within the jungle, and our guide responded with a laugh. Out of nowhere, from the innards of the jungle, another boy appeared, and the two friends greeted one another. The first boy pointed towards us, as if making an introduction, and the newcomer smiled. He was young and poor and friendly, a skinny Dayak with a machete. But I was losing faith in my ability to read people's smiles. I nodded back, and asked Budi what they were saying. 'I don't know,' he said. 'They are speaking the Dayak language.'

Ten yards further on both boys stopped and pointed with their *mandau*. There, sticking out of the sludge of the jungle floor, was a skeleton.

It was half buried in leaves and sodden clothes, but it was immediately obvious that it was human. Its bright white bones made me think of specimens in school biology labs.

Two hundred yards away there were five more skeletons.

All of them were women. You could tell from their clothes, cheap artificial fibres in gaudy colours which even the jungle could not digest. In three months, the natural shuffling action of the insects and vegetation had cleaned every scrap of flesh off their bones. Here was a line of delicate vertebrae, here a shoulder, here a nest of curved ribs. There was no smell, other than that of the earth and the leaves. None of the skeletons had skulls.

There was a child's purse, empty, with a pattern of yellow kittens. There were patterned nylon shorts, and underwear, with pelvises inside. Suddenly our guides no longer seemed remotely like potential muggers capable of murdering and robbing us; they seemed what they were, undernourished teenagers doing

us a favour. We asked them what had happened to the heads of
the six women.

'From when we first saw them here, they had no heads and
no hearts.'

A few minutes' hack away, amid another soup of muddy
clothes, there were two skulls. They were adult, but close by
there was a pair of elasticated baby's knickers. The boys said
that two weeks after the killings, soldiers had come here and
poured petrol on the skulls and burned the remaining flesh off
them.

I tried to imagine the terror in which these women had died.

They had fled into the jungle with their children, just as a
precaution perhaps, until their men could sort out the trouble
in town. From here they would have heard the shots and smelled
the smoke of their houses burning. Had they understood what
had happened when no help came? Perhaps the braver ones
among them walked back into Salatiga to have a look, and never
returned. How many nights did they spend waiting in the jungle?
Did they hear the *Whoo-woo-woo-woo* and know they were
being hunted? Did they know the Dayaks who killed them? Did
they think (as I was thinking): *This is a joke. You don't cut
people's heads off any more.* Or perhaps they understood it very
well.

Five of them had died together at this spot; the sixth one had
died alone. Had she escaped, or fallen separately in an earlier
encounter? They were killed by men, no doubt, who cut off
their heads and ate their hearts, but they were not violated and
nor was the mosque where their husbands had prayed. Now
they were like their houses, ruined but undisturbed by the side
of the road, ignored except by curious visitors, while the grass
rose up through their ribs to hide their bones.

Budi wanted to take a vertebra away as a souvenir, but I made
him put it back. We walked back to the road.

We shook hands with the rubber tappers. I felt guilty and
ridiculous for having suspected them of leading us into a trap.

We offered to drop them back in town, but they preferred to walk. I tried to give them money, but they refused to take it.

On the way back to Pontianak we dropped in at Andreas and Anselmus's house, where someone was waiting for us. He was the most frightened of all the people I met in Borneo.

For several days, the two priests had been trying to persuade him to see me, but from the moment we walked through the door he seemed to regret the decision. He sat on the far side of the fruit-peel-strewn table and nodded nervously as Anselmus explained to Budi the strict conditions on which he would talk to me. In anything I wrote, his identity must be masked completely. I promised that I would obscure not just his real name, but his profession, his age, his ethnic origin, and even his appearance. Later, when he had relaxed, I began as a tease to haggle with him over this, and won the right to the following details. He was Indonesian (but not Dayak), he was in his late twenties, and he had a thin moustache and a digital watch. The day before I left Pontianak, the man telephoned Budi to inform us of the pseudonym by which he wished to be known: Bernard.

Bernard lived locally, and he had something to show us, in a brown envelope which he pushed across the table.

The envelope contained photographs.

The first few showed burned-out houses, some with smoke still rising from them. On 7 February, a week after the trouble broke, Bernard had driven east towards the interior, shooting two rolls of film along the way.

The pictures showed roadblocks made of upturned tables, with slogans daubed in red on sheets of plywood: *Madurese, Criminals of West Kalimantan; Salatiga Won't Take Madurese Any More; Get the Hell Back to Madura.*

In Senakin, Bernard had arrived in the middle of a Dayak rally. The photographs showed a crowd of a few hundred. They were wearing T-shirts and jeans. They were carrying rifles and *mandau*, and there were feathers tied to their heads with red ribbons, and ribbons on their spears. They held banners bearing anti-Madurese slogans. In one photograph, the crowd held its arms aloft, as if punching the air. In another, the mouths of the Dayaks were open, as if shouting aloud. Behind them you could see the green hills. A group of men stood on the roof of a white bus.

'This was the first time that I felt afraid,' said Bernard.

The Dayaks were from the interior. The men on the bus were members of the regional assembly, sent to calm them down. They were visibly failing to achieve this. 'The Dayaks were all ready for war, and they were possessed, they weren't acting normally,' said Bernard. 'They were completely silent, and then someone screamed, and they all screamed together – "Whoo-woo-woo-woo!"' Standing separately from the local politicians was a group of men under a red sun umbrella. One of them had a red headband, and was speaking into a microphone. This was the *panglima*. 'I have seen politicians speaking to election rallies,' said Bernard, 'and they are nothing compared to the *panglima*. These people would have done anything he said.'

The next pictures were of burned-out houses in Pahauman containing skeletons – one perfect, the other just a curved backbone, like a huge white centipede. Then there was a decapitated corpse lying on the road in a pair of bright blue and red shorts. The corpse's balls bulged in the crutch of its shorts. In one of the shots, the corpse appeared to have a head, but this turned out to be his innards which were piled up on his chest where the heart had been torn out.

Next was a shot of a ditch by the side of the road, where two heads lay side by side. They were reddish orange, as if badly sunburned, the colour of people returning from a beach holiday, and what features were visible had become stylised by decay. A pair of dark eye sockets. A rubbery ear, beneath a slimy sideburn. They looked like pumpkins prepared for Hallowe'en, and left out in the garden for too long.

I asked Bernard if I could make copies of the photographs,

but he was afraid. These prints had been developed quickly, before the authorities had got a grip on the situation, but by now there were spies in the photo labs, he said. A friend of his who had gone back for more copies had had his negatives confiscated, and been visited by the military. If I was going to use them, I would have to take the prints.

Bernard was a poor man, with a sick wife. It hurt his pride to ask for money, but he needed it desperately. In the end I paid him five hundred pounds, and we shook hands on the deal with big awful grins on our faces.

In the car, I caught myself giggling, a strange cold kind of giggling, as I fingered the envelope of prints.

Budi and I drove home, and he told me about his wife and young children, and the anxiety of February when Pontianak was full of rumours of ethnic war and imminent Dayak attack.

His elderly mother lived on her own some distance from Budi's house. His wife's maid, a Dayak, had left the city and gone back to her village in the interior soon after the trouble started. There was a big Chinese population in Pontianak, more secure there than in Java, where Chinese shops and businesses were still burned down or stoned from time to time. But there was a casual, institutionalised discrimination that had kept Budi out of the state university (his academic record had been faultless, but he had failed to pay his bribe), and made it necessary for him to take on a Malay name. Budi's name was like the white shirt and black trousers that he wore every day, the long hours he worked, and the mathematical precision with which he recalled facts and events – an extra effort of adaptation that had to be made to keep up with the rest, to start from where the darker-skinned competition had found itself from the beginning.

We passed a poster which, although I couldn't read it, plainly warned of the dangers of Aids: a giant octopus wrapped its tentacles around the globe, above a stylised illustration of a condom. There had been two cases of Aids in Pontianak, Budi knew, both of them prostitutes of whom there were fewer now than in the past. There used to be a big red-light area: four hundred girls worked there. 'It was so cheap,' said Budi, rather to my surprise. 'Five dollars or less – four dollars. Four dollars – imagine! But it was a low-class place. A lot of fights in there over the girls, because people were drunk. But now it's gone. There were a lot of Muslims, Madurese in that area, and they burned the place down just last year.'

So business had moved to more upmarket venues including, it turned out, my hotel. There I would pay seventy-five dollars; at the cheaper Hotel Flamboyant, twenty-five. For some reason, Budi's knowledge of these venues surprised and slightly disconcerted me. There was a pause.

'You must have had a lot of Asian girls, yeah?' said Budi.

I mumbled non-committally.

'You know what? Javanese girls are a lot more . . . romantic than Chinese girls. They know what we like, they're not awkward, they know how to make love. Chinese girls, they're shy, bashful. They don't know what to say.'

I offered the unconvincing theory that this had to do with the traditional roles offered to women by the respective cultures: Chinese sitting at home with their feet bound with bandages, Javanese dancing erotically in front of their Sultans.

'You're right perhaps,' said Budi, 'but you know what? You can have your own opinion about the Madurese, but Madurese girls' – he exhaled in admiration – 'you should try it. *They know fucking*. It's amazing. I never used to believe it – my friend told me about it, but I thought, "Women are women – it's all the same hole." But he was right. It's not so easy to get it here, especially at the moment, but in Jakarta there are places you can go, massage parlours. I never believed it myself. But it's true.'

I learned later that this is a common belief among Indonesians: Madurese women, it is said, have mastered a technique of strengthening the muscles of their vaginas which they flex dramatically during intercourse. The secret is passed down from grandmothers and mothers and older sisters.

'It's like they're sucking you *inside them*,' said Budi, taking his eyes off the road. 'How do they do it? You're inside them, but they're sucking you.'

It was the durian season, and the villages were full of trucks and tables loaded with the smelly green pods. Even with the windows closed and the air conditioning on, the stink penetrated the inside of the jeep. I had never eaten them before, and the long drives and conversations were punctuated by the recycled taste of my durian burps.

One night we were driving back late through a burned-out settlement on the outskirts of Salatiga when we saw a light by the side of the road. Budi slowed and stopped in front of an unburned house, the only one intact within half a mile. Even I could work out the Indonesian words scratched with charcoal on to the walls: *JAVANESE, We are from JAVA*, they read, *NO MADURESE HERE*. We got out and found a family sitting at a wooden table around a moth-embattled candle.

They were the poorest people I had seen in Borneo. The man was hollow-chested, wrinkled and sickly thin. He and his wife were not old, but they looked more like the grandparents than the mother and father of the children who sat on the ground in grubby T-shirts. Their house contained nothing but a few rags on the floor. They gave us tea and told us what had happened here, and didn't smile or giggle once. I wondered about the life they must have had back in Java, to have exchanged it for this.

Like plenty of people they had sensed the trouble coming, and cleared out of town for a few days. But they had forgotten to mark their home with the slogans on the walls, and the Dayaks had assumed that anywhere left abandoned was Madurese. When the man returned, he found his house burned like all the others around it – the place they were living now had not originally been theirs.

All the Madurese who had stayed behind had been killed. Even their cows were killed, and there were 'hundreds' of heads on open display. Six of the family's neighbours were lying on the road, without heads or hearts, including a woman of eighty.

'How could you tell who they were, if they didn't have heads?' I asked.

'They were my neighbours,' the man said. 'I saw them every day.'

'Were you angry?'

'No,' he replied. 'I was only scared.'

A few more children and friends arrived and joined us around the candle, all of them with the stunned look of the very poor. They all started talking, in their quiet voices, and Budi was having trouble keeping up.

'I saw four or five children. No heads of children, but the body without a head.'

'When the Dayaks killed people, they put the heads in the road, and then gathered them together in one place.'

'They carried them there in a sack . . .'

'. . . the house of the leader of the Dayaks.'

Then one of the daughters ran up to her father and whispered something in his ear. Everyone fell quiet, and the mother began rapping her palm on my notebook and frowning at me. I slipped it into my bag, as the beam of a torch flickered on to the walls of the house. Two figures strode up from behind us.

The torch was pointed directly on to Budi and then on to me. The two newcomers looked at one other and laughed, and I was able to make out their faces. They were young men with long black hair down to their shoulders. They wore shorts and baseball caps, but were bare-chested; on his left side, each had a scabbard containing a *mandau*. One carried a thin hunting rifle, the other a bamboo spear. They laughed again, and sat down beside us.

The one with the rifle sat on the margins with his cap pulled down over his face, but his friend was chatty and bantered with the girls as they brought him tea. He was asking questions which, for some reason, Budi was reluctant to translate for me. There was an explanation of who we were and where we had come from. I heard the words 'England' and 'tourist'. Finally I managed to break in.

'What are you doing out so late?'

'Hunting.'

'What are you hunting?'

'Animals.'

'Have you found any?'

'Not tonight.'

He had a handsome face and glittery eyes. He and his friend were Dayaks, he said, who tapped rubber in the jungle near here. He came from Menjalin; he knew Father Kristof. His family lived a mile or so down the road in Salatiga, a wife and seven children. He was very proud of his children and told us their exact ages, from fourteen down to one year and four months. He liked the Chinese, he told Budi. His sister was married to a Chinese.

'What about Madurese?' I asked.

Budi chuckled anxiously as he translated the question, and there was more unconvincing giggling over the reply.

'He does not like Madurese people,' said Budi. 'He says that they were thieves here, and if they are allowed to escape to Pontianak they will just become pickpockets there. All Madurese people must leave Kalimantan.'

'Where are the Madurese who used to live around here?'

'Some of the bodies were taken away by the police, but around here there are still a lot of bodies in the forest. Nobody dares to take them out of the jungle.'

I said, 'I'm sorry if this is a rude question, but you must have killed a lot of Madurese?'

'He says that he never killed them himself.'

I asked if it was true that Dayaks were immune to bullets, and he laughed.

He chattered on about his sister and his Chinese brother-in-law, who was a businessman. After half an hour, we were such good friends that he shook us by the hand, and even allowed me to pose alongside him in a photograph. (At the sight of the camera his friend receded deeper into the shadows, with his cap pulled further down over his eyes.)

Budi's hands were shaking when we got back into our car. Much of what had been said remained untranslated, but he confirmed what was obvious: that the two men were hunting for Madurese who might have somehow escaped and secretly returned to the site of their former homes. They had seen our car by the road, and been suspicious. 'That was why they were so surprised to see us,' said Budi. 'They said, "We thought you were niggers."'

Budi asked them what they would have done if we had been niggers.

'We would have killed you,' they said. 'Dayaks don't like niggers. All the niggers must leave Kalimantan.'

'He said that he himself hadn't killed,' said Budi. 'But maybe he lied to us.'

I thought: he lied. They were killers. I had never seen war, but I imagined that a certain kind of war depended upon young men like these, and that you found them all over the world, and throughout history, in Cambodia, Bosnia, Rwanda, in every civil and ethnic war. Young men proud of their daughters and sisters who hunt other humans for pleasure. They were frightening, but there was nothing mysterious about them. We drove back fast towards the Equator, less afraid of Dayak magic, but altogether more afraid.

THE BEST PEOPLE

One

Later, people who had heard about the Dayaks and the Madurese in Borneo would say, with smiles of doubt upon their faces, 'So, then – did you actually *see* it?'

'I saw the victims of it,' I would reply. 'I saw their bodies in the jungle. I talked to people who'd seen it, and I saw photographs.'

'But you didn't actually see it with your own eyes. You know . . . *eating.*'

And I had to admit that, no, I hadn't seen it myself.

It was difficult to believe; there were moments when I had doubts about *it* too. An American professor once devoted an entire book to the argument that cannibalism was a myth, propagated by Western anthropologists as another means of elevating 'civilised' man above his 'savage' inferiors. After my newspaper stories from West Kalimantan, there were indignant letters from well-meaning human rights organisations, campaigners on behalf of indigenous peoples, who simply refused to believe that any of it had happened.

Two years passed, and change came quickly to Indonesia. Suharto was forced out, but with the new political freedom came violence. In half a dozen places, people were dying in unconnected local conflicts, and the killings in Borneo began to be forgotten. Then one day, unexpectedly, I went back to West Kalimantan and almost became a cannibal myself.

In the middle of March 1999, a moment of profound anxiety for Indonesia, when the nation itself seemed to be breaking up and slowly sinking, a remarkable gathering took place in the centre of Jakarta. It was held in the Hotel Indonesia, the country's oldest luxury establishment, which for forty years had served as the meeting place of the Jakarta elite. Within the hotel was a world of air-conditioned respectability; outside, around a large fountain at the centre of a traffic-stricken roundabout, dwelt a shifting population of street children, beggars, banjo players and prostitutes. And straddling the road in between, as I passed by chance one afternoon, was a crowd of astonishing people. They yodelled and whooped as they crossed the road; some of them joined hands and stamped their feet as they dodged the cars in an improvised dance. Drivers wound down their windows to have a look; the buskers and street children stared.

Half were barefoot or bare-chested, or both. There was at least one battle spear, a couple of hunting bows, a dozen *mandau* and a score of the ritual daggers known as kris. There were shirts of iridescent batik, sarongs in regionally patterned checks and stripes, and loincloths of straw and cotton. A band of Dayaks bore lozenge-shaped war shields; a group from Irian Jaya wore bird of paradise feathers in their headdresses. There was only one object that they all carried in common: flapping around each neck, in a laminated skin of transparent plastic, an identity pass bearing a name, a photograph and the words *Congress of the Indigenous Peoples of the Archipelago*. The event would continue for the next week, the Hotel Indonesia was the venue, and these were the delegates arriving for the opening ceremony.

The lobby of the hotel had been filled with stalls selling island produce – baskets, blowpipes, drums, fetishes and bowls. There were more than five hundred delegates and their supporters, members of dozens of different ethnic groups from across the islands: frizzy Papuans from Irian, ebullient Bugis from Sulawesi, laconic Badui from West Java. The printed agenda listed the seminars and workshops which were to be convened over the next week. There would be discussion of land rights, customary law and political empowerment; there would be debates and resolutions, and a ten-point list of demands. Indonesians were enjoying more freedom than they had had at any time in the last thirty years, but the congress's communiqué was still bracingly assertive and bold. 'If the state will not acknowledge us,' the document concluded, 'then we will not acknowledge the state.'

There were a few foreigners at the Congress too, members of the organisations which had been so upset by my writing on West Kalimantan. I encountered one of them in the hotel lobby, a British woman who had accused me two years earlier of inventing details of the killings.

'We need to talk,' she said, after we had been introduced. 'I've got a few bones to pick with you.'

'Bones?' I said.

We agreed to meet the following afternoon.

It was getting dark when I returned to my own hotel. I examined the souvenir which I had bought from the stalls in the lobby – a packet of the wood which Father Andreas had shown me two years before, the one which repels the blows of the *mandau*. Then I switched on my computer to look at the latest news.

It was a time of violence all over Indonesia. In the past few weeks, vigilante militias had killed independence activists in East Timor, soldiers had killed independence activists in Irian Jaya, guerrillas had killed soldiers in Aceh, and Christians and Muslims had killed one another in the Spice Islands. In Jakarta, mysterious bombs had been exploding, and in East Java, masked 'ninjas' had murdered and cut to pieces hundreds of men and women accused of witchcraft. But the item which caught my eye this evening was about West Kalimantan.

JAKARTA (AP) Two days of bloody clashes between rival ethnic groups armed with knives and swords killed at least 43 people in a remote corner of Borneo island in Indonesia, police said.

More than 500 houses were burned and several of the

victims were dismembered. One man was decapitated, his head paraded through a village by a screaming crowd, a witness said.

There was a flight to Pontianak the following day. I cancelled my appointment with the woman who had bones to pick, and telephoned the airport.

Two

It was Friday afternoon when I landed in Pontianak, and Budi came to meet me at the airport. 'Hello, Richard,' he said, as we shook hands. 'I think that I know why you are here.'

He had brought with him an envelope of articles from the local paper. The large-scale massacres, he explained, had begun only that week, but lesser killings had been taking place for almost a month. In February, a Madurese passenger on a bus north of Pontianak had refused to pay for his ticket. The driver, according to the paper, had 'glowered' at him, so the Madurese had drawn his dagger and stabbed the man in the abdomen. News of the incident spread quickly among the surrounding villages; in the following week, scores of Madurese houses were burned down and a dozen bodies turned up, some of them decapitated and mutilated.

'Just like two years ago,' I said.

But Budi shook his head.

This time the injured bus driver and those who avenged him were not Dayaks, but the people known as Melayu or 'Malays' – native Muslims who inhabited Borneo's ports and coastal villages. But then four days ago, just before the opening of the Congress of Indigenous Peoples in Jakarta, a Dayak man had also been killed near a Madurese settlement in the interior.

The situation could not have been worse. The scene was set for a slaughter. Along the coast road, three hours north of

Pontianak, the Melayu were mobilising, setting up roadblocks, and sweeping through Madurese settlements. In the interior, the Dayak war parties were also gathering. And trapped in the middle were tens of thousands of Madurese.

Many of them had already fled, and were living as refugees in Pontianak. But thousands more were still in their villages, and the Melayu checkpoints prevented any evacuation by road. The Madurese were gathering on beaches in the hope of escape by boat, and even there their enemies were closing in on them.

'Maybe this will be worse, much worse than 1997,' said Budi, as we drew up at the hotel. 'Two days ago forty-one were killed. Yesterday they said it was sixty-two, and maybe the real number is much higher.'

The killings were concentrated 120 miles away, near the town of Singkawang. Budi went out to find a car and a driver; in a time like this, he explained, he did not want the responsibility of driving as well as being my guide. We met again early the next morning, and set out north from Pontianak.

'The road is so quiet,' Budi said, after we had been driving for half an hour. 'There used to be a lot of buses here, but now everyone is staying at home.' To the left, tracks led down to beaches and the ocean, and on the right was the low green of the jungle. Small outcrops of limestone, isolated from one another like the islands of the sea, loomed out of it and then disappeared behind us. We passed a candy-coloured Chinese temple, and next to it a dilapidated old house with a thatched roof and red lanterns hanging down from the eaves.

In Singkawang we dropped our bags at the hotel, and then set out again on the road north. Ten minutes outside town was a military post where the soldiers lazily waved us through. There was no sudden shock or transformation; the atmosphere of abnormality gathered imperceptibly. The road beyond the town was still quiet, but every few miles young men were to be seen, standing or strolling aimlessly along the side of the road. Several of them carried *mandau* on their belts. I was tired after rising so early, the scenery was monotonously green and even, and I began to nod off in the back of the jeep. It was in this state of blurred tension, between sleep and wakefulness, that I registered the approach of two boys on a motorbike, driving towards us in the opposite direction.

The boy at the front wore a white T-shirt and hunched forward into his handle-bars; his passenger was bare-chested and leaned perilously back. In his right hand, he carried a black sack which he swung around his head causing the bike to wobble. It contained something heavy. Both of the boys wore yellow headbands. They were yelping and hooting and travelling much too fast.

Two miles further on, we stopped at a village where a crowd was milling about in front of a mosque.

They carried knives, pitchforks and metal-tipped spears. There were many more headbands of yellow and red, and faces daubed with red and white paint. The crowd – mostly young men and boys, with a few women and older men – was pressing up against what looked like an old oil drum in the middle of the road; as our jeep pulled up, they clustered around the drum, as if to protect it from sight. A dozen people walked towards the jeep, and there was glaring and muttering when I stepped out. A fat man in a T-shirt and a yellow headband stepped forward, shaking his head and speaking sternly.

'Put down your camera,' hissed Budi. 'Leave it in the car. They want no photograph.'

The crowd was drifting away from the oil drum in twos and threes, and gradually surrounding us and the jeep. I said to Budi, 'Tell them who I am and why I'm here.'

He hesitated, and then began speaking to the fat man. I thought to myself, 'Why *am* I here?' but then Budi had finished, and the crowd was looking at me. It was my turn to speak again.

'Ask them what they're doing over there,' I said, gesturing towards the oil drum. 'Can we have a look?'

The fat man frowned as Budi put the question. Behind him,

the crowd was murmuring to itself. People were smiling at me, and giggling naughtily. I heard certain words in Indonesian, muttered over and over again. Later, I asked Budi what they had been saying. The phrase was: *Show him.*

The fat man led the way towards the oil drum, and the crowd parted on either side. The thing sat on top, wrapped in an elegant green cloth – I thought of the woven sarongs which I had seen at the Congress only two days before. Very delicately, he unwrapped it, and the crowd gave out a chortling sigh.

It was the head of a man in his forties or fifties. His eyes were half open, and his dark skin was turning grey. There was an open gash on his cheek, and a deeper one beneath his lip. Through his nose someone had twisted a cruel metal hook. A laugh went up as a lit cigarette was pushed between his lips. The boys tweaked his face, and patted his head; women came up to stare at him with curious expressions. Later, I saw a man with a machete carving his head like a joint of meat, and passing pieces of his scalp around as souvenirs.

The wounds were clean and bloodless. A man who introduced himself in English as the local schoolmaster explained that he had died early that morning. His name was Ali Wafa, and he was a *kyai*, or local Muslim preacher from the nearby village of Semparu.

'There is another head of a man from the same village who was killed this morning,' Budi said. 'Remember those boys on the motorbike back there? They were carrying it in a bag. They have been taking the heads up and down the road to show them in the villages.'

'Who are these people?' I asked.

'They are Melayu mostly, the people from this village. The ones with the yellow ribbon on their heads are Melayu, and the ones with the red are Dayak.'

'Why did they kill this man?'

The schoolmaster said in English, 'Because he was a bastard. He was an evil bastard. He was the leader of the Madurese.'

The rest of the village had escaped to a small island just off the coast, where they were waiting for boats to carry them to safety. There was only one place left now where the Madurese still held out, and when the schoolmaster spoke its name the young warriors repeated it, and shook their weapons in the air.

'Sambas!' they said, laughing. 'Sambas! Sambas!'

'Sambas is further north of here,' said the schoolmaster. 'Maybe in Sambas there will also be a war tomorrow.'

I said to the schoolmaster, 'Doesn't the army try to stop them?'

'The army is too few,' he replied. 'And they are afraid.'

Three young men thrust their way to the front to take a look at us. They wore cocky smiles; with a lurch, I realised that the red on their faces was partly paint, and partly dried blood. One of them had a black plastic bag tied to his belt, which bulged unpleasantly, as if it was filled with liquid.

'What's in there?' I asked.

'Bread,' the young man replied, and the crowd snickered.

The dizzy tiredness which I had been feeling in the car came over me again. I said to the schoolmaster, 'Who is the leader? Who is the *panglima*?'

'No, no,' he said, and smiled indulgently. 'That is the Dayak people. We are Melayu, and we have no *panglima*. We are Muslims.' He nodded towards the mosque.

Budi and I stood next to one another looking at the head. It was noon and the sun was directly overhead. Neither I, nor the head, nor the crowd around it cast any shadow.

There was a pause. The schoolmaster smiled enquiringly as if more words were expected of me. Then the three cocky young men walked over to the oil drum and wrapped Ali Wafa's head up in the green cloth. A motorbike was wheeled over, and the three of them squeezed on to the single seat, kick-started the engine, and wobbled off down the road.

'Do you have any more questions?' said the schoolmaster. I couldn't think of a single one.

Budi and I climbed back into the jeep. The driver looked pale. Through the rolled-down window the schoolmaster shook our hands and said, 'For myself, I cannot agree with killing, but there has to be a solution to the Madurese people because they cannot live alongside others. If this was not done, then the problem would just get worse. The Madurese people will become stronger, and then there will be no control. It is better for them to go back to their own island. There will be peace when they leave.'

On the way back to Singkawang we came upon a gang of boys who were playing with the other trophy from Ali Wafa's village. It was split at the back and the brain could be seen. Nearby, in a field, a group of men were slaughtering a cow with a machete, hacking through its neck with powerful swings. The cow made no sound and did not struggle. It fell heavily on to its knees and then on to its side, as the blood ran on to the earth.

Sambas was fifty miles from Singkawang, but even at that distance it was obvious that something awful was happening there. Our driver heard the rumours early the following morning; as I was eating my breakfast, he timidly approached to announce that he would not be able to drive us that day. By the time we found another jeep it was after nine, but not a shop or business in Singkawang was open. 'Sambas?' said the officer at the army checkpoint, and when we nodded he shook his head disbelievingly as he raised the bamboo. It was 21 March 1999, a Sunday.

There was no ordinary traffic on the road. The only vehicles were motorbikes, carrying two or even three riders, and buses and large trucks with slatted wooden sides. Each was packed with Melayu dressed raggedly for war. They clung to the roofs of the buses and the running boards of the trucks. They raced one another with crazy speed and the warriors leaned out and waved as they overtook us, shouting, 'Sambas! Sambas!' and pointing up the road.

People fell into two categories that day: those who could not be induced to go near Sambas, and those who could not get there fast enough.

At a town called Pemangkat, we stopped and photographed a group of warriors. It was appalling to see how young they were. The atmosphere was closer to that of a school outing than a war party, an outing which had been hijacked by a gang of horribly over-excited bullies. At the sight of the cameras they pranced and posed rapturously. Most carried small sickles, some had *mandau*, a few had longer swords or spears, and one carried a hunting rifle. With care and ingenuity they had fashioned uniforms for themselves with ribbons and bandannas, scarves and balaclavas. One young boy wore a strip of red cloth covering his face into which he had cut two eyeholes. In his T-shirt and his shorts, with his bad teeth and his childish grin, he looked like a naughty boy dressed up for Hallowe'en.

Beyond Pemangkat, we passed rows of burned and smouldering houses by the side of the road. Distant columns of smoke rose up from the jungle, each one of them representing another Madurese village. The new driver knew all their names and pointed them out as we passed: Selekau, Setimbuk and, far down towards the sea, Segaru, the island where the Madurese refugees were awaiting their Dunkirk. Had the boats come to rescue them in time? Or had the Melayu gone in, and 'finished' it, as they had promised?

Ten minutes before Sambas thick billows of smoke were visible, rising from a point close to, but outside, the town. We passed through an army checkpoint; the soldiers were doing nothing to stop the trucks of arriving warriors. Budi asked the name of the place from where the smoke was billowing, and the officer told us it was a Madurese hamlet named Suka Ramai. 'It is a strange name,' said Budi. 'Suka Ramai. The words mean "I love noise" or "I love trouble".'

Sambas was a small market town, the usual agglomeration of wooden homes and low concrete commercial buildings shaped around a square. The metal shutters on the first-floor shops were all drawn down and padlocked. Not a single person was to be seen outside. At a T-junction on the edge of town, a massed body of men had gathered: older men than the imps in Pemangkat, big, burly men with long knives and a dozen rifles between them. To the right, a narrow road led towards Suka Ramai.

Half a dozen reporters and cameramen were already standing uncertainly at the junction. We stopped the jeep and cautiously walked towards them.

A man on a motorbike emerged from the direction of the smoke, and came to a jerky stop. In one hand he brandished a curved sword and in the other he held out an object attached to a short length of string. It was pink and delicate and abstract-looking, and it took several seconds to piece together the visual information and to understand that it was a human ear.

The man dismounted, kicked out the stand on his bike and sat on it facing us. A cameraman and two photographers took up positions in front of him; he brandished the ear like a medal, and held it still so that they could focus their lenses. He wore a yellow headband daubed with paint, and there was blood on the sleeve of his jacket and on the blade of the sword. There were fine beads of sweat on his lip, and he was shouting into the cameras in a barking, staccato manner. Was this the state of possession, the battle trance about which I had heard so much? He was a handsome man, with frowning muscular brows and shapely lips. As he spoke I noticed his teeth, which were very white and evenly spaced. I stared at the small dainty ear and began to feel as if I was falling into a trance myself.

'What does he say?' I whispered to Budi.

'He says, "We don't care about your race. We don't care about your religion. Christian, Muslim, Buddhist, Dayak, Melayu, Chinese or Buginese – all of them are welcome here. We just don't want Madurese. All the Madurese must leave."'

'Ask him what is happening up there.'

Budi asked. 'He says go and see for yourselves.'

'*Silahkan, silahkan*,' said the man with the ear, pointing up the road, towards the smoke. Go ahead. Be our guest.

A mile of fields lay between Suka Ramai and the spot where now we stood. The road across them ran dead straight. The cameramen and reporters exchanged hesitant glances. I had never before felt simultaneously such extremes of eagerness and reluctance. My body felt light, as if I might float away from the earth. It wasn't fear, because there was a weird absence of any personal threat. It wasn't suspense, for it was obvious what was happening up the road. But it was impossible to turn back now.

The driver refused to take the jeep any further. As we began to walk silently towards I Love Trouble, another truck overtook us and the warriors packed into the back cheered and waved their blades. A thin man on a bicycle passed by in the opposite direction, with a little girl perched on the handlebars; both of them waved and smiled. The surface of the road was in good condition; we passed one smooth patch which was sticky with blood.

A scattered group of warriors appeared from the direction of the village, jogging towards us out of the smoke, waving their weapons. A man carrying a spear ran up to me, grinning delightedly, and shook my hand. 'Anti-Madura!' he shouted. 'Madura, no! No Madura!'

Now there were hundreds of young men streaming down the road past us. They were all smiling, and panting with exertion and excitement. More of them stopped to talk.

'Ask them where they come from,' I told Budi.

'Pemangkat,' said one boy in a T-shirt bearing a map of the London Underground. 'But I haven't been there for seven days.'

'What have you been doing?'

'We have been hunting the Madurese people.'

'What do you do if you find them?'

'We kill them directly, then take the head and chop it.'

'Why do you chop the head?'

'It is our tradition.'

Then a boy in a white vest was walking towards me, holding a human arm, severed below the elbow. All of the fingers and much of the skin had been stripped off the hand. Bone and muscle bulged out of the other end.

When the warriors had gone, Budi said, 'It is not their tradition. It is a Dayak tradition, but they are Melayu.'

Soon I could smell the smoke of the burning houses. There were perhaps a dozen houses in Suka Ramai, and all of them were in flames. There had been a hundred Madurese holding out here, and at least a thousand Melayu in the raiding party. A few of the Madurese had stayed behind to put up a fight; after two of them were shot, the others had run off into the jungle. Some of the raiders had stayed in the village to chop up and divide the two bodies; the rest had crossed the fields to hunt down the fugitives in the forest. But they had made a clean escape, and the tired, thirsty Melayu were returning to the burning village. We were arriving at the tail end of the hunt; the fun was over for the day. A battered pickup halted beside us, and a Chinese man began unloading boxes of bottled water and handing them out to the warriors.

There was nothing else to do, so we walked back along the road. I felt obscurely disappointed, as if the point of the afternoon had passed me by. We climbed into the jeep and drove back into Sambas to find water ourselves.

In the market square a few of the young warriors were standing around, and a single shop was open. There was a stand selling the kebabs called *sate*; nearby smouldered the embers of a fire. Among them was a charred human femur. Budi noticed it at the same time as me, and he suddenly looked stricken. His lips trembled and he was on the edge of tears.

'Let's go, Richard,' he said in a low, strangled tone.

I walked quickly to the shop to buy water and cigarettes.

As I was fumbling for the money, a tall man in a yellow headband walked over from the *sate* cart. On his belt hung a rusty handgun, as well as two of the bulging plastic bags I had seen the day before. In greasy fingers he held a piece of grey, fibrous, partly cooked meat impaled upon a stick of wood. He pulled off a piece with his teeth and chewed it. His face was a foot away from mine.

He held the kebab out to me, and smiled. '*Silahkan.*' Please eat.

The other boys in the square had gathered round and were laughing. '*Silahkan! Silahkan!*'

'No, thank you.'

Budi walked up, looking agonised. 'Please, Richard, let's go.'

The man continued to push the meat towards me, talking excitedly.

'Tell him no, I don't want it.'

But he wouldn't take no for an answer, as he waved the stick of meat in my face.

I experienced again the sensation of light trance, and of gravity failing around me. I thought about how easy it would be to take the meat, and to eat it. I thought about the animals which I had eaten over the years: horse, dog, monkey, snake, snail, slug. I remembered in particular the monkey, which had been grilled over a fire in a jungle village. Its meat had been tough and gamey, but afterwards I had seen a relic of it: a simian right arm, hand and portions of a ribcage. The skin was charred, but patches of fine grey fur were still visible and the hand had ten delicate fingernails, like the nails of a newborn baby. How far was a monkey from being a human? How close was I to being a cannibal? My dreaminess deepened as I pondered the consequences of my actions in the next two or three seconds: *I, a cannibal* . . . But the piece of meat looked cold and unappetising. I needed to drink water before I could think about eating.

'Ha!' said the kebab man with a cackle. He pulled the meat away and stuck it into his mouth, and I felt my knees going cold with relief.

There were so many questions I could have asked. I asked the first one that came into my head.

'Delicious,' he said, when Budi had translated. 'Like chicken.'

We walked back to the jeep, and the kebab man followed us, with a group of young Melayu, all of them laughing and jabbering and pointing behind them.

'Oh *no*,' said Budi quietly.

'What is it?'

'They've got more . . . meat. They want to show it to us. They want us to eat.'

'Let's just go.' But the hands of the Melayu kebab man were on my shirt and he was tugging me back from the open door of the jeep. 'No thank you,' I said, trying to keep a smile on my face as I unpicked his fingers. 'No thank you. Let go.'

The driver was frowning and sweating, as we struggled to close the doors. Then the engine wouldn't start. Twice, it rumbled and grated and then died. Budi was muttering something, perhaps even a prayer. Outside, the kebab man and his friends were tapping on the window, and bouncing ecstatically up and down. Then the engine started up, and we began to reverse slowly into the road. The men outside were miming the action of a pair of chopsticks over a bowl of rice. They were shouting words I understood: '*Makan! Makan!*' and '*Silahkan!*' They chased after the car as we drove away.

Makan. Silahkan.

Dinner time! Be our guest!

Three

I saw my sixth and seventh heads on Tuesday afternoon in a Dayak village an hour's drive from the town. They were visible from a few hundred yards away, standing on oil drums on either side of the road, with a crowd of about two hundred people milling around them. Most of the onlookers were men, but there were young women and children there too. 'What do you want to do?' said the man who was accompanying us, a Dayak leader in his fifties. I said that I wanted to have a look.

We walked up towards them, past the warriors with their spears and red headbands and hunting rifles. Even in big cities in Indonesia, people shout greetings when a foreigner passes by, but these people looked at me with indifference. The heads had been taken just a few hours before, and they looked . . . they looked like all the other heads I had seen.

They were a middle-aged couple, a few years younger than my own parents. Their ears and lips had been shaved off with machetes, giving them a snarling, subhuman look. The wife's nose had also been removed, and a cigarette had been pressed into the cavity. Her eyes were clenched tight shut, and above them an atrocious wound had been cut deep into her forehead. Why did I take photographs of the heads, knowing perfectly well that no newspaper could ever print them? Was it simply in order to document the event? Or were there baser, more prurient motives?

I had never worked in such conditions before, and nor had anyone I knew. The experience produced two contradictory reactions. The first was relief, together with a guilty pride, in finding myself able to confront horror without being overcome by nausea or fear. The second reaction took the form of troubling questions, which nagged me at odd moments. Why was I not more upset by this? What was wrong with me? I don't know what to call such an emotion, but it is something close to shame.

Two years earlier, when few people understood the scale of what had happened between the Dayaks and the Madurese, I had spent a fortnight in Borneo searching for cannibalism and headhunting. I had found witnesses, photographs and skeletons in the jungle, but not the thing that I secretly knew I was seeking. Afterwards, I wrote long newspaper and magazine articles – tens of thousands of words, all about failing to find a severed head. In March 1999, in the space of four days, I saw seven of them, along with a severed ear, an arm, a hand, numerous pieces of heart and liver, and a dismembered torso being cooked over a fire by the side of the road – and I find myself at a loss over what to say. The most devastating thing about black magic is not the blood and darkness, but the gaping, profound banality.

By the time the attack on I Love Trouble was done, hundreds of Madurese had been decapitated and eaten, 10,000 had fled as refugees to Pontianak, and there were almost none left alive in the settlements along the coast. But another road ran west from Singkawang and into the forests of the Dayak interior. It was here, everyone said, that the killings were now taking place.

Dayak leaders in Singkawang were adamant that this was a conflict between Melayu and Madurese; the Dayaks, they insisted, were staying out of it. But the driver of our jeep, whose name was Petrus, travelled along the jungle road one afternoon to visit his brother and Dayak sister-in-law. 'You should see what it is like,' he said when he returned. 'You've never seen anything like it.' Petrus was a chubby, smiling man, a Christian from the eastern island of Flores. He had many friends among the Dayaks, he said, and could provide some useful introductions. As we were setting out for the interior on Tuesday morning, he smiled at me again and said, 'It is unbelievable up there. Have you got the guts?'

The landscape was quite different from that of the coastal road: instead of low scrappy undergrowth, the trees on either side were thick and looming, and the limestone hills beyond them were rough and high. Within fifteen minutes of leaving Singkawang, we were driving past deep jungle. We passed a military barracks with pillars carved in the shape of Dayak shields; a few hundred yards on was a Christian cemetery cut out of the forest, with wooden crosses and whitewashed stone walls. 'Now we are in the Dayak area,' announced Petrus. In Borneo, I was always conscious of crossing boundaries, visible and invisible doors which would open silently and then close behind me with a click.

Two wooden barrels flanking the road marked the entrance to a village. There was a butcher's shop with cuts of beef hanging from meat hooks, and a food cart with a crude Union Jack painted on the side. Then the road turned a corner, and immediately ahead were three hundred Dayak warriors with rifles and headbands.

Petrus slowed the jeep to a halt, and leaned out of the window. A Dayak with a spear approached warily, then smiled as he recognised Petrus. The two clasped hands, and Petrus gestured towards me with words of explanation. The man's T-shirt also bore a Union Jack.

'It is because they like English football,' Petrus said. 'Dayaks love football – Manchester United, Tottenham Hotspur.'

Two miles further on, there was a roadblock of bamboo poles balanced across two tables. On each of the tables was a scraggy head. One of them was mutilated unrecognisably and rubbery-grey in colour. The other was that of a boy, barely a teenager, his eyes open and his skin smeared with blood.

There were more smiles and handshakes for Petrus, and more polite nods to Budi and me in the back.

A few miles further still, there was another checkpoint, and another head. There were no warriors here, so Petrus simply manoeuvred around the obstacles and through the narrow gap. At one point, the side of the jeep brushed with a bump against the table on which the head rested. The head was that of a young man. It wobbled uncertainly on its stump of neck; for a moment of horror, I believed that it was going to topple and roll on to the ground. Why should the thought of the severed head falling be worse than the fact of the head itself? But it quickly ceased wobbling, and we edged safely through to the other side.

In the town of Semelantan we visited the district office and heard the story of Martinus Amat, the Dayak whose death provoked the killings in the interior. The district chief was a Dayak, and next to him sat the local army chief, a Melayu major. They were friendly and open, with occasional moments of evasiveness and embarrassment. They were acutely conscious that within their community they had lost all control.

'There are two versions of what happened to Martinus Amat,' said the district chief after we had introduced ourselves. 'This is the first one.'

Martinus was an eighteen-year-old from Semelantan. He had been one of a group of Dayaks in the back of a pickup truck as it had driven to Singkawang a week before. Close to the village of Jirak, according to the other passengers, a group of men stopped the truck, and began shouting angrily at the occupants.

'They kept asking, "Where is the fat Melayu?"' the district chief said.

The Dayaks in the back of the pickup leaped out and fled, but when Martinus jumped he hurt his leg and couldn't run away. He was set upon and beaten, and the beating killed him. 'It happened on the 16th of March at 2 p.m.,' said the district chief. 'It was midnight when I heard and by that time he was dead.'

Within Semelantan and the surrounding villages, at least, nobody had any doubts about what had happened: once again, a blameless young man had been murdered without provocation by a gang of Madurese. Even the Madurese themselves made the same assumption about the identity of the killers. The district chief collected Martinus's body from the army hospital at 9.30 on the morning after he died. Along the road, Madurese families were already stacking up their possessions and boarding buses, in certain anticipation of revenge.

'I went to the house of Martinus's family,' the district chief said. 'I handed over the body, and tried to cool them down. I was away for less than an hour. But when I got back, the Madurese houses in Jirak had already been burned down by a mob.'

The second version of the story was virtually the same as the first – the stopping of the pickup, the search for 'the fat Melayu', the death of the boy. The difference was the identity of the men who killed him. There was one friend of Martinus's who had stayed by the truck and been there when he died; after it was too late, when the burning and killing were well underway, the district chief had talked to him at length. The boy said that the attackers had been shocked when they realised that Martinus had died from his beating. They asked the boy where Martinus lived, and when he told them that he was from Semelantan the men looked upset. They apologised for what they had done. They gave the boy cigarettes, and then they ran away.

'I'm not completely sure because I wasn't there,' said the district chief. 'But, from what I heard from that boy, it was Dayaks who killed Martinus.'

He stopped speaking for a moment as we absorbed this information.

'They were Dayaks,' said the major. 'They were looking for a Malay man – perhaps he owed them money. They thought that Martinus was the Malay, and they beat him up to scare him. But by accident he died.'

The district chief said, 'It was Dayaks killing a Dayak. But no one wants to hear this now.'

He shook his head and smiled. The major stared at the floor with folded arms. Nobody spoke for a while.

'How many of the Madurese do you think escaped to safety?' I said.

The district chief looked at the major, but he didn't return the look.

'Some,' he said eventually.

'How many are still hiding in the forest?'

'Hundreds. Hundreds and hundreds. They are hunting them down now.'

'And how many are dead?'

A pause. 'There are people killed,' he said, with strain. 'But I don't feel authorised to tell you how many.'

'It's very difficult to know the exact number,' said the major.

'Sometimes, a man will be carrying a hand, and he'll say, "I killed one." Another will be carrying a leg, and he'll say, "I killed one too." But the hand and the leg may be from the same body. So we count the number of heads.'

People in the villages reckoned that more than two hundred Madurese had been killed so far in the district of Semelantan, and that they were still being killed, at the rate of about thirty a day. Along the road, every few hundred yards, we encountered small groups of young Dayaks, stepping into or out of the jungle, armed and excited. These were the hunting parties, and the hunt was continuing. Even when we couldn't see them, we could hear the sound of their cries through the trees, the chilling, childish *Whoo-woo-woo-woo-woo!* Before we left Semelantan, Petrus stopped at a stall and bought forty packets of *kretek* to hand out at the checkpoints. Within an hour and a half, all the cigarettes had gone.

The further we travelled into the jungle, the poorer the Dayak villages became. Evidently, we were crossing another boundary here, into a harsher and more unpredictable realm. A man named Tomas, the leader of a Dayak community organisation, accompanied us to smooth things over with the hunters, although for much of the time he was the most nervous person in the jeep.

I counted up the number of heads I had seen since arriving in Borneo on Saturday. There had been five. Why was I travelling into the forest and what did I expect to find there? I didn't know any more.

It was in a village called Montrado that I saw the sixth and seventh heads, the middle-aged husband and wife, facing one another across the road on separate oil drums.

After I had looked at them for a bit, Tomas came up and said, 'Do you want to see some Madurese?'

I shook my head.

'But these people are alive,' said Tomas. 'They are the last living Madurese in Montrado.'

They were sheltering in the house of the Dayak chief – two families of eight people altogether, including four children. I glimpsed them as we were led inside – dark, hollow faces peeping around a door at the back. The chief, whose name was Elias Ubek, told us the story of how he had saved them the night before. 'I am the leader of these people,' he said, 'and I cannot cool them down. Last night I almost became a corpse myself.'

The killings in Montrado had been going on for three days. Elias Ubek reckoned that there had been 170 Madurese families here, and that seventy people – about a tenth of the population – had been murdered so far. But those were just the ones he knew about.

Elias was a skinny man with lank, murky hair and a jaundiced tinge to his skin. His small plaster house was the biggest in the village. The cramped room in which we sat contained bamboo furniture and devotional trinkets; one wall was hung with a lurid tapestry of the Sacred Heart. 'Some are shot, some are hacked,' Elias said. 'They don't care about women, children. They kill wives, husbands, they kill the children. Sometimes they pour petrol on them and burn them while they're alive. I must have seen about six or seven children myself. Two of them were babies. Three or four months old. They chopped their heads off too.'

The people whom Elias saved had been caught the day before. 'One of them is a Javanese family – the woman was widowed, and she remarried a Madurese. The other family has Chinese blood. So they are not all pure Madurese themselves. Still they tied them up, and they were about to do them in, when some of our people recognised them and told them no. But the one who wanted to kill them, the leader, he isn't a local man. He came from Darit. Those Dayaks are so violent – sometimes the local people try to stop them, but they are uncontrollable. They are unconscious, it is a supernatural spirit. They eat many of them.'

Elias poured out tea into cups with pictures of Jesus on the side. 'I went out and untied the people they were going to kill and brought them quickly in here. The mob was so angry. I told them that if you want to kill them you'll have to kill me first.'

The army command in Singkawang had been told about the Madurese, and had promised to send a truck to pick them up. A convoy was said to be making its way even now, but it was being harried along the way by the Dayak warriors. 'I face such difficulties here, until these people are evacuated,' said Elias. 'I haven't rested for three days and two nights. I think that many of the Dayaks here hate me now. They despise me because I am against the killing. But that's the risk. I've got to resist their anger.'

Beyond Montrado, the road was lively with traffic. A few hundred yards along the road, we watched a hunting party disappear into the jungle on the right, and a little later two boys rode past on a bicycle, with a severed hand bobbing from the handlebars at the end of a piece of string. At the next corner, I found myself parting with a 10,000-rupiah bill – a 'loan', as it was called, to a tall young man with a transparent bag of liver tied to his belt. The Dayaks who were waving us down here all had questions, about me, about the other occupants of the jeep, and about the reasons for our journey. Word had got around that treacherous Dayaks were collaborating with the enemy in order to frustrate the hunters; it was necessary to reassure them that there were no fleeing Madurese in this jeep.

For the next three miles the road was deserted. Then there was a T-junction where a number of small fires were visible at the side of the road. About a dozen Dayaks were tending to them busily. Knives and *mandau* could be seen; above the flames, they were erecting frames of sticks for cooking. Behind them were a number of pink objects on a low stone wall. As we passed I saw two legs, a limbless trunk. Something else, perhaps an arm, was being positioned over the flames.

The Dayaks were absorbed in the preparations for the barbecue, and they ignored the jeep.

'Don't stop, Petrus,' I said.

Five minutes later, we were waved down again and as the jeep slowed a young warrior opened the door, smiled apologetically and jumped into the back. This is great, I thought. First, I give a cannibal a tip – now I'm giving them taxi rides.

Our cannibal was a teenager. He was shirtless, and wore neat jeans and worn trainers. In his hand he carried a sheathed *mandau*, with a red-painted handle carved into the shape of a horse. It looked brand new, the kind of thing you would buy from a tourist craft shop. I thought of the *Whoo-woo-woo-woo-woo!*, the wail of the Dayaks on the trail of a flagging victim, like Apaches in a Western. My new friend looked like nothing so much as the participant in a giant game of cowboys and indians.

He was chattering with excitement about the things that he had seen and done. He told us that the man whom they were cooking on the road had been caught that morning. 'We killed it and we ate it,' he says, 'because we hate the Madurese.' He had taken part in four killings himself. 'Mostly we shoot them first, and then we chop the body. It tastes just like chicken. Especially the liver – just the same as chicken.'

I asked him about the heads of the children and babies which Elias Ubek had seen in Montrado, but he shook his head and laughed. 'We don't kill babies! If we find a baby we give it to other people. In fact, we found a kid and a baby and we saved them.'

'How old does someone have to be before you will kill them?' I asked.

'Around thirteen or fifteen,' he said.

'Why do you kill them? Why don't you just send them all away?'

'Because we hate them.'

Twenty minutes down the road, he got out at his village. He was bubblingly grateful. We had saved him a tiring walk at the end of a long, exciting day. A bit later on, Petrus spoke up. 'You know, I've been all over this country – to Sumatra, to Java, all over eastern Indonesia,' he said, 'and these people – they're the nicest, the friendliest, the best. There's no one like them.'

He was perfectly serious, and what he said was true. There couldn't be any doubt that this was evil in its most bestial form. But these were not evil people, and this was not an evil place.

Four

Most of the photographs I took in Borneo could never be published, but at one of the checkpoints, between Pemangkat and Singkawang, I made an effort to frame something printable. A group of Melayu boys were playing with a head on an oil drum. The routine was familiar: the patting and poking, the cigarette stuffed up the nose, and the keepsakes of skin and scalp. Two young brothers were in charge of the head, and they were delighted to show it off. For five minutes, I snapped them as they clowned with their atrocity. Then they grew bored and begged some cigarettes from the driver. I left them by the jeep with Budi and walked back down the road.

My idea was to take a shot from behind. There would be no doubt what was depicted – the head of a decapitated man on an oil drum – but without the slashed mouth and lidless eyes, and the ribbons of tissue trailing from the neck. I had knelt down and was raising the camera, when the younger of the brothers spotted what I was doing. He raised his hand, ran forward, then picked up the head and turned it round through 180 degrees to face me. I walked round to the other side, and tried again. The same thing happened. The boy was trying to be helpful. He couldn't understand why I should avoid the face of the dead man. He wanted to give me the very best view of this magical object that was bringing him and his brother so much excitement and delight.

There were moments, when the hunt was underway and

immediately after a kill, when the more murderous among the warriors became abstracted and withdrawn; at those moments, it was easy to believe in spirits, or at least in bloodlust. But among most of them the overwhelming mood of those few days was jubiliation. Piled into their buses, with their motley colours and their chants, they were like fans of a triumphant football team, a team which after long years of undeserved obscurity had suddenly, through courage and persistence, achieved a famous victory. In Montrado, an old woman approached me as I was looking at the heads, and repeated a single phrase: 'At last, at last, at last . . .' Rather than exultation, there was relief – that a wrong had finally been set right, and a threat that had hung over the population for years had been decisively removed. This was the strangest, and the most pitiful, thing about being among cannibals in Borneo: not how angry, but how happy they were.

I gave up trying to take my photograph and looked at the boy with the head. He was about twelve years old, his brother fifteen. In their lifetimes, the purging of the Madurese and the coming to their village of this trophy were the grandest, the noblest, the most glamorous events they had ever known. Something had changed; justice had been achieved. How poor an existence these people had, that this hairy lump on an oil drum should be an emblem of morality and hope.

Beside a burning house on the road to Sambas, a boy with a yellow headband said, 'These were all Melayu fields once, but the Madurese took them over. They use violence, and until now we have never used violence in return. When they use force against us our dignity rises up. And so we burn their houses. We take our heart's revenge, and we don't want them to come back.'

A Melayu man holding a Madurese head by the hair said, 'People have wanted to do this for such a long time, such a long time. The Madurese have a different society from us. They are so different from the Chinese, the Melayu, the Bugis. Many,

many times we have told the police about this, about the problems we face with these people. But nobody listens. So there is no alternative. The Madurese have to go.'

I never got to know a Madurese – for obvious reasons it was impossible in West Kalimantan at that time. The closest I got was the faces peering round Elias Ubek's door, and later the thousands in the displacement camp in Pontianak – unsmiling and uncomplaining, making do with small boxes of noodles and bags of wheat, as helpless and baffled as refugees anywhere in the world. But everyone else I spoke to in Borneo agreed that, as a community, they were impossible to live with.

They were clannish, aggressive and predatory. They resorted to violence at the slightest provocation. They were poor, of course – but everyone in Borneo was poor. 'They cannot exist peacefully alongside other people,' Budi said. 'Chinese, Melayu, Dayaks – we can get on together. But Madurese just love to fight and steal.' Hearing this often enough, you begin to believe it. But it also sounds unpleasantly like the kind of consensus that has built up at various times about Romany Gypsies, or about Jews.

And yet in the war against the Madurese, there was no trace of the beliefs which inspire other ethnic conflicts – no doctrine of superiority, no urge to expansionism or memory of historical injustice. The notion of a Melayu nationalist or a Dayak supremacist was ridiculous. There were no propagandists or ideologues; there were scarcely any leaders. Even tribalism did not explain it, for there was nothing tribal uniting the Melayu with the Dayaks and the Buginese.

The Indonesian word which I heard over and again was *adat*, usually translated as 'traditional law'. It is *adat* which is violated when somebody steals durians from the tree that has always belonged to your ancestors, and waves a sickle at you when you remonstrate with him. 'In the eyes of Dayaks,' a Dayak teacher said, 'when people do not respect our *adat*, they become enemies, and we don't consider our enemies to be human any more. They become animals in our eyes. And the Dayaks eat animals.'

The army convoy reached Montrado that evening. One of the trucks parked directly in front of Elias Ubek's house, and lowered its tailgate. The Dayak warriors had been waiting all day. They crowded up around the truck, three or four hundred of them, jeering and whooping. The soldiers in the truck screamed at them and pointed their rifles. But it was they, and not the Dayaks, who were afraid.

One by one, the eight Madurese ran out of Elias's house and leaped into the arms of the soldiers who dragged them up into the trucks. Every time, the crowd jeered and spat.

When all of them were inside, huddling under blankets on the floor, the convoy turned round and set off back to Singkawang. The sun had already set. There were twelve trucks, each containing about a dozen soldiers – 150 men to protect a handful of Madurese.

Near Jirak, the convoy was ambushed. Gangs of Dayaks began firing from both sides of the road, and the soldiers fired back. The warriors were armed with hunting rifles, home-made blunderbusses, slings, and bows and arrows. The soldiers carried automatic assault rifles. 'The Dayaks had no chance,' said a photographer, who was riding in one of the army trucks. 'They were standing a few feet away pointing their pop-guns. The soldiers were protected by the trucks. They could take their time, they were aiming directly at them.' It was late that same evening, and the photographer and I were sitting in the hotel in Singkawang. It was my last night in Borneo.

The photographer said, 'One of the Dayaks had a huge bird mask. It looked like the head of an eagle, with a great feather head-dress. I saw it standing by the road, walking up and down during the shooting. Then it was running away back into the forest.'

By the time the Dayaks had retreated, four of them were lying dead on the road. Not a single soldier or Madurese was hurt.

THE RADIANT LIGHT: JAVA 1998

KRISMON

In Yogyakarta, in the spring of 1998, a student at the university gave me a copy of the *Prelambang Jayabaya*, the greatest and most famous of the prophecies of ancient Java. King Jayabaya – or Joyoboyo, or Djajabaja, or Jaya Abhaya – lived in the twelfth century, and the verses which bear his name began to circulate six hundred years later. 'The Nostradamus of Java,' said my student friend, whose name was Nuri. And sure enough, the prophecies of Jayabaya had the same vague yet nagging suggestiveness, which enabled people in every age to believe that they were witnessing their fulfilment.

> One day shall come a cart without a horse,
> An iron necklace will circle Java's shores,
> Then shall a boat fly in the sky,
> Then shall the river cease to flow:
> And these shall be the signs that the time of
> Jayabaya is at hand.

Cars, railways, aeroplanes, dams... Far from being welcome advances, to the Jayabaya poet these were omens of doom. The verses embodied a recurring theme in Javanese thinking, the belief that peace and prosperity, by their nature, could never last. If Europeans viewed history as progress, to Javanese it had always been a process of cyclical repetition. An Age of Gold was followed by an Age of Darkness, and then by another Age of Gold. Their alternation was inescapable, a principle of the universe more powerful than any man.

The poem described the disasters that beset the land during the Age of Darkness. Crops failed, bringing famines and epidemics. Pirates and brigands flourished. Violence and hardship forced entire populations out of their villages and on to the road. Unnatural and impious behaviour prevailed, between parents and children, men and women, the rulers and the ruled, even among animals.

> The earth will shrink and every inch be taxed,
> Horses will gorge themselves on chilli paste,
> Women will dress themselves in clothes of men,
> And these will be the signs that the world turns upside down.

> The rains will fall out of their natural turn,
> The corrupt will spend their fortunes lavishly,
> The king who breaks his promise will lose power.

> Then holy temples will be scorned with hate,
> And persecution crush the innocent.
> The pure of heart will with misfortune meet.
> The ministers will become common men,
> The little folk will rise up to be lords.

I met Nuri in Gajah Mada University, Yogyakarta's most famous campus. As we talked, in the shadow of a banana tree in front of the university offices, a mass of students was gathering for the biggest demonstration to have taken place in the city for more than thirty years. The girls wore tight jeans and blouses, and on their heads the *jilbab*, the white Muslim headscarf. The boys wore T-shirts and university blazers in bright primary colours. Most sat on the grass talking, or stood smoking under the trees. Teams of students with paint and markers put the finishing touches to banners spread out on the grass.

There were at least 10,000 demonstrators that day. They began their march early in the morning, and the speeches and chanting went on all afternoon. Amien Rais, the closest the movement had to a national leader, was a professor at Gajah Mada. 'Students are an objective political force in this country,' he said later. 'What happened in the Philippines and in Iran has given us inspiration to mobilise People Power.'

At nine o'clock, when the students began their slow procession, the chants were seemly enough: reject Suharto, and lower prices. An hour later, they were mispronouncing the president's name as the Indonesian equivalent of 'Arsehole-harto', and by noon, they were shouting 'Hang the President'. Confined to the narrow paths and roads of the campus, they seemed a multitude. As they finished their march, the demonstrators produced an effigy of Suharto, with limbs of stuffed stockings and a crudely painted face. They set fire to him on the grass, and cheered and whooped as the smoke rose. Then, after a final round of chants and slogans, they began quietly to disperse.

In old Java, nothing was without meaning and everything could be interpreted. A bridge collapsed, killing the servants of a minister: that man's days at court were numbered. The wild animals of the forest were seen wandering in the city: the city would fall to its enemies. Earthquakes, volcanic eruptions, eclipses and comets were recorded in the chronicles, along with the disasters which they presaged – and, inevitably, in the telling of their stories the historians proved themselves right. But what would have been recorded in the annals of Java in the last years of the twentieth century?

In 1996 – the thirty-first year of Suharto's New Order – Megawati Sukarnoputri, daughter of the old president, Sukarno, was forced out by the government from the leadership of the opposition democratic party. Her supporters were enraged, and mounted a peaceful protest, the protest which I had seen in the party headquarters on my first visit to Indonesia. The headquarters was raided by commandos with concealed knives. The capital rioted.

In the thirty-second year of the New Order, 1997, thousands of Madurese were decapitated and cannibalised by Dayaks on the island of Borneo. During the campaign for that year's election, there were violent disturbances across the land. Suharto's party won, but the people sneered at his victory. In the wet season no rain fell. Crops failed, and the jungles of Borneo and Sumatra burned in uncontrollable fires.

Smoke from the Indonesian fires choked the people of Malaysia, Singapore, Thailand and Brunei. Cars crashed on the smog-choked roads, and ships collided in the sea lanes. A passenger plane flew into a smoke-covered mountain while descending to an airport. A few weeks later another jet crashed in a vertical dive into a jungle swamp.

The Indonesian rupiah began to lose its value. Banks closed down. The stock market plummeted after rumours, false as it turned out, that President Suharto had died. The year 1998 began with food riots in East Java. Nine out of ten companies on the Jakarta Stock Exchange were found to be technically bankrupt. Young political activists began disappearing; it came out later that they were being kidnapped and tortured by the army. Demonstrations began in universities in half a dozen Javanese cities.

The currency had become almost worthless. Indonesia was an international laughing stock. And the Indonesian government flailed, boldly announcing economic reforms one day, and cancelling them the next morning.

For the first time in thirty years, people cried openly for new ministers and a new president. But in the middle of March 1998, during the country's worst turmoil for thirty years, Suharto was reappointed president for the seventh time by a gathering of a thousand carefully chosen supporters. It was this 're-election', this cynical refusal to face reality, that infuriated the students of Yogyakarta. As the president's tame parliament was cheering his swearing-in speech in Jakarta, in Yogya he was being burned in effigy.

Javanese history was full of moments which had been identified as the beginning of the Age of Jayabaya – the reigns of evil kings, the last days of Dutch colonial rule, and most recently the events of 1965 and 1966 when the anti-communist massacres had brought an end to the Old Order and the beginning of the New. Nuri had pulled the English translation of the *Prelambang Jayabaya* from the Internet; he smiled apologetically as he handed it to me. But for many people in early 1998, there was nothing ridiculous in the notion that the time of madness was at hand.

I had flown back to Jakarta ten days earlier. In Tokyo, where I boarded the plane, the ground was covered with snow. Landing in Jakarta was like arriving for the first time: the wet, cocooning warmth which penetrated the stiffest air conditioning, the lingering smell of clove *kretek*. But one thing had changed, and with it everything else: money.

Since the previous summer, after a similar catastrophe in Thailand, the Indonesian rupiah had collapsed. Formerly, one pound had bought about 4,000 rupiah; now it was worth 16,000. As a visiting foreigner, in other words, I had become four times richer. In international terms, Indonesians had become four times poorer. The cost of foreign goods, the cost of settling a bill with a foreign supplier and, above all, the cost of the foreign bank loans with which so many Indonesian companies were indebted – all were four times more expensive, and as the rupiah slipped down every day, the costs went up. Most big Indonesian companies were already ruined, and more and more people were losing their jobs. This was the *krisis monetar* – the *krismon* – and the government was powerless to stop it.

At the traffic lights in Jakarta, the mobs of vendors who pounced on stationary cars had been swollen by the newly unemployed and by immigrants from the countryside. As well as the usual newspapers and cigarettes, they thrust forward a new article of merchandise: a glossy poster bearing the names and portraits of each member of Suharto's new cabinet. Among the new ministers was the president's daughter; Suharto's golf and fishing buddy had been awarded the trade portfolio. 'But here – here is not the worst,' friends in Jakarta told me. 'The countryside, East Java – that's where you must go to see the people who are really suffering.'

To travel in such a time was to experience what it might have felt to be a tourist after the collapse of the mark in Weimar Germany. The cost of aviation fuel had driven the price of air travel beyond the reach of any but the rich, and the domestic flight which I took out of Jakarta was less than a quarter full. More alarmingly, aeroplane spare parts had also become unaffordable; the flight was an hour late in taking off, as the engineers delved into the engine, making do with what they had. That night I arrived in the East Java town of Malang and checked into its best hotel. My room, furnished with antiques, opposite a palm-shadowed swimming pool, cost the equivalent of only fifteen pounds sterling. Later, when I checked the latest exchange rate, I discovered that the rupiah had declined still further: I would actually be paying more like twelve pounds. When I settled my bill, the rate had gone down again.

I paid in cash, with bricks of 50,000-rupiah notes, all of them freshly printed by the panicking central bank. Each bore the smiling face of Suharto and the title by which he liked to be known: *Bapak Pembangunan* – the Father of Development.

All year, as the price of basic household necessities had gone up, riots had been breaking out in small towns and villages in East Java. For a week, I visited them with a young guide from Malang named Vinny. East Java is a wide province; hours of driving separated one stop from the next. Sometimes we spent all day in Vinny's jeep, and it was during these long drives, half dozing, with the window open and the air flapping across my face, that I came to love the beauty of Java. In the mountains, the air cooled and the road curved close to the slope above precipices of jungle. But for most of the time, the way was flat and straight, with a continuous procession of people and animals. At these times, Java felt like one continuous village strung out along hundreds of miles.

The bigger houses had whitewashed walls and brick-red roofs. Straggly palms lined the road in front of them. The bases of the trees were painted in bands of white, and the shadows they cast fell rhythmically across the moving car. Every few miles was a small mosque with its shiny dome, and a public monument of inspirational character: a family group, standing stiffly and staunchly with crudely painted faces; a charging soldier, bayonet out-thrust. Behind and between the houses, rice fields were visible in shades of green and yellow, and beyond everything stood the looming, deep-green forest.

A well-tamed river ran by the road, feeding the irrigation channels between the paddies. A woman walked beside it, carrying a plastic water bottle in one arm and the hand of her young son in the other. A bicycle trundled past with a large, unvarnished door precariously balanced upon it, and a man walked in the opposite direction pulling a wet-eyed ox at the end of a heavy rope. On the outskirts of one village, a line of cars dawdled behind a procession. Vinny started to overtake and then braked with a sudden jerk.

In front of the cars six men in shorts and T-shirts carried a coffin. One man held a green parasol above it. It was draped with a shiny cloth and strings of white flowers.

The man with the parasol beckoned Vinny to overtake.

Vinny worked for a tour company in Malang which made its money from organised ascents of East Java's great volcanoes. In the past few months, he said, the work had dried up. Well-off Indonesians, who made up the bulk of the visitors, simply could not afford it, and foreigners, for whom such holidays had become absurdly cheap, were scared off by reports of the rioting. Vinny had a basic school education. His English, which was wittily fluent, was self-taught. He despised Suharto with a casual contempt, and he moved in a world in which everyone else was cynical about him as well.

The elections, he said, were a cheat: many people voted for the ruling party, but only because they had been intimidated by their village head or local army commander. Most of them were weary of Suharto, but they hated his 'cronies', especially his sons and daughters, even more. 'Indonesia is a republic,' Vinny said, 'but really it's more like a kingdom, with Suharto as the king, and his children as the princes and the princesses. If you are a friend of Suharto, you can have any position in the government. If you are his child, you can have any business contract you like. The corruption is so high. But here in the countryside, the people are still poor.'

'Then why have they tolerated Suharto for so long?' I asked.

'Because they are afraid,' Vinny said.

'But what are they afraid of?'

'They are afraid of the past.'

'Of what in the past?'

Vinny glanced sideways at me and smiled. 'You should ask the older people that question,' he said. 'But the past is past. We have to do the right thing now, for the present. We have to step into the future.'

The car slowed again. In the middle of the road was an oil drum and around it young boys were holding battered tins which they pushed into the open windows of passing cars. 'They are collecting for a new mosque,' Vinny said. 'But I don't like to give because you know that the money will not really go to the mosque, but to these boys.' The oldest of them approached with his tin, a tall, skinny boy with dark rings beneath his eyes. Vinny shook his head, and steered the car slowly around the oil drum. And out of nowhere, on this quiet road between trees, a passionate anger possessed the young collectors. The smaller ones shouted shrill insults. The oldest one laid his skinny hand on my arm where it rested on the open window, and gripped so tightly that the skin was marked by a bruise. Vinny shouted back at them, accelerated with a screech, and drew to a halt half a mile down the road under a huge, overshadowing banyan tree.

'Stupid,' said Vinny as I rubbed my arm. 'Are you OK?'

'Why were they so angry? Just because we didn't give them money?' A green and red butterfly flew into the jeep and settled on the wheel.

'Something,' Vinny said, brushing it away. 'Something. I don't know what.'

The countryside around Trenggalek, a small town at the western end of East Java, had been poor enough before the *krismon*. But this year, planting had been delayed by the drought. Imported rice had become unaffordable because of the rupiah, and everything in the shops was expensive because of the cost of the diesel oil needed to transport it to the remote villages. People who had lost their jobs were returning from the towns and increasing the burden on the villages. Pockets of this area, it was said, were the poorest places in Indonesia and people were reduced to substituting rice with corn and cassava.

'The cassava stops them from becoming sick and starving,' said a man called Hardjiyo. 'But compared to when they eat rice, they have no energy, no power.'

Hardjiyo worked for the Trenggalek branch of the democratic party, but he was a different kind of activist from those I knew in Jakarta. There the party was run by smart English-speakers with diplomas and designer spectacles. Hardjiyo wore jeans and a T-shirt and had simple political ambitions: every five years he did his best to persuade a few more people in Trenggalek not to vote for the ruling party.

We picked him up in front of his small party office, and he guided Vinny out of the town. On the way we passed a bank with a poster bearing the government's latest slogan: I ♥ rupiah. 'It's true that we love rupiah,' Hardjiyo said. 'The problem is that rupiah don't love us.'

We drove along narrow lanes through villages of plaster and bamboo. 'Do you see chickens?' Hardjiyo asked. 'Not so many chickens these days.' A large chicken-breeding farm had formerly stood nearby, he said. But the ingredients of the chicken feed were imported, and overnight they had become unaffordable. After a few weeks of agonising, and not entirely in his right mind, the owner had burned down his chicken sheds with the chickens inside them. Tens of thousands of chickens had been barbecued at a stroke. And so the price of eggs had doubled.

Hardjiyo pointed out the fields of despised cassava plants, with their red stalks and rotary leaves. 'If a woman eats only cassava, she sometimes cannot produce milk for her baby,' Hardjiyo said. 'But the powder milk is too expensive now. There are plenty of sick babies. Last week, a friend of mine buried his baby.'

'How do the people here feel?' I asked. 'Are they angry?'

'They are very angry, but there is no riot. They are very, very angry, but here it won't happen like those other places. Because the people have too little. When you are hungry it is difficult to make a riot. And they are afraid.'

'What are they afraid of?'

Hardjiyo smiled.

We reached a village called Sumurup and went to the house of Hardjiyo's friend, Jamari. He was a carpenter who also kept a small rice field. His wife and two little sons were cheerful enough, but it was clear that their lives had been transformed in the past few months. Jamari's particular complaint was the fourfold increase in the price of batteries for the electric lights that lit his workshop after dark. But nobody was buying his simple chairs and tables anyway. The family lived off a gruel of one part rice and three parts cassava. It was grey and lumpy and had a nutty, slightly muddy taste. It left them feeling listless, sleepy and inactive. 'It makes us feel bored,' said Jamari's wife.

Once, the people of Sumurup had profited from plantations of clove trees, the essential ingredient in *kretek* cigarettes. But the business had been ruined six years earlier when Suharto's most hated son, Tommy, had been awarded the monopoly right to buy cloves from farmers. Within two years, thanks to Tommy's fecklessness and greed, the market had collapsed. Now the price of cloves was rising again, but all the villagers had sold their trees long ago.

'What people hope is that the president will change,' said Jamari. 'But they will not express what they feel because they are afraid.'

For the third time that day, and with little hope of a direct answer, I said, 'What are you afraid of?'

'We are afraid that 1965 will happen again,' Jamari said without hesitation. 'We're afraid that if we speak out, somebody will come and take us away during the night, and perhaps they will kill us.'

He led us down a lane to the village cemetery. It was here that members of the Indonesian Communist Party, the PKI, used to hide when the soldiers and militiamen came to the village, and here that many of them were dragged into the open and killed.

It had begun in November 1965, a few weeks after the mysterious coup attempt and Suharto's rise to power. In the group of villages around Sumurup, 150 people had been murdered, about one villager in forty. Several had died in Sumurup itself; even thirty-three years later, Jamari could still remember each of their names. He took a pencil out of his shirt pocket and slowly wrote them in my notebook: Paiti, Musati, Sutomo, Karni . . . There were nine names altogether.

'Karni I saw myself,' he said. He pointed towards a flat worn stone between the cemetery and the lane. 'It was there. I saw it with my own eyes.'

The killers operated in two ways. Some people found themselves formally arrested by soldiers who visited their homes and took them away to the barracks to be questioned. After a few days, the detainees were handed over to the anti-communist vigilantes, and taken away to a lonely spot to be killed. But many of the murders took place close to the victims' homes. In Sumurup, a gang of about a hundred young men arrived one night, members of the notorious Muslim youth organisation, Ansor. They came in army trucks and there were soldiers with them. But the soldiers took no direct part in what followed.

'They came looking for Sutomo and Karni, but they could not find them,' Jamari said. 'They came again the next morning, but they weren't at home. Sutomo they found in the rice field, and they killed him there. Karni was hiding here in the cemetery. He was well hidden. But people who didn't like him told Ansor that he was here.'

'They shouted out that they wouldn't harm him,' he said. 'And so he came out from the place where he was hiding. But they carried him here, and beat him with sticks. They held him up' – now he mimicked the movement of a man being hauled up by his armpits – 'and cut his throat with a machete. They brought the body to the cemetery and dug a hole and buried it.' He turned to Hardjiyo. 'Their leader was Y——'

Hardjiyo nodded. 'Mr Y——is still living near here,' he said. 'He is an ulema. He became a member of parliament, for the ruling party.'

We stood looking down on the worn stone by the road. I asked what kind of a man Karni had been.

'He was a very kind man,' said Jamari. 'All the ones they killed were kind. Karni was the village secretary. Musati, too – he was a teacher. Even if they were PKI, they never seemed like a threat to anyone. Everyone knew what they believed, it was no secret.'

'What happened to their families?'

'The families of those people were very afraid. Always, they believe that the army will think they are also involved. Most of them went away to some other village. Karni's wife stayed, but she lost her mind, and then her relatives took her away.'

Hardjiyo was younger than Jamari, and would have been a child at the time of the killings. But he nodded his head. 'You had to join the crowd,' he said. 'If you didn't, you were a suspect. No one even tried to stop the killing, they were too afraid. Even after this time the people are still afraid.'

But conditions were so different now, I said. Communism was finished all over the world, and there was no demagogue like Sukarno today. Surely too much had changed in Indonesia for anything like that to be repeated? Vinny began translating this, and Jamari interrupted him. 'Anything can happen in this country,' he said. 'People are suffering, and as long as they suffer like this, nothing is certain. This crisis makes everyone so dizzy.'

TIME OF MADNESS

It is often said of a national leader who falls from power that he has 'lost his magic'. In the case of Indonesia, or at least the island of Java, this is literally true.

In Javanese tradition, politics is an aspect of the supernatural; any man who seeks to rule the earthly realm must also control the hidden powers which exist beyond it. I had seen in Borneo that, where people believe in the power of magic, magic becomes real. But the war charms of the Dayaks were crude compared with the mystical cult of the kings of Java.

Over the centuries Java had been Buddhist, Hindu and finally Muslim, but in each religious epoch certain convictions remained. The Javanese king was not merely the representative of the divine, but the one and only link between man and the gods. The two worlds reflected one another; disorder in one was matched by disturbance in the other. The ability to maintain harmony between the seen and the unseen – this was the essence of being a king.

Royal legitimacy took a distinct, visible form: the divine light called the *wahyu*. In Javanese chronicles and puppet plays, the *wahyu* was described in various ways. Sometimes it came in the form of a vision (the dream of a sky with seven moons) or a divine being (a child as small as the handle of a dagger, shining like the sun). But most often it appeared as light: a star, a luminescence, lightning – sometimes accompanied by thunder – or a dazzling ball of white, blue or green radiance, streaking across the sky.

The *wahyu* was the visible token of greatness and charisma. It transfigured its possessor, who shone with radiance, dignity and authority. The *wahyu* might be present from birth: one king had absorbed it in the womb, when the hovering light touched the head of his pregnant mother. Another, Pangeran Puger, acquired it from his dead brother, Amangkurat II. 'The story is told that the [dead] king's manhood stood erect and on top of it was a glittering shine, only the size of a grain of pepper,' the chronicles record. 'But nobody observed it. Only Pangeran Puger saw it. Pangeran Puger quickly sipped up the light. As soon as the light had been sipped, the manhood ceased to stand erect. It was Allah's will that Pangeran Puger should succeed to the throne.'

Power was also concentrated in sacred heirlooms and regalia: holy lances, crowns, cannons, carriages, the gongs of the gamelan orchestra, and the ritual daggers, or kris. Supported by such talismans, and by means of a constant and ongoing spiritual effort, the king sustained not only his own position, but the stability and well-being of the whole world. The titles taken by the Javanese rulers indicated the responsibility which they bore in tethering down human existence: *Paku Alam* – the Nail of the World; *Hamengku Buwono* – the Sustainer of the Universe.

'Power is the ability to give life,' the Indonesia scholar Benedict Anderson wrote in a famous essay on the Javanese kings. 'Power is also the ability to maintain a smooth tautness and to act like a magnet that aligns scattered iron filings in a patterned field of force.' But kingly legitimacy could be lost as well as won.

The greatest threat to the power of the king was the weakness known as *pamrih*. The word suggests a combination of selfishness, arrogance, indulgence and corruption. *Pamrih* might reveal itself in an excessive fondness for women or wealth, beyond what was necessary for the glory of the state. A king who showed favour to a particular faction or to the members of his own family also displayed *pamrih*.

Once infected with the worm of corruption, disaster was only a matter of time. There could be no struggle for power; the king's authority and legitimacy, once compromised, were lost for ever. Scholars and holy men would recognise the coming disaster, and warn the king against it. Typically, his reaction was violent and cruel: the arrest of the critics, their torture, humiliation and death. And this brutality, the slaughter of the wise and innocent, was another sign of *pamrih*, another proof that the king had abandoned the virtues of a king and that the *wahyu* was deserting him.

No one was better equipped to understand the fickle cycles of Javanese history than President Suharto. Magic and violence had overshadowed the first half of his life.

He was born in 1921 in a village a few miles outside Yogyakarta, the cauldron of Javanese culture. To the north of Yogya was the smoking shape of the god-mountain Merapi, Java's most active volcano. To the south was the Indian Ocean, abode of Nyai Lara Kidul, goddess of the Southern Seas and divine consort of the Sultans of Yogyakarta. The royal palace itself, and the arrangements of the halls and pavilions within it, were a symbolic diagram of the Javanese universe, filled with music, dance and puppetry.

After his ascent to power, there were rumours that Suharto himself was an illegitimate child of the palace who had been foisted on a peasant family soon after birth. Whoever his true father was, Suharto's childhood was painfully disturbed and unhappy.

Soon after his birth, his mother disappeared. She was found, days later, in the dark room of an empty house in a state of trancelike withdrawal. When the baby was a few weeks old, his parents divorced and, for the rest of his childhood, Suharto was passed among a succession of aunts, uncles and family friends. Three times he was kidnapped by one parent or the other. He moved house nine times before he left school.

The happiest time of his childhood was his apprenticeship to a man named Daryatmo, whom Suharto would often consult in later life. Daryatmo was a Muslim preacher, but he was also famous as a *dukun*, or white witch. The *dukun* could exorcise haunted houses and drive out demons from those who were possessed. People visited him for advice on marriage, business, farming, and for the herbal remedies which Suharto helped him to concoct out of roots, leaves and herbs.

Suharto went to school until he was seventeen, but he had little interest in book learning. The lessons that remained with him were those which he absorbed from the world around him: the mysticism of Daryatmo, and the moral code of the *wayang gulit* puppet plays. The stories of the *wayang* originated in the Indian epics, the *Mahabharata* and *Ramayana*, but over the centuries they had been transformed by the native traditions of Java. Their heroes embodied the Javanese ideals of chivalry, loyalty and duty. Throughout his life, Suharto expressed himself through the aphoristic teachings of the *wayang*.

Never be taken by surprise.
Never be overwhelmed.
And never trust too much in your own power.

Riches without wealth,
Force without arms,
Strength without sorcery,
Victory without humiliation.

The Second World War, and the Indonesian revolution which followed it, transformed Suharto's life. He served successively in the home guard of the Dutch colonial administration, the police force of the occupying Japanese and the guerrilla militia of the Indonesian independence movement. By 1950, at the age of twenty-nine, he was a lieutenant colonel in the newly-formed army of the independent Republic of Indonesia. Over the years he acquired a reputation as a tough, cautious, reliable and rather uninteresting officer – a natural deputy, but the temperamental opposite of the fiery independence leaders of the older generation. After independence, Suharto moved quietly up the command ladder, in the chaotic Indonesia of the 1950s and early 1960s.

One man dominated Indonesian politics throughout this time: Sukarno, the founding president, the *proklamator* of Indonesia's independence. Bung – or 'Big Brother' – 'Karno, as he was known, was a man who revelled in the gift of Power. In his rambling, electrifying speeches, his spine-tingling denunciations of the colonial West, in his many marriages and affairs, at mass rallies and press conferences and diplomatic functions, Sukarno shone. He looked like a matinée idol, with his cream suits and his limousines. He thrived on contradiction, confrontation and tumult. Meanwhile, prices rose, debt increased, productivity fell and people went hungry. There were riots and rumours of coups. It was obvious that the country was falling to pieces and beneath the political frenzy – the demonstrations, the contention of political parties – was a sense of foreboding.

On 30 September 1965, a group of colonels, including members of Sukarno's palace guard, kidnapped and murdered six of the country's most senior generals and dumped their bodies in a well. They claimed to have been acting to foil an imminent right-wing coup attempt against Sukarno, but within hours their movement had collapsed in confusion. With the death of the generals the unknown, unfancied Suharto found himself catapulted into a position of leadership. With unflinching cool, he rallied the army, overcame the rebels and arrested their leaders with scarcely a shot fired.

The truth of what happened on the night of 30 September and 1 October has never been established. But in Suharto's version of events there was no doubt. The coup was the work of the Communist Party which was intent on enslaving Indonesians, as it had already enslaved the people of Russia,

China and Eastern Europe. All over Indonesia, a campaign of killing was organised against real and alleged members of the PKI. It was one of the great massacres of history; in the space of a few months, hundreds of thousands of people died. 'Nothing the Dutch imperialists had done in 350 years of depredations in the archipelago,' wrote Benedict Anderson, 'matched the speed, scale, and ferocity of Suharto's *matanza* against his own people.'

The worst thing was that they did it to themselves. The massacres were not a scheme imposed from above by the powerful upon the weak. The army provided lists of names, trucks, a few weapons, and occasionally assisted in the executions. But most of the killings were carried out by ordinary Javanese farmers, fishermen, craftsmen, teachers, ulemas, government clerks and students – by hand.

After the 'Gestapu' – the creepy Indonesian acronym by which the stifled coup came to be known – Sukarno faltered. Publicly, he tried to shrug off its significance, thereby inviting suspicions that the murder of the generals had not completely taken him by surprise. Suharto, meanwhile, moved with the certainty of a man whose time had come. Thousands of communists were rounded up in Jakarta, and photographs of the corpses of the murdered generals were dispatched to regional military headquarters. The PKI's enemies in the army and the mosques had been waiting for their opportunity for so long that a direct order was unnecessary.

Wherever they occurred, the massacres took on a local character; beyond the urge to purge the communists, they became the means of working out old political, religious and ethnic hatreds. In the eastern islands, with their large Catholic and Protestant populations, Muslims murdered Christians. In Bali, the killers were Hindus, and in West Kalimantan they were Dayaks who headhunted Chinese. No one knows how many people died; respectable estimates range from a few hundred thousand to a million, most of whom died during the last twelve weeks of 1965.

Given the scale of the killings, it is remarkable how little reliable information about them has survived. Those foreigners who had not fled the country were confined to Jakarta; among Indonesians, the subject quickly became a taboo, and even now men as open as Jamari were difficult to find. But a few contemporary accounts survive.

The killings were often carried out at night, by the light of paraffin lamps. The victims were generally murdered in the open air, in secluded places on the outskirts of villages: paddy fields, rubber plantations, banana and coconut groves. Sometimes they were tied to trees or to one another, or lined up beside specially dug graves or the banks of rivers, into which their corpses were tipped. Often they were tortured. Rape and castration were not unknown and the mutilated bodies were sometimes left out in the open on public display. Guns were rarely used; in most cases the victims were killed by hand. They were strangled with nooses, beaten with sticks and iron bars, brained with rocks, soaked in petrol and burned alive, or slashed to death with sickles, swords or machetes. In Cirebon on Java's north coast, the local anti-communist militia constructed a town guillotine.

There was a symbolic, even ritual, element to many of the killings. The communist leader in Bali was named I Gde Puger. He was a notoriously corrupt man, famous both for his greed and his corpulence, so, before shooting him in the head, his killers cut the fat from his body. Elsewhere, the mutilation of the victims was explained in magical terms, as a means of rendering the dead imperfect to prevent them from achieving harmony with the universe.

Before going about their work groups of vigilantes often became entranced. In Bali, they were possessed by the spirit of Shiva, Hindu lord of destruction. Communist prisoners there were sometimes given the choice of execution or something called *nyupat*. 'One should not speak of murder but rather of *nyupat*,' one Balinese official explained. 'That is the shortening of someone's life in order to free them from suffering, and to

give them a chance to be reincarnated as a better person.'
Witnesses described the eerie sight of prisoners walking calmly
to their deaths, already dressed in white burial robes.

The PKI in Java drew its strength from poor villagers whose
practice of Islam was profoundly mixed with old rituals and
magic. In many places, suspicion of communism mingled with
the fear of black magic. The communists were demons, less than
human, and they were killed accordingly.

From a contemporary account of the killings in East Java:

A young boy . . . son of Pak Tjokrohidardjo, who was a
member of the local PKI committee in Singosari
Kecamatan, was arrested by Ansor. He was then tied to a
jeep and dragged behind it until he was dead. Both his
parents committed suicide.

Oerip Kalsum . . . was a member of the PKI. Before being
killed, she was ordered to take all her clothes off. Her body
and her honour were then subjected to fire. She was then
tied up, taken to the village of Sentong in Lawang, where
a noose was put around her neck and she was hacked to
death.

Suranto, headmaster of the high school in Pare . . . went
to meet his wife, nine months pregnant . . . They were
beaten until they fell unconscious and were then killed.
The man's head was cut off and his wife's stomach was
cut open, the baby taken out and cut to pieces. The two
bodies were thrown down a ravine to the east of the
market in Pare. For a week afterwards, their five children who were all small (the oldest was eleven) had no
one to help them because the neighbours were warned
by Ansor members that anyone helping them would be
at risk.

Children often died with their parents, but in parts of East Java bands of young orphans roamed the countryside, scavenging like dogs. The Brantas River, which ran through East Java, became clogged with corpses – farmers constructed bamboo gates along its banks to keep the bodies from floating up the irrigation channels. In the port city of Surabaya, the British consul woke one morning to find bodies washed up at the bottom of his garden.

The few foreigners who remained noticed a remarkable thing: that, among Indonesians, no one was surprised by the slaughter. 'One of the most astonishing experiences of visitors to Djakarta at the height of the mass killings was the apparent indifference among even the most sensitive people,' wrote one journalist. 'They would eagerly retail rumours which had come in, hot from the foundry, about decapitated human bodies blocking the streams in Semarang, about human heads ornamenting avenues of wooden spikes along the road to Solo, about entire villages being mown down by a single sweep of the anti-communist militia. But, though there was concern and sympathy for the families of the dead, there seemed to be little horror or senti-mentality . . . This sense of the inevitable is a deeply engrained and familiar trait among the Javanese people.'

One day in March of 1998, Vinny and I stopped in the town of Blitar, the childhood home of old President Sukarno, and the place where he was buried. Sukarno had lost his power quickly after the killing of the generals. By March 1966, he had signed over authority to Suharto who was appointed acting president the following year, and full president in 1968. Sukarno lived under house arrest in Bogor, a safe distance from Jakarta, and died there in 1970, unhappy and forgotten.

But now, in 1998, he was enjoying a revival. The chaos and corruption of his last years were forgotten; people remembered him as the proclaimer of independence and founder of the nation. Since being deposed as leader of the democratic party, his daughter, Megawati Sukarnoputri, had become a national hero, and her own gathering power owed much to memories of her father. Thousands of people were coming every day to be photographed next to his grave, and teams of vendors sold Sukarno posters and T-shirts. Among the items on display were photographs of the gravestone itself, a rippling boulder of polished black stone. Clearly visible in the patterns of light on the stone were the face, eyes and mane of a *singa* – a great, male lion. The man selling the pictures told us that the lion was Sukarno's *wahyu*, come back as a sign to Indonesians during this time of tribulation. But one of the T-shirt vendors said it was just a coincidence, a random likeness created by the flash on the shiny stone.

We visited Sukarno's childhood home, a simple house now turned into a museum. On the wall were old photographs: Sukarno the open-mouthed demagogue, jabbing his finger in the air; Sukarno the film star, with his lovely wives and sexy grin; Sukarno the statesman, smiling and shaking hands with the leaders of the world. The display made no reference at all to his lonely end and the horrors which preceded it.

At the back of the house hung a cage with a green bird, and a large frame containing a greying piece of paper bearing hand-written words in Javanese. The glass was stained and there were ancient cobwebs trapped beneath it. There was a date at the bottom: 1964, a year before the coup and the killings and the end of Sukarno.

Vinny and I stood side by side scrutinising the document.

'What is it?' I asked.

'It's a poem. It is not by Sukarno, but I think that he may have written out this copy.'

'What does it say?'

It was an extract from a famous lament by a poet of the late nineteenth century named Prince Ngabehi Ronggawarsita. Its title was 'Poem in a Time of Darkness'.

TIME OF MADNESS

The lustre of the realm
Is vanished to the eye,
In ruins the teaching of good ways,
For there is no example left.
The heart of the wise poet
Is so coiled about with care,
Beholding all the wretchedness,
That everything is darkened,
The world immersed in misery.

The King – kingly perfection;
The Prime Minister – first in truth;
The regent – constant of heart;
The courtiers – meticulous;
Yet none can act to stay
The time of doom.

In this time of madness
To join the mad is unbearable
Anguish to the suffering heart.
Yet not to join
Means losing all,
Starvation at the end.

STRENGTH WITHOUT SORCERY

The New Order created in the late 1960s by President Suharto was seldom as brutal or arbitrary as Cold War dictatorships in other countries of the developing world. In Indonesia, political opponents died or disappeared from time to time, and there were reports of torture and mistreatment in custody. Many thousands of people, accused – or merely suspected – of communist sympathies, were jailed for decades, and most of them never faced trial. But to the casual observer there were few obvious signs of oppression. Within Java and the main islands – excluding, that is, the brutal anti-guerrilla operations in East Timor and Aceh – opposition to the government tended to end in exile or imprisonment, rather than torture or execution. The relative mildness of New Order made it all the easier for the democratic governments of the West to get along with Indonesia.

Suharto was a subtle and self-effacing man, with a gift for indirectness and for controlling events without ever appearing to be directly responsible. But he was a killer. The events of 1965 were his talisman, the evil spirit which protected him and his regime. Whatever edifices of progress might be constructed over the next thirty years, beneath them all was a pit in which lay the bodies of those who died in the anti-communist massacres. All Indonesians understood this. And rather than face up to what they had done to one another, they thrust the memory from sight, retreated from politics and for the next thirty-three years left Suharto alone.

The New Order was born in extreme violence; the threat of

violence was implicit throughout its history; and it ended with an eruption of violence that reverberated long after its founder had gone.

But the most striking thing about the first three decades of the New Order was how boring they were. Suharto came to power in one of the most angry and polarised countries on earth. Within a few years, politics had been abolished, conflict outlawed, ideology had been replaced with consensus, and rhetoric had given way to bureaucratese. This was Suharto's greatest achievement: to tame the frenzied bull which Sukarno had ridden, and transform it into a dozy, cud-chewing cow.

The changes were gradual rather than sweeping, accomplished by means of tinkering adjustments to existing arrangements. Suharto had no grand vision to unveil but within five years of edging out Sukarno he had flooded parliament with his own supporters, created a feared network of spies and established the army as the most powerful institution in the country. The rabble of political parties which had contended under Sukarno were 'streamlined' to three. The government funded them, appointed their leaders and barred them from political activity outside the official election campaign periods. 'With the one and only road already there, why must we have so many cars, as many as nine?' Suharto asked. 'Why must we have wild speeding and collisions?'

This was the tone of voice in which the New Order explained itself: indulgent, simplistic and infuriatingly smug. It justified its actions in the name of 'the people', whose interests it alone was equipped to understand. At the same time, the people were not to be trusted, and constantly needed to be protected from themselves. This became obvious above all during elections, the five-yearly 'Festivals of Democracy', each one a huge and subtle fix, from the pre-screening of the parliamentary candidates by the government to the vote-counting process. Further padded out with government appointees, the assembly thus created would elect the president a year later. No one ever stood against Suharto, and there was no debate about his candidacy. The speed record was set in 1973 when he was renominated and re-elected in the space of eight minutes.

Suharto called this fraud 'Pancasila democracy', after the 'Five Principles' espoused by Sukarno at the founding of Indonesia. In themselves, the Pancasila were unobjectionable, a set of ideals under which Indonesians could unite whatever their race and faith: belief in one God; just and civilised humanity; national unity; democracy through deliberation; and social justice for all. But on this simple foundation, the New Order built a vast fortification in which it locked up Indonesian politics for thirty years.

'Pancasila democracy endeavours to strike a balance between the interests of the individual and those of society,' Suharto explained. 'Its characteristics are its rejection of poverty, backwardness, conflicts, exploitation, capitalism, feudalism, dictatorship, colonialism and imperialism.' This was the intellectual core of Pancasila: support for good things; opposition to bad things; and Daddy Knows Best.

A vast Pancasila literature was spawned, along with an indoctrination programme to which all schoolchildren, soldiers and everyone in an official position had to submit. Pancasila man, properly constituted, placed loyalty to the state above all religious, ethnic or regional loyalties. He was obedient to authority, and always willing to surrender his individual rights. He cherished stability, security, development and, above all, consensus – meaning, in effect, that he agreed with everything that Suharto decided. He abhorred Western-style democracy, and was on constant guard against the return of communism, still lingering like anthrax spores in the Indonesian soil. But the strength of Pancasila was its flexibility. It could mean anything Suharto wanted, and it magically transformed the meaning of familiar words and concepts. Just as Pancasila democracy was an elaborately packaged dictatorship, so a Pancasila teacher – if he was doing his job – was a propagandist, a Pancasila journalist was a toady, and a Pancasila civil servant was a compliant lickspittle.

The New Order rested on a nullity, a denial of ideas and imagination, and the damage it did to the country is difficult to measure. 'I think that it is Suharto's worst crime,' said the human rights lawyer, Adnan Buyung Nasution, 'that he has made Indonesians afraid to think, afraid to express themselves.'

Pancasila was authoritarianism dressed up as platitude, but it also possessed something mysterious and even mystical. The Five Principles were less an ideology than a revelation, self-justifying and self-fulfilling. 'They became holy formula protecting the nation,' wrote the anthropologist Niels Mulder. 'They were . . . turned into objects the possession of which legitimated the regime and blessed the course it sailed. They became like a *wahyu*, a divine mandate. After all, when in the possession of the right mantras, a ruler can do no wrong.'

'No country can be considered alive if it does not contain conflict,' Sukarno had declared, in outlining the Pancasila in June 1945. But in the universe of the New Order, conflict of any kind was against the rules. Suharto simply could not understand it when people opposed him. In his intellectual universe, dissent was nothing to do with differing points of view; it was a matter of stupidity, ignorance and bad manners. 'If people differ in opinion,' Suharto counselled in his autobiography, 'I suggest that they deliberate until a consensus is reached. Don't disagree just for the sake of argument even when you've been proved wrong. We do not abide by this sort of attitude here.'

But when Suharto's grandfatherly suasions failed, and when memories of 1965 were not enough, the New Order did not hesitate to lock up and to kill those who offended it.

Hundreds of thousands of alleged communists were arrested after the Gestapu coup. A decade later tens of thousands of them were still being held on the fetid prison island of Buru. Throughout the New Order, non-communist opponents of Suharto were arrested and harassed in ways large and small. Those who led opposition could be held indefinitely on grounds of 'subversion', or sentenced to years in prison for 'insulting the president' or 'sowing hate'. On the few occasions when frustration expressed itself in open dissent, the response of the security forces was often violent. Hundreds of demonstrators were shot dead in the port of Jakarta in 1984. In Java, as many as 10,000 gangsters and petty criminals were summarily executed by Intels in a campaign to crack down on urban crime; their bodies were often left out in the streets as an example. The further from Jakarta, the more brutal the repression. Against the independence movements of Aceh, Irian Jaya and East Timor, torture and execution were routine and hundreds of thousands of people died. In these territories, the New Order operated ungloved and unmasked – racist, genocidal and unaccountable.

By the standards of most of his countrymen, Suharto lived well, but not in the opulence usually associated with corrupt dictators. His house at 8 Jalan Cendana, or Sandalwood Street, was one of the best addresses in Jakarta, but it was that of a successful professional rather than a plutocrat. Those who visited it described number 8 as simple and modest. 'It's as you'd imagine the house of a senior government official,' one civil servant told me. 'If you didn't know, you'd never think it belonged to a president.' The front door opened on to a low-ceilinged room carpeted in brown and filled, not with treasures, but with souvenirs and gewgaws. A stuffed tiger sat on one side; a glass cabinet contained painted plates; a small table bore photographic portraits of the family. Cultured Indonesians who had been there sometimes described it as kitsch. 'There are these meaningless artefacts around the house,' said Sarwono Kusumaatmadja, who served for ten years as a member of Suharto's cabinet. 'The colours don't match, the sizes don't match – it's like entering a curio shop. It's rather disconcerting to see this very proper, dignified old man sitting there, and look around the room and see all these nonsensical trinkets.'

In his modest and regular habits, his privacy and his starchy morality, Suharto was everything that Sukarno was not. He rose before dawn, took his lunch at home and went to bed at midnight. He didn't like alcohol, but accepted a drink occasionally to put foreign guests at ease. His greatest indulgence was an occasional cigarette which he smoked wrapped in a corn cob, like a peasant. Throughout her life, he remained faithful to his wife, the plump and stalwart Madam Tien ('I think "free love" is not good,' Suharto revealed. 'I myself have been able to curb myself in that regard.') He rarely wore his military decorations, and displayed no personal vanity. 'He wears a suit but tacky, awful taste,' an elegant, foreign-educated Indonesian diplomat once told me. 'Double-breasted, but very badly cut, so that he looks like a chauffeur.'

Before 1965, Suharto had never been abroad and even as president he made few overseas trips. His only recreations were golf and deep-sea fishing. He read little, apart from Indonesian newspapers and official reports, and he was a dull public speaker. Suharto never raised his voice or lost his temper, never showed sadness or trepidation or excitement. Even at moments of the utmost tension, he was rarely without his famously faint and ambiguous smile. His closest aides, the men who worked alongside him every day, were unable to judge his mood and thoughts. And yet, in the private evening meetings which he held at his home, he had a compelling presence. Battle-hardened generals, men with advanced degrees from the world's most famous universities, dissolved into inarticulacy in his presence. A former minister, Juwono Sudarsono, described 'the density of his silence'. 'He would stare you in the face and create a sense of awe,' he said. 'It was his presence and his stare. He looked right through you. Every five years, a thousand people met in a congress and there was not one who was brave enough to stand up and say, "Enough!"'

Even towards his closest friends, Suharto was ruthless. Old and loyal advisers would find themselves suddenly barred from his confidence without a word of explanation. Afterwards, they found their reputations eaten away – Suharto's autobiography is filled with barbed subtleties about the incompetence of one old friend and the emotionalism of another. He survived as he did because he was alone, and because he allowed nobody to come close to a position from which they might threaten him. In thirty-three years of power he never faced a serious challenge – never once. The president was the state, the state was him, and by 1998 it felt to many people as if the end of Suharto would be the end of Indonesia itself.

All his life Suharto was close to visionaries and mystics, and seems to have regarded himself as one of them. Tales of his magical gifts had circulated since the war against the Dutch, when the guerrillas under his command became convinced that he was immune to bullets. A later story explained why Suharto, alone among the country's senior generals, had not been killed by the Gestapu plotters. He had been advised by a seer, it was said, to spend that night 'at the confluence of two waters', and had taken one of his sons fishing at a place where a river joined the sea. Suharto played down such rumours to Westerners and Western-educated Indonesians, but among Javanese he encouraged them.

In his autobiography, he made a distinction between the cultivation of supernatural stunts – fortune telling, flying, immunity to weapons, and the like – and the deep spiritual truths apprehended through meditation. He pooh-poohed the rumours that he depended on *dukun* to make important decisions. 'If we were in the middle of a war and were seeking a *dukun*,' he wrote, 'we would be killed by the enemy first.' But he made clear that both kinds of mystical power – the superficial and the profound – truly did exist. The point was that Suharto relied on nobody. It was not that there were no sorcerers and seers, but that the president, with his far greater and more penetrating powers, was superior to all of them.

His Muslim faith was not that of Arabia, but the ancient

mystical practice of Java, the religion of meditation and the legends of the *wayang*. Suharto, it was said, used to slip away from Jakarta in his helicopter to meditate in the limestone caves on Central Java's Dieng Plateau. In 1974 he went there with the Australian prime minister, Gough Whitlam, of all Western leaders the one with whom he had the closest rapport. It was during this visit that Whitlam agreed to turn a blind eye to Indonesia's imminent invasion of East Timor; as a sign of his gratitude, Suharto took him into the Cave of Semar, sacred to Java's greatest native deity.

In the plays of the *wayang*, Semar is represented as the equivalent of a Shakespearean clown, a fat, farting dwarf who provides light relief from the heroics of his knightly masters. Semar the servant mocks the pretensions of the *wayang* heroes; at the same time he is the most powerful of all the gods. The ambiguity of the slave-god appealed to Suharto, the peasant-president. The document in which Sukarno had signed over his presidential powers in 1967, the birth certificate of the New Order, was called *Surat Perintah Sebelas Maret*, the Letter of Instruction of the 11th of March. Running together the first syllable of each word produced the acronym by which it was always known: Super Semar.

Mystical divination is a business in Java, and there were many *dukun* keen to claim a close relationship with the president. But two names stood out. The first was Suharto's wife, Ibu Tien, a remote descendant of the royal house of the city of Solo. Tien, it was said, had inherited magical gifts; there were many who believed that the waning of Suharto's powers began with her sudden death in 1996. The other was Sudjono Humardani, the man with best claim to the title of Suharto's witch.

Sudjono was a general who became Suharto's unofficial business manager. He was also an adept of Javanese mysticism, with a passionate belief in Suharto's magical destiny as the 'Just King' of Java. He kept a notebook of supernatural observations which he would pass on to Suharto. He had a collection of magical kris, and he concocted potions and elixirs. Early on in the New Order, Sudjono went on an important diplomatic mission to the United States with a man named Umar Khayyam, a poet and academic whom I met once in Jakarta. On the flight, Sudjono showed Umar a small case filled with glass vials of liquids and powders.

Some were for good health and the treatment of various disorders. Others were aphrodisiacs, for men and for women. Sudjono had a dirty sense of humour and clearly intended to have some fun in America. 'Sudjono said, "This one is a very good one. It will make any women moan!"' Umar told me. 'Then I said, "What's that one?" and he became very solemn.'

The bottle contained sand from a holy place in Java. It was Sudjono's intention to sprinkle it secretly in the White House. In this way the magic of Java would work its influence in the citadel of American power, and the New Order's diplomatic mission would be guaranteed success.

The Javanese arrived in Washington, went to the White House, and held their formal talks. When they were outside again, Sudjono smiled at Umar and held up the empty bottle. 'I don't know how he did it, and I didn't see it myself,' Umar said. 'But he poured the sand into the carpet of the White House.' And until the very end, the New Order enjoyed the unfailing support of the United States.

What did Suharto himself really believe? Sarwono Kusumaatmadja thought that his Javanism was just a political tool. 'He told me that he gave the impression that he was superstitious, because Indonesians are superstitious, and they want a president who is superstitious too,' Sarwono said. 'But then he knew me and my background – that I was educated, scientifically minded, and that I wasn't having any of that mysticism.' Was Suharto being honest about his cynicism, or just flattering Sarwono with his own rational view of the world? Was it, in fact, another form of manipulation?

Even after he slipped from favour in Cendana, Sudjono

Humardani believed that the president shared his faith. But a few years after Sudjono's death, Suharto's autobiography came out. 'About Sudjono Humardani, I had heard people say that he knew more about mysticism than I did,' Suharto wrote. 'But 'Djono used to do the *sungkem* [pay homage] to me. He regarded me as his senior who had more knowledge about mysticism . . . I just listened to make him feel good, but did not take in everything he said . . . So those who thought that 'Djono was my guru in mysticism had it wrong.'

His Javanese friends were saddened and surprised by these remarks about Sudjono. But it was so characteristic of Suharto – the insistence on his own superiority and independence, the belittling of his old friend even in the grave.

After the mystical banality of Pancasila, and the concrete power of the army, came the third pillar of the regime and the one in which Suharto took the most pride: development. Inflation, poverty, infant mortality and population growth were dramatically reduced under the New Order. Literacy, life expectancy, GDP and foreign investment all went up. Within a few years, foreign engineers and bankers began visiting Jakarta once again, and Indonesia was building factories and clinics and electricity grids. Suharto revelled in these achievements; he was never happier than at the inauguration of a new power station or on the production line of a condom factory.

Indonesia's political and intellectual poverty, the repressive security apparatus – these were accepted because, economically, Suharto was a hero. However unhappy Indonesians were with their leader, there was no doubt that, under him, most of them had become better off. Political scientists call this 'performance legitimacy', and one of them formulated what he called 'Suharto's Law': as long as people feel themselves getting richer, they will tolerate a stunted society. The question is what happens when they start to feel poor again. And from the beginning, the New Order's economic achievements were being corroded from within.

Suharto had little taste for personal wealth, but throughout his life he enriched his friends and family by rewarding them with state contracts. As a young officer, he had been temporarily relieved of his command after being caught out in small-time sugar-smuggling with his *dukun*, Sudjono. Over the next forty years a small group of relatives, ex-army men and Chinese entrepreneurs were handed billion-pound monopolies for oil, roads, bridges, power plants, gold, cloves, teak, pulp and cars.

There was General Ibnu Sutowo who brought the state oil company close to bankruptcy. There was Muhammed 'Bob' Hasan whose timber concessions stripped thousands of miles of forest in Borneo and Sumatra. Then there were the children, known to all by their family pet names: the boys Sigit, Bambang and Tommy, and their sisters Tutut, Titiek and Mamiek. Suharto – guilt-stricken, it is sometimes said, at having been absent for so much of their childhoods – indulged them endlessly; compared to the children, the older cronies were models of honour and restraint.

Towards the end of Suharto's reign, it was estimated that there were 1,251 separate companies in Indonesia in which members of the Suharto family held a significant share. The family's total wealth was reckoned at 90 million pounds. Behind each of the children and the major cronies were echelons of sub-cronies and sub-sub-cronies who fanned out in their wake. No one with crony status had to risk his own money, because state banks would provide loans without collateral to anyone with political connections. Without them, it was impossible to do any large-scale business.

The outside world continued to heap praise and encouragement on the Father of Development, although it is hard to see how Suharto could have failed to improve a country so rich in resources, and so underdeveloped, as Indonesia. But the truth was there for anyone who genuinely wanted to know.

In July 1997, after the collapse of the Thai, Malaysian and Philippine currencies, international money stopped believing in

Indonesia. Currency traders, foreign and local, began selling the rupiah which plummeted in value. Suharto raged against the fickleness and cynicism of the financial vultures who fed on economies for quick profit. But the fund managers were only responding, as vultures do, to the smell of decay.

THE SACK OF JAKARTA

On the grass oval in front of the Sultan's palace in Yogyakarta, I decided that I was going to get married. It was dusk, a Monday evening in May, and prayers were beginning in mosques across the town. On the green, boys were dismantling the tents and roundabouts of a travelling fair which had stopped overnight. I had spent the afternoon pacing up and down, a solitary foreigner in a city emptied of tourists. Now I felt peaceful. I thought of a face and the smell of clean skin, and I knew what I wanted to do.

Back in the hotel I made telephone calls and reservations. I flew back to Jakarta, in the last available seat of the last flight. Seated beside me was a Javanese businessman who had spent the day in Yogya playing golf. He was in his sixties, plump and amber-skinned, and he wore an intricate batik shirt of orange and gold. I asked him his opinion of the political and economic situation and he said that, although things were, admittedly, very bad, there was nothing to worry about. He knew President Suharto personally, he told me, and the president knew what he was doing. He asked me my nationality and my age. He asked me how many children I had.

'Are you married?' he asked.

'Not yet.'

In Jakarta, I dined with a group of television journalists, all making their own plans to leave Indonesia now that the cities were quietening down. Nervously, I told them about my decision. I would fly back, unannounced, and present myself and

the vision which had come to me in front of the Sultan's palace
– a vision of calm and certainty, of a life together after too long
apart. There would be no more long-distance phone calls, no
more doubt and hesitation. But I was biting my nails, and
smoking again. It was late by the time I went to bed, and the
air in my small hotel room was hot and thick.

I woke up when it was still dark, my throat dry and my confidence broken. I dialled the familiar telephone number, lying in
bed with a cigarette in my fingers.

Forget about him.

Give me this chance.

Please, let me come to you.

Two hours later, after it was light, the airline office opened.
There was plenty of time to cancel my flights.

So I would leave Jakarta a day later than I had intended, and
for the Asian city where I lived as an expatriate, not the European
one which I thought of as my home. The day gaped emptily
before me. I paced up and down, as I had done in front of the
Sultan's palace, and told myself over and over what a mistake it
would have been, and how fortunate I was to be free of responsibility and obligation. I watched the television news, and stared
aimlessly at the map of the city spread out over my bed. The
hotel room was more humid than ever; the air-conditioning unit
on the wall generated only noise. I pulled out a notebook and
dialled the mobile telephone number of my television friends.

They were already driving round the city, looking for campus
demonstrations. They were only mildly surprised to hear from
me.

'You decided not to go? Come and find us. We're at Trisakti.
A lot of students, a few police. Looks like there could be trouble.'

I gathered the necessary objects into my rucksack and hurried
out on to the street. Even as I busied myself with my notebooks
and mobile phone, as I pressed the button to summon the hotel's
lift, and stood in the fumy street waiting for a taxi, I was

conscious of hurt leaking slowly into the corners of me, like the spreading of a stain. Trouble, authentic trouble, the excitement and distraction of a true crisis – that, I sensed, was all that could save me from my heart pain now. But it had become obvious in the past few days that the crisis was receding. Suharto was struggling but, for the time being, at least, he was safe. The climactic confrontation was not going to come this month. It was too much to hope for.

In the city of Medan in Sumatra the previous week, the students had marched for three days, demanding democratic reform and relief from the newly announced rise in the price of petrol. One boy had been killed when he tumbled off his motorbike during a rally. The students blamed the police for his death, and the next day they marched out of the campus, where they were joined by thousands of Medan's poor. Riots and looting followed. Mobs attacked the homes and shops of local Chinese and ten people were killed.

In Yogya, two days later, a crowd had paraded down the airport road, toppling lamp-posts, smashing walls and burning cars. An innocent bystander, a man by the name of Moses Gatotkaca, had been beaten to death by the police, and in Bogor an Intel officer had been killed by a hurled rock. By now the unrest had spread across the country – to Borneo, Sulawesi, Irian Jaya and the outer islands.

During the two months since the demonstrations had been going on, the character of the slogans had changed dramatically, and euphemism – once instinctive – had been abandoned. *Hang Suharto* was commonplace in the regional cities – *Fuck Suharto, Suharto is a Dog* or *Suharto is the Child of Satan* were gaining currency. In Yogya I had seen crude images of Suharto in hell, being humiliated by demons; or Suharto as the devil himself, cramming the bodies of workers and farmers into his beak. And yet the protests remained confined to students. National politicians, like Megawati Sukarnoputri, observed from the margins.

The boldest, like Amien Rais, gave rhetorical encouragement at best. The senior army officers, in whom many Indonesians secretly placed their hopes, appeared unwaveringly loyal. And, despite the humiliation of the *krismon*, and the abject fumbling of his government, Suharto himself was as infuriatingly serene as ever.

In Jakarta, the stalemate was especially obvious. Whether it was Suharto's physical presence in the city, or the presence on its streets of so many of his praetorians, the Jakarta students were deeply cautious. The fear of Intel infiltration was as great as ever; the marches were strictly confined to campus. Even the protest banners were impersonal and abstract: *Lower Prices*, they urged, and *Students Demand Democracy and Reform*. There was talk of escalation, of raising the pitch and tempo of the demonstrations – but not yet. The Jakarta students chose their big days, and there was nothing to suggest that this was going to be one of them.

Trisakti University was on the road that ran to the airport; it was the first time I had heard the name, and until that day nobody else in Indonesia had paid it much attention either. Gajah Mada in Yogyakarta and the University of Indonesia in Jakarta: they were the activist, the 'hot' universities. Trisakti was a private institution, and therefore expensive, and it was secular, without the focused religious identity of the Islamic schools. Its students were fashion-conscious children of government officials, businessmen and army officers, the last people one would regard as heroes and martyrs. Trisakti University was a place for well-off posers. But nothing was more fashionable in Indonesia these days than protest.

It was obvious from the moment I got out of the taxi that this was an exceptional demonstration. Trisakti was bulging and bands of students were arriving all the time from other universities. Speeches were buzzing through the megaphones inside the campus, and thousands of people were spilling over its walls and into the road. Students wearing headbands and blazers were perched in the trees and on the crossbars of the big metal gates. As well as the usual scrawled libels on Suharto, they held long banners, carefully and neatly stencilled with democratic slogans. It was the biggest demonstration to have taken place in Jakarta for years.

A six-lane road, one of the main routes into the city, ran past the gates of the university; elevated above it was the motorway that led to the airport. By lunchtime, both were blocked by the overspill from the campus, and a small group of police was deployed across the road in two thin lines. They carried transparent plastic shields and wooden batons, but they were outnumbered; when the crowd surged, their lines staggered and buckled. But reinforcements soon began to arrive, and the atmosphere quickly became threatening.

A riot unit of Kopassus, the feared special forces, appeared in big open-topped trucks, carrying automatic rifles. The special riot police – known as the BriMob – arrived, wearing black body armour, and carrying canisters of tear gas and gas masks in green pouches. Three squat black armoured cars trundled up, with mesh over their windows and roof-mounted water cannons.

The demonstrators were left with a choice: go back into the campus, or remain on the street, sandwiched between the two lines of troops.

The students remained on the street.

Cameramen and reporters were arriving and forming huddles as they greeted one another. Everyone was thinking the same thing.

'This could turn nasty.'

'If they start firing, Suharto's finished.'

'Or *they're* finished.'

But it was never easy to feel afraid on such occasions because – despite the presence of so much armour and weaponry: shields, visors, truncheons, daggers, belts of cartridges, rifle muzzles, armoured cars – everyone on both sides of the lines was so humorously and unselfconsciously relaxed. Apart from the committed few – the sloganeers and banner-bearers at the front of the crowd – the students were all smiling, and when they were not smiling they were laughing aloud. The sight of foreigners, especially sweating, harried journalists barking into mobile phones, made them laugh. Cameras made them laugh too, and whenever one was brandished they would call their friends and throw their arms around one another in a happy huddle. En masse the soldiers and the police were grim, but individually they smiled back when you greeted them. None minded having his picture taken; no one stopped us passing from one side of the police lines to the other.

At one point I broke away to take a close look at a Tactica, one of the black British-made armoured cars which had broken up so many democracy demonstrations in Indonesia. The use of these vehicles was something of a scandal back in London; I was crouching down to take a photograph when a policeman appeared from behind the monster, frowning and asking me questions aggressively in Indonesian. I spread the palms of my hands and smiled.

'From *Inggris*,' I said, pointing to the vehicle, and then to myself. 'Me, too: from *Inggris*.'

He stopped frowning immediately.

'From *Inggris*? Good, good,' he said, and he patted the side of the Tactica like the flank of a great horse. He shook my hand, and we stood smiling together with shared pride in this brutal machine from my home country, thousands of miles away across the sea.

Before I arrived at Trisakti that morning, the students had held a rally demanding Suharto's resignation and calling for political reform. They wanted a new president, a new parliament and new election laws, and speeches outlining these demands went on for two hours. When the speeches were over, they burned an effigy of Suharto. This was a bold, but not unprecedented, gesture. The Triskati students, however, had an innovation of their own:

before its immolation, the Suharto mannequin was defaced with a little black moustache.

'Hang Suharto! Suharto is Hitler!' screamed the students, as the flames rose.

Most risky of all, the students were planning to march out of their campus and down the road, to present a petition at the national parliament. By quarter past one, more than five thousand had gathered in the campus, and more and more of them were spilling out on to the street. The police were refusing to let them pass. The shouting and sloganeering were becoming noisier and more aggressive. The leaders with the megaphones were trying to persuade the students to sit down. After long negotiations, the protesters finally agreed to move back: a no man's land of twenty yards was established between them and the police.

At 1.27 p.m., as I recorded it in my log, the students sat down on the road. For the first time I noticed dark clouds, close overhead.

At 1.28 p.m., without any warning, the police charged forward and snatched the space which the students had yielded.

There was immediate uproar: all the students were on their feet, jabbing their fingers and bellowing. They had made a concession, in good faith and in the interests of lowering tension, and the police had taken advantage of it. From within the campus, where still larger numbers of people were watching over the wall, came a booing jeer.

At 1.29 p.m., the demonstrators' anger was boiling over in chanting and fist-waving. The lines of police and special forces stiffened. Sensing the surge in tension, the cameramen and photographers scuttled forward.

At 1.30 p.m., the rain began.

Everyone cheered.

It was the heaviest kind of tropical rain, and it transformed the atmosphere completely. In such rain, you have a choice: either seek shelter close at hand, or resign yourself to getting as wet as you will ever be when fully clothed, short of jumping into a swimming pool. Within a few minutes the scene outside Trisakti had been transformed from a tense confrontation to water play.

A few of the students tried to rekindle outrage against the police; many people ran inside or simply gave up and went home. But most stayed and laughed beneath the rain, as their anger was washed away. The banners grew heavy and sagged. The cameramen swaddled their cameras in protective polythene. People held newspapers, books and scarves over their heads. In all that crowd there were no more than three umbrellas, and a dozen people struggled for shelter beneath each one – one of them, bright yellow, was decorated with the ears of Mickey Mouse.

After the rain had stopped I climbed the pedestrian bridge which led over the road. It was blocked by police in black body armour carrying rifles and sticks. I told them that I wanted to photograph the scene on the road below, and they had me take pictures of them too, smiling with thumbs up, posing with their guns clutched against their chests.

I bought fried dough and oranges and ate them standing beside the Tacticas. It was almost twelve hours since I had woken up in the dark. I felt very tired and found myself thinking about the woman who was not going to become my wife and whom I might not see again. Most of the correspondents were leaving now. I turned down a couple of lifts back into the city.

The students and police officers continued negotiating and by late afternoon they began once again creating a space between them. The confrontation had been averted; the demonstration was coming to an end. I walked for fifteen minutes along the closed road and picked up a taxi at a busy intersection. My hotel room was oppressively hot, but I took off my damp clothes and fell asleep immediately.

An hour later I woke up with bitter voices in my head, the fresh memory of disappointment and humiliation. I had thought to have sidestepped my personal pain, sublimated it in the drama of a greater public moment. But the moment had not been great enough. It was the middle of the evening, lunchtime in Europe, and time for me to start writing an account of a large but disciplined demonstration by Indonesian students, which had ended peacefully.

I switched on my computer, and logged on to the news wires. After reading a few lines, I immediately rang the mobile phone of a friend who worked for Reuters. He said that it was true: in the last few minutes, the police had opened fire on the students at Trisakti University. He was in his car, stuck in traffic, and trying to get through to the hospital.

Four students were killed during the demonstration at Trisakti. I saw them that evening, in the Sumber Waras hospital, a few hundred yards from the university.

It was immediately obvious that something awful had happened. Inside the hospital entrance, young men and women were standing around, speaking quietly in small groups. Some of them had bloody elbows and noses from the police batons. They looked stunned, and several of the girls were crying. The reporters formed a huddle around one woman, as she read out the list of four names, all of them young men, students of Trisakti, shot dead two hours ago: Hendriawan, Hafidin Royan, Hery Hartanto, Elang Mulya Lesmana. The woman spoke in a whisper, and the rest of us too talked in hushed voices. The moths flapped against the naked bulbs, and the women cried. I wrote the names down in my notebook with a sensation of clarity and excitement.

One of the students led me down the corridor and through the wards. The deeper that we entered, the more people I saw weeping.

In a small blank room were four beds, with the body of a dead student on each one.

The bodies were covered with sheets, and the sheets were

specked with blood. On each bed someone had placed a piece of paper bearing the deceased's name, age and university faculty. Friends of the dead boys were standing around the beds, crying, or chanting prayers from the Koran.

Two young women entered the room, and the sheet was pulled back from the face of Hendriawan, the economics student. His eyes were closed, and his lips were parted. He wore a red headband, and behind his left ear was a blood-soaked bandage. One of the girls reached out to touch his face, and flinched when she felt how cold he was. I took three photographs as she did that, as she touched her friend's cold face.

Another student took me to the bed of Hery Hartanto, and lifted the sheet. His eyes were half open, and he had tangled hair and glassy skin. Hery Hartanto was a member of the engineering faculty. They said that he had been shot in the chest, but his chest remained covered up. There was a lot of blood on the sheet, but his face was unmarked.

I took two photographs of Hery Hartanto before I was led out of the room.

Outside, more and more people were arriving to see the bodies of the dead boys. I saw a diplomat I knew; he was carrying a mobile phone and made frequent calls to his capital, 'so that M——' – his foreign minister – 'knows what to say'. He had just walked around the university campus which was quiet and deserted now. In his hand he held out the cases of two spent cartridges.

The end of one was round and regular; this, he said, was a rubber-tipped round. The police used these openly, firing them into the air and occasionally into crowds, when blanks failed to break up a demonstration. They had a narrow calibre, and hard blunt tips; at close range they could certainly kill. But the mouth of the second cartridge had crinkled indentations. 'You see the difference?' said the diplomat. 'That one is a blank – this one is a live round. This is the proof. They were firing live rounds.'

*   *   *

On the night of the killing of the students at Trisakti, something decisive happened among the Indonesian journalists who had been in the hospital that evening. Over the last six months, the newspapers had become bolder by the day, their criticisms less abstract and more direct – but television, by and large, had lagged behind. The next morning, though, the TV breakfast news showed everything: the peaceful demonstration, the rain, the sudden shooting, the weeping friends, and the scenes from the hospital. The papers ran close-up photographs of the dead boys on the front page. All of Indonesia was seeing what I had seen the night before and every flag in Jakarta was flying at half-mast.

There was a memorial ceremony at the university. It began early: by eight o'clock there were more than five thousand people gathered in the flower-heaped campus. All the most famous and prominent members of the Indonesian opposition arrived to give speeches. Their message was the same: continue your demonstrations; ensure that they are peaceful; they did not die in vain.

The speakers drove out of the gates to cheers. Some of the students followed them to the cemeteries where the funerals were to be held, but most remained in the campus. There were a few songs and speeches, although none of the passion of the day before. The students had had the stuffing knocked out of them, but outside the campus a new crowd was gathering. They were boys and men from the *kampongs*, the poor, urban villages, which nestled alongside the skyscrapers, shopping centres and universities of central Jakarta. By the time the funeral rally was over, there were hundreds of them milling around on the roads in front of the campus, and calling out for the students to join them.

'Come out!' they shouted. 'Let's take revenge on the police!'

Soon teams of youths were yanking the metal railings out of the central reservation and using them to block the road. Then trees were being pulled down with ropes, and one group of boys began heaving decorative plant pots from the pavements and smashing them. Someone had commandeered a rubbish lorry and drove it under the elevated motorway. The teenage hijackers jumped out and scuttled away, cackling. An orange glow was visible in the cab, and soon the whole truck was burning with black smoke.

Within a couple of hours the intersection by the university was entirely blocked by several thousand people. It was strangely difficult to judge their mood. There were family groups of women and young children here now, and the *kampong* dwellers had been joined by office workers in smart shoes and company uniforms. Most of them just stood around watching the smoke rise from the truck and waving cheerily at the students. But several big groups of young men were indulging in ambitious acts of destruction. One mob looted and burned a petrol station which sent more black smoke up into the air. After that, lots of people carried petrol bombs in their hands which imparted an edge of menace to the whole atmosphere. Street signs and lamp-posts were pulled down: I watched one man demolish a set of traffic lights by bashing it repeatedly with a No Parking sign. A few hundred riot police and marines appeared unobtrusively and formed lines across the road, but they were badly outnumbered and made no effort to disperse the crowd. One place, however, was well guarded – a pink shopping mall and hotel opposite the university which were owned by a crony family. There the police formed tight lines and fired shots into the air when the crowd got too close. Everywhere else they looked sheepish and ill-prepared, as if nobody had told them what to do.

A bank was stoned and broken into. Computer terminals were dragged out into the road and set on fire. What were the police doing? Where was the army? Yesterday, a crowd of well-behaved students had been ruthlessly cut down: what fate could these delinquents expect? But the crowd seemed to understand that the police were not serious. It was extremely tense and strangely unthreatening.

There was a roar of gears, and a big open-backed truck lurched at speed down the main road. Its windscreen had been smashed, and cheering youths wearing coloured bandannas were clinging on to the outside. One by one they leaped off and the driverless truck careered on down the road, scattering rioters and policemen. It trundled to a stop, and soon it too had been set on fire. A horrifying body lay on the road nearby, a boy who had slipped as he jumped off the lorry and whose head had been run over by its wheels.

Darkness fell. With the trucks and the petrol station still glowing and smoking, the crowd began gradually to break up and to go home.

When Jakarta began to burn, Suharto was not even in Indonesia. In an extraordinary gesture of confidence, he had flown out the previous weekend to a conference of Islamic leaders in Cairo. However much they hated him, Suharto made Indonesians feel secure. His absence made a giddy situation more unpredictable still. Twenty-four hours earlier, Jakarta had been a place of anger and frustration, but order. Now anything seemed possible. Purges, coups, massacres. Tanks on the streets, bombardment from the sea, fire from the sky. Nothing would have come as a surprise.

The next morning I climbed into a taxi with a group of colleagues and drove towards north Jakarta. Every building that possessed shutters had them pulled down and padlocked. Freedom Square, the vast square field facing the presidential palace, was empty of people, apart from small and scattered detachments of police. North of the square, a street called Gajah Mada led through Chinatown and towards the docks. Beyond here the taxi driver refused to go.

The looting had begun early. Gajah Mada was a long and very straight road; a sewer-like canal ran down the middle of it and there were shops and offices on both sides. The sky was overcast and, as we walked north, sections of the street were obscured by billowing smoke. For several hundred yards, there was nobody to be seen. Then suddenly, out of an alley, several dozen people ran whooping, each of them carrying a brand new pair of shoes. They whooped even more loudly when they saw us, and jumped up and down waving their shoes in the air. Then they whooped away into the smoke.

We walked on as the smoke thickened and cleared. A pair of women trotted in the opposite direction grasping between them a large frozen joint of meat. Beyond them was a crowd of people, a thousand or more, and close to them was the source of the smoke: half a dozen burning cars, some of them tipped on to their sides. The crowd was standing in front of a shuttered building with a sign outside advertising electrical appliances. Men were running up to it and launching flying kicks at the shutters, which squealed metallically. Then three of them lumbered up carrying a heavy metal street sign which they used as a battering ram. There were all kinds of people here, from little boys in shorts to old men and women. The onlookers counted the blows of the battering pole.

'One! Two! Three! Four!' As the shutters split open there was a general cheer.

Within moments, two of the young men emerged carrying cardboard boxes with pictures of televisions on the side. And soon the onlookers – the young couples and schoolchildren and old ladies – were clambering inside themselves, and tottering out again with whatever they could carry.

All along the road the same thing was happening. At the Hollandia Bakery people ran in and out carrying boxes of cakes and buns. A frozen-food shop had already been stripped, the source of the joints of meat. Two little boys of about seven years old walked by in their school uniforms. One was carrying a book of blank receipts, the other a plastic bag of disposable safety razors. Suddenly there came a commotion of running and cries.

'The marines!' people were shouting. 'The marines!' A few scarpered down side streets. Most just put down their loot and stood at a nonchalant distance from it.

Eight young marines walked up with their rifles at the ready.

They moved slowly, spread out across the street in a wide line, and passed the electrical shop and the smashed offices. A little further on was a furniture showroom out of which a group of men and women were manoeuvring an awkwardly shaped table. Absorbed by their task, they had no idea that a patrol was coming. As they guided the table through the broken shutters, one of the women tripped and fell at the feet of the marines. Seeing them, she stood up and screamed, but the captain spoke softly to her and raised his hand in a calming gesture. The woman smiled and giggled, and the captain shook her hand. It was obvious then that the marines were more nervous than any of the looters. They went steadily on their way and as they walked a man shouted out: 'Long live the marines!'

Everyone responded, raising their fists in the air. 'Long live the marines! Long live the marines!'

People ran up and began shaking their hands. The marines looked pleased and sheepish and tremendously relieved. A group of cheering looters walked alongside them as they moved up the street. Behind them, the bursting of shutters and breaking of glass took up once again where it had left off.

We spent about four hours in Chinatown. As the day wore on, we hired motorcycle riders to give us lifts down the side streets and further north towards the docks. There was burning and looting all over Jakarta. It continued all day and throughout the night.

The mess was extraordinary. Paper, cardboard, glass, metal, plastic, wood, cloth, foliage and food crunched, snapped and squelched underfoot. By midday, there were more people than ever on the streets, most of them bearing loot of one kind or another. Some people had opened their stolen boxes and set up impromptu market stalls on the pavement. But looting was already giving way to destruction. I saw TVs with their screens kicked in, pyres of CD players, and watched one man carefully set fire to an industrial floor-sanding machine. Most of these people were half-hearted thieves: over the next two weeks, thousands of conscience-stricken looters returned their spoils to the owners of the ruined shops. Even on the day itself, the acquisitive urge was surpassed by the urge to destroy.

A big shopping centre caught fire slowly. For a long time it exuded black smoke in thickening billows, then the exterior concrete began to blacken and char; finally, the inner walls and partitions of wood and plaster fell away, and flames were visible. The building made unexpected noises as it burned: deep crunching sounds and mysterious crackling pops. The fire had started in a McDonald's on the ground floor: the yellow plastic arch of the famous logo slumped and drooled in the heat like one of Dali's melting watches.

We attracted a lot of attention on Gajah Mada Street. There was a dangerous, skittish atmosphere; the crowds were prone to sudden panics and surges. As a car burned itself out or a shop was emptied, a cry would go up and hundreds of people would all sprint in one direction, towards a new spectacle or away from an imagined threat. Sometimes the spectacle was my friends and me: a circle would form, and people would shout questions and wave the things they had looted, and beg to have their photograph taken. But then the excitement would take on an edge, we would be poked and jostled, and we would have to push through the circle, smiling all the time, to climb on to the waiting motorbikes and drive away.

It was hard to get much sense out of those who were actively looting. People would explain their actions by saying that they had come 'to support the students' and 'to tell Suharto to resign'. They parroted the students' slogans about reform, and the evils of corruption and nepotism. But many of the younger men had a crazed air about them, almost as if they were on drugs. There were numerous exchanges of the following kind.

Journalist: Why have you come out here today?

Rioter: Fackin Suharto! Fackin fackin fackin fackin fackin Suharto!

Journalist: Why are you against Suharto?

Another rioter: Suharto bad. Suharto bad man. Bad, bad man, Suharto.

Journalist: But why . . . Hey! That's my camera!

A few television crews were mugged that day; many had narrow escapes. One colleague told me how, faced with a demand to hand over his mobile phone, his camera and all his money, he had had the idea of punching his fist into the air and shouting, '*Hidup Rakyat!* Long live the people!'

'Long live the people!' shouted the happy crowd, to the irritation of the muggers, who were morally obliged to join the chorus. 'Long live the people,' he shouted again and again, and then, 'Long live the journalists!' And soon everyone took this shout up too, and he was able to march back to his car at the head of the friendly mob and drive safely away.

I had begun to feel nervous in my small, cheap hotel, so I moved to the Mandarin Oriental where most of the foreign press was staying. My room was on the eighteenth floor. From the window, late in the afternoon, dozens of columns of smoke were visible in every direction.

The Jakarta police would eventually release a helpful set of figures describing the material damage. According to this official reckoning the riots destroyed 2,547 shophouses, 1,819 shops, 1,119 cars, 1,026 private homes, 821 motorcycles, 535 banks, 486 traffic lights, 383 office buildings, 66 buses, 45 workshops, 40 shopping malls, 24 restaurants, 15 markets, 12 hotels, 11 police stations, 9 petrol stations and 2 churches.

Some 1,200 people died in Jakarta alone, many of them trapped in burning buildings; 2,000 more were arrested. There were smaller but equally intense riots in Surabaya, Medan, Solo, Palembang, Pekanbaru, Bandar Lampung, Boyolali, Karanganyar and Sukohardjo. The destruction was not indiscriminate. The rioters were drawn to symbols of oppression and inequity: the gleaming shopping centres full of unaffordable foreign brands; car and motorbike showrooms; the homes of New Order toadies.

The Social Affairs Ministry where Suharto's daughter Tutut had recently been installed was burned, and so were the booths along the airport road where Tutut's company collected the tolls. But those who suffered most were the Indonesian Chinese.

The home of Liem Sioe Liong, one of Suharto's oldest and wealthiest friends, was ransacked and torched. But the Chinese who suffered the most were petty traders and shop-keepers. Theirs were the CDs and VCRs and laptops being looted in Gajah Mada. Many of them died in their homes, when the shops below them were set on fire. There were persistent stories, difficult to substantiate, about teams of young men who broke into the upstairs apartments and raped the female occupants.

It was an extraordinary, unclassifiable spectacle: a political protest, a pillage and an ethnic pogrom. Has anything like it been seen in modern peacetime: a capital city sacked by its own people?

It is the conviction of most Indonesians that the May riots were not spontaneous, but were deliberately engineered for political reasons. There is some evidence for this belief. For a start, there was the inertia of the security forces, after their brutal and unprovoked intervention at Trisakti. Then there was the eerie speed with which the rioting took hold in widely scattered parts of a huge city. Consistent stories emerged of agents provocateurs who arrived early in the morning and encouraged local people to start looting shopping malls and showrooms. These accounts described the arrival of military trucks carrying well-built young men dressed in civilian clothes, but with close-cropped military-style hair. They would set fire to tyres or rubbish in the street to draw a crowd, and then start throwing stones and breaking windows. Then they would produce crowbars and cans of petrol, and break open shutters and start fires. And once the looting was well underway they would quietly disappear.

The provocation was assumed to have been carried out by

one of two rival factions. One was led by the defence minister and chief of the armed forces, General Wiranto, the other by his enemy, Lieutenant General Prabowo Subianto, commander of the Strategic Reserve. Wiranto was Suharto's former adjutant; Prabowo was his son-in-law. Wiranto was a secular nationalist; Prabowo was associated with Muslim hardliners. One general or the other, depending on which theory you believed, ordered the killings at Trisakti and started the riots. Perhaps the purpose was simply to humiliate his rival. Or perhaps it was to discredit Suharto, and create a situation in which a new strongman (Wiranto or Prabowo) would be needed to 'restore order'. Indonesians love conspiracy; wherever they look, they glimpse puppet masters. Perhaps that is a natural consequence of decades of powerlessness under a corrupt dictatorship. But it is also part of the Javanese sense of fate, the conviction that history moves on its own predestined path, uninfluenced by ordinary men.

Certainly, there were rivalries among the generals, and there may have been provocateurs at work that morning. But the accounts of them were always second-hand and it was days after the riots that they began to circulate. I saw nothing of them, and nor did anybody I spoke to during those three days.

The sack of Jakarta was pitifully easy to understand on its own terms. Poor Indonesians had plenty of reasons for destroying their city; the reasons had been accumulating for years. That was why as the riots wore on, more and more of the looters shed the look of naughty surprise which many of them had worn in the morning. Instead, they took on the air of people doing something quite natural and understandable, the only way, under the circumstances, that they could be expected to behave.

News of the killings at Trisakti and riots reached Suharto in Egypt, but it wasn't until the second day that he decided to return. In a speech in Cairo, he said that he 'had no problem' about stepping down 'if the Indonesian people no longer have confidence in me'. 'I will not stay on through the force of arms,' he said. 'Not like that. I'll become a *pandito*, bringing myself closer to God.' A *pandito* is a Javanese sage, one of those whose meditation and austerities bring spiritual harmony to the kingdom. From time to time, Javanese rulers had abdicated to become *pandito*. And now, at this moment of crisis, Suharto was explicitly using the language of kingship and mysticism.

He landed at the military airbase in the early hours. A convoy of a hundred cars and armoured vehicles escorted him back to Sandalwood Street. The road to the civilian airport, meanwhile, had been taken over by bandits who stopped travellers to the airport, robbed them at knifepoint, and stole their vehicles. There was more looting the following morning, but the atmosphere in Jakarta had changed. For a start there were tanks all over the place, more tanks than I have ever seen – on corners and at the big intersections, and circling the roundabout in front of the hotel.

Two days after the shooting at Trisakti, I climbed on to the back of a motorbike and drove towards east Jakarta where smudges of smoke could still be seen. We reached a shopping centre which had been thoroughly burned the day before. Air force troops in orange berets were guarding the shell, but people walked freely in and out. They were congregating around plywood trays filled with what looked like charred pieces of wood. A man squatted on his heels, holding them up for inspection. And close up you could see that they were body parts, fragmentary and barely recognisable: a wrist, an elbow joint, something that might be a thigh or a buttock, and a clenched pair of burned human hands. On the wrist was a metal watch, so little damaged that you could make out the time: 12.04.

Hundreds of people had burned to death in shopping centres all over town. The remains were being gathered up that morning, and they were transported to the mortuaries by the sackful. Cipto Mangunkusumo Hospital received hundreds of bags which were roughly reassembled into 239 bodies. Only fifty were in a state to be identified. The rest were tipped two days later into a mass grave.

THE WAYANG

By the weekend, the rioting had spent itself and a weird calm settled over Jakarta. Finally, someone had given the order to flood the city with tanks and soldiers. There was no more looting, but the only significant traffic was in the direction of the airport where thousands of expatriate families queued for flights to Singapore. In the Mandarin Oriental an antic atmosphere prevailed.

All the normal guests had left and the place had been taken over by journalists, each demanding Internet access, fax facilities, supplementary telephone lines, satellite television and room service. Camera positions had been set up on the roof, and Indonesian academics and politicians could be spotted in the lobby on their way up to be interviewed by the correspondents. The hotel's elegant Italian restaurant was as raucous as a student common room.

With so little to see on the streets, the only thing to do was to sit at the telephone and speak to people who might have some idea of what was going on. But nobody knew. One of his former cabinet ministers told me that Suharto was about to declare martial law. A distinguished political scientist insisted that he was safe for several months at least. There were rumours that Suharto's children had fled – to Britain, Singapore or Australia. Everyone assumed that a mighty struggle for power was going on between the two rival generals, Wiranto and Prabowo. One of them, it was said, was planning to force Suharto out in a coup; the other wanted to save the old man by brutally repressing the students. Or else they were beating out an agreement to join forces in defence of Suharto – or jointly to oust him. As to which general inclined in which direction, there was no agreement. All we could do was look out for signs, and hope that we would recognise them when they came.

A formation of tanks, moving from one divisional headquarters towards another? A lone helicopter taking off from the presidential palace? Bodies dangling from lamp-posts? A letter, printed on the gilded notepaper of the Mandarin Oriental, was pushed under the doors of the guest rooms.

Dear Sir/Madam

As we all brace for a possible escalation in the social unrest we would like to advise you where to assemble in the event of a possible emergency.

The assembly point is Pelangi Terrace, which is the pool deck located on the fifth floor of the hotel. Please note that in such an event the fire alarm will continuously ring, the lifts will be grounded and the emergency exit staircases only can be used.

It would be appreciated if you could turn off the lights when leaving the room and close the curtains.

Kind regards

Jan D. Goessing
General Manager

It was impossible to relax, or to talk about anything but the riots and the students and Suharto. There was an air of menace, an overwhelming sense that something was about to happen, suddenly and violently, and that if your attention lapsed, even for a few moments, you ran the risk of missing the whole thing.

At his home on Sandalwood Street, Suharto was receiving visitors from parliament, the army and the mosques. His callers were tactful and indirect. They chose to 'explain the aspirations of the students' rather than explicitly asking the president to resign. In response, he agreed to repeal the price rises and to reshuffle his cabinet.

It was obvious by now that he had to go. As long as he stayed, Indonesia would never recover. He was more than an obstacle to the solution; he had become the problem. But the demonstrations and the riots had not been enough to persuade Suharto himself of this. He was clinging on.

Amien Rais, the professor and student leader from Yogyakarta, announced a mass demonstration for the following Wednesday, a national holiday which commemorated the birth of the Indonesian nationalist movement. A million people, he promised, would gather to pray and demonstrate peacefully in Freedom Square, in front of the presidential palace and in the shadow of the National Monument. After the shock of the riots, there was a dawning sense of destiny, of history in the making, and of trepidation. People said that National Awakening Day would be Indonesia's moment of People Power, its Velvet Revolution, or its Tiananmen Square.

On Monday morning a big crowd gathered at the University of Indonesia campus in central Jakarta. The students wanted to drive in buses and trucks to the Indonesian parliament and enter the building to present their grievances. Having sat out the riots, they were taking back the initiative. It was a bold and dangerous move.

The Trisakti shootings, after all, had taken place less than a week before, and in an atmosphere far less tense and uncertain than this. The students were accompanied by a group of retired generals, academics, poets and politicians, many of them former members of the New Order who were now openly calling for Suharto's resignation. Officially, they were lending moral support to their juniors; actually, they were human shields, intended as a discouragement to any trigger-happy troops.

It was an exceptionally hot, still and humid day. The students boarded the buses, dressed in the bright blazers of their various universities, and the banners and posters hung limply in the soggy air. Watching the students, it was striking how different they were in appearance from the rioters of the week before – tender faces, healthy, well-fed skin. I followed the convoy on the back of a motorbike and dismounted at a safe distance to approach the gates of parliament on foot. There was a great crowd of coloured blazers and khaki and blue uniforms, but no clear lines between them. As I drew closer it became clear why. The gates of parliament were open. The police and the soldiers were letting the students in.

They were letting in journalists too. In March, when the People's Consultative Assembly had met here to re-elect Suharto, you had needed two sets of identity cards to enter. Today, a camera and a notebook were enough to get waved through. There were thousands of students inside already, and more were arriving all the time. Many of them, it became clear, had travelled in trucks provided by the army. This last piece of information took some time to absorb. The police and the army, who had killed demonstrating students at Trisakti on the previous Tuesday, were now inviting them into the parliament to press the case for Suharto's resignation.

Physically, the parliament consisted of two parts: a large white 1960s shoebox containing offices and, beside it, the green-roofed structure which contained the parliamentary chamber. It took the form of of two domelike hemispheres joined at the edges, which had been variously compared to the humps of a camel, the cups of a brassiere and a pair of upturned green buttocks. A line of soldiers stood at the top of the steps, sealing off the entrance into the buttocks. Everywhere else, the students walked freely.

In front of the parliamentary buildings was a broad open area of lawns, ponds and fountains. Boys carrying megaphones marshalled the students into groups according to university: the yellow blazers here, the scarlet blazers over there. The bolder among them were entering the parliamentary office block and starting to explore. I followed them into a large open hall with staircases and lifts. Members of parliament were coming out of their offices to see what was going on, to find themselves surrounded by groups of students, politely setting out their demands. After several wrong turns I found myself in a gallery looking down on a windowless chamber. Dominating its dim, beige interior were the wings of the great golden Garuda of the Republic of Indonesia, flanked on either side by the official portraits of Suharto and his deputy, Habibie. This was the Second Committee Chamber of the People's Representative Council. The gallery was filling up with students – they were being allowed to wander wherever they liked. At the podium, a man in black *pitji* was speaking in front of an audience of a few dozen MPs. It was Amien Rais. A student in a green blazer interpreted what he was saying for me.

It was a familiar message. Parliament and elections must be reformed. The judiciary must be strengthened. Politics must be opened up once again and patronage abolished. No more corruption, collusion and nepotism – the slogan of the students. 'By using meritocratic principles, with God's help, we may be able to save this country,' he was saying. 'At the moment, every-thing depends on the president, and we can't afford this any more.' The only thing remarkable about this was the setting, inside the guts of Suharto's toy parliament. Students were arriving on the balcony all the time. Each one of them, hearing Amien Rais's words, looking from the MPs to the speaker at the podium, the podium to the portraits on the wall, registered an expression of amazement at the juxtaposition: *him,* saying *that,* to *them, here.*

'I have talked to labourers, fishermen, housewives and students, and they have a single demand,' Dr Rais was saying. 'Suharto has to step down. Anything else is cosmetic. A cabinet reshuffle is just cosmetic. There can be no political reform without a change of national leadership. We are running out of time.' He jabbed his finger at the portrait on the wall. '*He has to go*, and the sooner the better.'

In Indonesian law 'insulting the president' is a crime punishable by imprisonment. For that week, though, it was a national sport. The scene in the grounds of the parliament was the equivalent of the All Indonesia President-Insulting Championships.

Thousands of students had arrived by now, and they teemed across the grounds. There were a few dozen soldiers, but all they did was watch and politely fend off the red roses that were being pushed down their rifle barrels. After a while they gave up even trying to protect the green domes, and the students crawled all over them as well. After weeks of wary demonstrations, it had finally become clear that there were no longer any rules. Having breached parliament, the students reasoned, it hardly mattered what they did once they were inside.

A mime artist, wearing only a loincloth and with his skin painted in the red and white of the national flag, acted out the struggle of Indonesia on the paths around the fountains. Another group dressed as mourners carried on their shoulders a cardboard coffin containing a symbolic Suharto. Presidential effigies suffered terrible indignities on the lawns. Sketches and poetry and songs were being performed to rhythms beaten out on thousands of empty plastic water bottles.

The hand-held banners were quickly seen to be inadequate for the vast space which the students now occupied, and teams were quickly at work with paint and sheets. Soon new posters, forty feet high and inscribed with entire political manifestos, had been draped from the windows and across the green cheeks of parliament. Sitting on the grass the blazered groups passed chants

back and forth among one another. There was the ever-popular
'Hang Suharto', and a new favourite, a children's nonsense
rhyme, adapted to refer to the most notoriously greedy of the
president's children.

> Bambang Tut!
> Bambang Tut!
> Akan galing!

> Bambang and Tutut!
> Bambang and Tutut!
> Their daddy is a dog!

There was also a song about the martyrs of Trisakti. The chorus
was translated for me as follows:

> My heroes have passed away,
> My flowers have faded away.
> The soldiers are all cockroaches.

A small number of the banners were in English, including
one which ambitiously combined the diminutive of Suharto's
name and the popular theme song from the film *Titanic*. 'My
"Harto" Will Go On . . .' it began in conventional lettering which
then changed into a dripping Gothic, horror script, '. . . To Hell!'
An accompanying cartoon depicted the president being graph-
ically dishonoured by demons.

Delegations of students and opposition elders came and went
all morning, converging on the office of Harmoko, the speaker
of the Indonesian parliament. Harmoko had lived the life of a
quintessential crony. Having led the toady journalists' union for
a number of years, he established a toady newspaper, then ran
the ruling party before being promoted first to information
minister and then to his present position. He was head of both

houses of parliament: the People's Representative Council, which drafted legislation, and the larger People's Consultative Assembly, which chose the president.

Constitutionally, he was third in the national hierarchy, after Suharto and Vice-President Habibie; it was no surprise that his home in the city of Solo had been stoned, looted and burned. But Harmoko had been badly shaken up by this, people said. Perhaps that explained what he did at parliament that afternoon.

Soon after lunchtime, Harmoko entered the parliamentary press room accompanied by his deputy speakers – each of them veteran toadies, seasoned beneficiaries of Pancasila democracy. Among them was the head of the armed forces faction, Lieutenant General Syarwan Hamid – the man who had organised the raid on the opposition headquarters in 1996 when the plain-clothes commandos had gone in at dawn with their knives.

The statement took only a couple of minutes to read. Afterwards, copies of it circulated among the students, and the soldiers let them climb up on to one of the tanks to proclaim it aloud. The news resounded across Jakarta; by the time I got back to parliament, an hour and a half later, the students were still jumping up and down in celebration. 'The Speaker and Deputy Speakers,' it began, 'who are concerned with the good of the nation, call on President Suharto to act with wisdom and erudition and do what is right: resign.' As Harmoko had come to the end of the announcement, the TV cameras showed the grinning Lieutenant General Hamid clenching his fist and punching the air.

Many of the students left parliament after that. They thought that the struggle had been won, but they were wrong. Word went about that General Wiranto was to make a statement of his own on the other side of town, at the Defence Ministry on Freedom Square. It was held in another windowless, colourless chamber, filled with journalists and diplomats. An hour after he was supposed to make his appearance, there was still no sign of

Wiranto. An adjutant entered and placed name cards in front of the seats where the commander-in-chief and his senior generals were to sit. Lieutenant General Prabowo's was not among them.

It was obvious to everyone that Wiranto was going to make an announcement of great significance. The ease with which the students had entered parliament, the capitulation of Harmoko, this long wait for the general's arrival (he was said to be at Sandalwood Street, talking with Suharto): surely all of this meant that the moment of crisis had now been reached? Wiranto suddenly marched in. Prabowo was with him.

Wiranto had a handsome, troubled face and walked tall and straight. Prabowo was stocky and piglike, and his face was sweaty. Wiranto went quickly into his statement, stood up with polite thanks, and walked out followed by his staff. Fifteen minutes of confusion followed as those who understood Indonesian quarrelled among themselves about what had been said, and those who did not stood around them helplessly.

But it became clear that Wiranto had offered nothing new or decisive. He had warned against the big demonstration which Amien Rais was planning for National Awakening Day. He excoriated the rioters, and promised that the armed forces would defend and protect the constitution and national stability. He expressed support for Suharto's cabinet reshuffle and a 'reform council' of academics and critics. He did not denounce Harmoko or his parliamentary statement, but pointed out that, without a full parliamentary vote, it was merely the opinion of individuals without legal force.

His words were mild, conciliatory and unconvincing. They diminished none of the tension. This was to be the pattern of the week: sudden waves of excitement which surged to a peak, only to dissipate into feeble ripples.

It was a thrilling time, and like many people in Jakarta I was experiencing self-conscious flushes of excitement at the momentousness of it all. A struggle was taking place between something old, murderous and corrupt and something new. One power was dying; another was fighting to get born. In a century of such changes in countries all over the world, this was the last time that it would happen. Such events are flattering to those who witness them; you feel that just by being there you are courageous.

Words, which until then had been historical abstractions, were taking on concrete form: uprising, revolution, People Power. I had always imagined such dramas proceeding according to a structure, with a stately and orderly rhythm. But there was no rhythm to these events at all. They were like the movement of traffic in a Third World city. They blared and screeched and ignored the signs. They were punctuated by collisions and dead ends. They kept you awake at night.

The next morning Suharto appeared at his palace where he met with a group of nine Islamic leaders. Amien Rais had pointedly not been invited, and nor had Megawati Sukarnoputri. But all of those present advised the president to resign.

Afterwards, he gave a speech which was carried live on the domestic and international news channels. It was a comically clumsy broadcast. The cameras began rolling before Suharto was aware of them, so for several minutes viewers all over Indonesia were able to watch him standing obliviously in the large palace room, grey-faced and podgy, killing time with his hands in his pockets. At one point, Suharto crooked his left arm and looked at his watch. A photograph of this gesture was used in newspapers and magazines across the world over the following days: the failing dictator, running out of time.

When he eventually delivered his statement, though, he did so calmly and without a trace of defensiveness. 'I have taken the decision as president to implement and lead the national reform immediately,' he announced, as if reform was a notion which he had come up with himself that morning in Sandalwood Street. He also had big news about the next presidential election: 'I will not be prepared to be elected any more.' A new president would be chosen after parliamentary elections. These would be held 'as soon as possible'.

When visitors called on Suharto, he told them, 'I've had it with being a president,' and 'I'm sick of the presidency.' It was the old pose which he had maintained before every election, when delegations from parliament would have to beg a reluctant Father of the Nation to allow himself to be nominated once again. *They* had asked him to do it, Suharto was pointing out now; he had never *wanted* the job anyway. It was only his overwhelming sense of duty which had compelled him to accede to the pleadings of the people – and now see what the ingrates were doing! Well, he was sick of it. He would quit. He just wasn't prepared to say when that would be.

At parliament, where they watched it on television, Suharto's speech went down very badly with the students. There were 30,000 of them here now, people said, and they had become both better organised and much more on edge. A group called the Voice of Caring Mothers was bringing in packed lunches and crates of water. Everyone who now entered was required to prove his bona fides to sceptical and sometimes aggressive stewards. Suharto's continuing stubbornness made the students' presence in parliament seem too good to be true. There were rumours that thugs from one of the toady youth groups were infiltrating the demonstrators to stir up violence among them as a pretext for a crackdown. People thought they could see snipers in the high buildings overlooking parliament, or at least the narrow red laser beams which they used as sights. When an army helicopter flew past, and hovered menacingly low overhead, the students screamed and cursed it with fury and dread.

Normal parliamentary work had come to a stop; the entire complex was now a playground for Suharto-baiters. They slept on the grass and washed in the fountain. In the chamber, they stood at the podium acting out impersonations of Suharto and Harmoko. There was no vandalism, only the squelching, rattling detritus of 30,000 people – discarded twists of paper containing cold rice and congealed chicken, and thousands and thousands of empty plastic water bottles.

Everyone was focused on the following day, National Awakening Day, and Amien Rais's million-man demonstration. Some of the students would remain in parliament, but most were to march early in the morning to Freedom Square. Schools, shops and offices would be closed. The supermarkets were filled with panic shoppers. By evening, the students were afraid of all kinds of things – of infiltration, of a murderous military raid in the early hours, of more riots provoked by tomorrow's march, of a confrontation with armed police. Distinguished professors and lawyers and doctors were coming to parliament by the hour to support and applaud the students. They would stand on the bonnets of jeeps with bandannas around their heads, and remind them of Manila in 1986 and Seoul in 1987, and of Timisoara, Prague and Berlin. Then they would take their bows, punch the air and drive home for the evening, leaving the students to think about tomorrow's march and about the student uprising which their sponsors had been so careful not to mention, the one in Beijing in 1989.

Before dawn, an army general, whom he refused to name, telephoned Amien Rais and warned him of another Tiananmen Square massacre in Jakarta if the rally went ahead. At 6 a.m., Dr Rais appeared on television and announced that it was cancelled. Twenty thousand people demonstrated peacefully in Medan that day, 30,000 in Solo, 50,000 in Surabaya, 100,000 in Bandung and in Yogyakarta the Sultan himself led a crowd of more than half a million. But in Jakarta, Freedom Square was deserted.

At breakfast time I drove by motorbike taxi down the empty main road which led up to the National Monument. Forty thousand troops had been deployed throughout the city, with 160 tanks. All the streets leading to Freedom Square had been sealed off with razor wire. There was no traffic apart from the tanks and no people except soldiers. The stillness and emptiness transformed the place. From behind the wire roadblock, I noticed for the first time the yellow blossom that grew in the trees in the square, and the voices of the birds in their branches. Since Dutch colonial times, this space had been the heart of the city, almost the symbolic centre of the archipelago, occupied twenty-four hours a day by Indonesians eating, drinking, sleeping, buying, selling, flirting and fighting. Never in its history can it have been so quiet.

There were soldiers at parliament as well. The road at the front was closed off, and it took an hour of pleading and cajoling to get in through the back gate. Many more universities had sent delegations to Jakarta for the march. After its cancellation they had come here instead, and the place was so full that it was difficult to move. The crowd, so focused and disciplined until now, had grown unmanageable and rather frightening. Even the Caring Mothers could not provide enough food and water. There were stories that parliamentary offices had been broken into and documents burned. The thought of being caught in this mass when a panic took hold of it – after shots had been fired, for instance – was appalling.

I found a vacant patch of grass, among the patchwork of blazers which the students had spread across the ground. They were eager to talk, and they were unanimous in their opinions. As the latest pamphlets put it: *Suharto, Go To Hell With Your Plan – Step Down Now.*

There Can Be No Reform Until Suharto is Replaced
Do Not Be Fooled by Suharto's Tricks
Suharto's Goal is to Avoid Resigning

News came from inside the chamber that the People's Consultative Assembly, the body which chose the president, was going to be summoned on Friday to a special session. The threat was made explicit by Harmoko himself: if Suharto hadn't resigned by then, he would be formally voted out of office.

I began talking to the students sitting next to me about Javanese superstition – about the luminous *wahyu* which fizzes through the sky at the passing of Power from one king to the next. They wore the yellow blazers of the University of Indonesia; most of them were medical students. They smiled at my questions but, as we talked, all of them came out with their own stories of magic. One girl, a trainee anaesthetist, had spoken just the day before to a noodle seller who had seen the *wahyu* at the height of the financial crisis three months ago. It had risen up out of Sandalwood Street and flown south. He had described it as 'a snake of light.'

'Gus Dur lives in that direction,' said the anaesthetist's friend – this was the nickname which everyone used for the blind Muslim leader, Abdurrahman Wahid.

'So does Megawati,' said a young man in 'Hang Suharto' T-shirt.

'Or it could have been going to Yogya,' someone else said. 'To Amien Rais.'

'No! Yogya is a long way.'

All the students were still smiling.

Then a boy in a bandanna asked, 'Do you know Jayabaya?'

'Yes, I do.'

'Do you know Sabdopolon?' Sabdopolon, he explained, was another Javanese prophet. His most famous prediction was that, five hundred years after being overrun by Muslim invaders, the ancient Hindu kingdom of Majapahit would return.

'When was the end of Majapahit?' I asked.

'Five hundred years ago.'

We all smiled again.

Then the second girl asked, 'Do you know the name of Moses Gatotkaca?'

Moses Gatotkaca had been the first victim of the violence of May 1998. He was a thirty-nine-year-old activist in Yogya who had been eating with friends at a roadside restaurant when one of the big demonstrations passed by. The police charged, he and his friends found themselves surrounded by thrashing batons, and Moses had been beaten to death.

'And you know where his name comes from?'

Gatotkaca, they explained, was a character of the *wayang*, a hero of the Pandawa clan, the army of good. He was staunchly loyal and patriotic – Sukarno had once described him as the model of the New Indonesian Man. Gatotkaca was killed by the evil King Karna, in the apocalyptic battle between the Pandawa and their enemies, the Kurawa.

'And Moses Gatotkaca was killed by Suharto,' said the first girl. 'One of the students killed at Trisakti was Elang Mulya Lesmana. Lesmana? You know he's a character of the *wayang* too?'

'Suharto knows the *wayang*,' said her friend. 'He loves the *wayang*. It is performed for him sometimes, privately, in his palace. He knows what those stories mean. What does he think to himself, what is his secret feeling, when he reads in the newspaper that he has killed a man named Gatotkaca and a boy named Lesmana?'

It was twelve days since Moses Gatotkaca had died in Yogya. It seemed to have been as many weeks. I thought of the Sultan's palace, and the decision I had reached there all those days ago, and of the woman whom I was not going to marry. If I had not lost my nerve and called her that morning, if I had flown back to Europe a few hours before the shootings at Trisakti, I would have missed all of this.

'When Suharto reads that in the newspaper he knows his time is up,' answered the boy in the T-shirt. 'He knows that it is finished.'

ASCENSION DAY

Suharto resigned soon after nine o'clock in the morning of the following day, Thursday 21 May 1998. I had woken at dawn, as usual. It was Christ's Ascension Day, another of those intriguing facts of which Suharto might or might not have been aware.

Already, the hotel was full of rumour. Suharto was to make another announcement and, having failed to find recruits for his reform committee, there were only so many things left for him to announce. I climbed into a cab with two friends and drove towards the palace to watch it in person. But the driver could not find his way through the roadblocks, and the announcer on the radio talked as if the statement was going to begin at any moment. We jumped out at the next hotel we saw – a small, cheap hostel, emptied of its backpackers – and watched it on the fuzzy television set in the café.

Just as before Suharto's last national address, there were delays. The TV picture cut between the empty room in the palace with its microphone stand and the excited announcers in the studio. When they had run out of things to say, a series of pop videos were screened, featuring warbling *dangdut* musicians. There was a smiling young keyboard player with white teeth and a crooner with an oiled moustache. One of the songs was called 'A Pair of Eyes', the next one was 'Three Nights'. 'It is a famous song,' said the man who was interpreting for me. 'Famous from the Sukarno time, from the 1960s.'

Then we were back in the palace, and Suharto was walking in and standing at the microphone. Muslim clerics and military officers with gold braid on their uniforms were visible behind him. There was General Wiranto, and Vice-President Habibie – and Tutut, the oldest daughter. Suharto was wearing his black *pitji* and a short-sleeved safari suit. He looked a little tired behind his spectacles, but his delivery was characteristically flat and unin-flected; only occasionally did he look up from his text. He was as calm and self-possessed as ever. He gave no impression of being in the grip of strong emotions, or of trying to suppress them.

Habibie, his eyes bulging with alarm, was sworn in immedi-ately as president. The frowning official of the Supreme Court held the Koran above his head as he read the oath. Then Wiranto gave a speech, and it was over.

Later on, I read the end of the New Order described as being 'like sex without orgasm'. It was as unmomentous a historic moment as could be imagined – perfunctory, anti-climactic and unconvincing.

Suharto began by speaking of his 'deep understanding' of the people's wish for change, and of the 'inadequate response' to his proposals for a reform committee. He requested forgiveness 'if there were any mistakes and shortcomings' in his leadership. He thanked the ministers of his outgoing cabinet. 'May the Indonesian nation remain victorious with Pancasila and the 1945 Constitution,' he said. At no point did he express sadness or regret.

The words which were picked over most closely were those which expressed the act of resignation itself. In Suharto's mouth, the abandonment of his office was transformed from a moment of humiliation into a confident assertion of power. 'I have decided,' he said, halfway through the brief address, 'that I have ceased to be president of the Republic of Indonesia as of the time I read this on this day, Thursday, May the twenty-first, 1998.'

He managed to make his defeat sound like an order, to be executed on the double, with vigour and dispatch. Rather than being pushed, he was making a bold leap. It was a *coup d'état* in reverse: Suharto, by the force of his will and personality, was unilaterally naming himself Ex-President.

'The utterance was self-executing in a way reminiscent of the power ascribed to the god-kings of ancient Java,' the political scientist Donald Emmerson wrote later, '– that merely by saying something, they could make it happen.' One of Suharto's favourite Javanese axioms was *victory without causing humiliation*. His resignation had achieved the reverse: a defeat which robbed his enemies of all sense of triumph.

We left the backpacker hotel and drove towards parliament in silence. Many of the roadblocks were still in place and the driver took an indirect route. We passed down a street where live animals were sold on the pavement. For a few days it had been deserted, but this morning the vendors were out again, sitting on their haunches in small groups, smoking and talking and listening to radios. They must have heard the news but they displayed no signs of excitement. I remember staring out of the window of the taxi at cage after cage of captive puppies.

The students in parliament had watched the broadcast, and marked it with scenes of conventional jubilation. Cheers, dancing, mass leaps into the fountain. Many people simply prayed; the flag which had been hanging at half-mast was raised to the top of the pole once again. But the euphoria did not last long. The students didn't like Habibie. Many of them hated him. He was, after all, one of Suharto's oldest friends. This was the weakness in their campaign: it had concentrated on removing Suharto without establishing any consensus on who should replace him. The credible candidates – Amien Rais, Megawati, Abdurrahman Wahid – were divided by rivalry and mistrust. The Constitution said that if the president becomes indisposed the vice-president must take over for the rest of his term. And that is what had happened.

There were fewer students than the day before, and their numbers were being diluted by ordinary Jakarta people, middle-class sightseers, who had begun arriving in family groups. Some of the students were resolved to stay where they were and to occupy parliament until Habibie, and even Wiranto, had also resigned. But most of them were leaving. Soon teams carrying black rubbish bags were about the grounds, making inroads into the drifts of plastic bottles. Wandering among them were the tourists, shaking hands with the students, posing with them for photographs and pointing out to their children the sights of this remarkable happening which seemed already to be slipping into history.

The next morning, large groups of youths from Muslim youth organisations turned up at parliament carrying pro-Habibie banners. There was taunting and stone throwing; a riot was narrowly avoided. It was clear that this was not a spontaneous demonstration, that it had been well organised, probably at the behest of the new leadership.

In the early hours of the morning after that, trucks of armed soldiers arrived and instructed the students to leave immediately. They made a show of refusing; there was a little shouting and jostling, but no blows, stones or shots. The protesters didn't seem surprised to see the soldiers; some of them looked almost relieved. And within an hour or so, they were forming lines, climbing into the trucks, and leaving parliament with barely a murmur.

The day after the resignation, I began to feel very sleepy and rather confused. The insomniac clarity of the past two weeks had blurred to a fog. What exactly had happened, after all?

Suharto had been replaced by his most loyal retainer. Habibie promised reform, but when he appointed his new cabinet, half of the ministers, and all the senior posts, were unchanged. In the speech he had given immediately after Habibie's swearing in, Wiranto had promised to support the new president, to protect the nation, and to 'safeguard the security and honour' of Suharto and his family. And so the man whom the students had vowed to hang continued to live undisturbed in Sandalwood Street.

Most remarkable were the many things which had *not* happened. There had been no crackdown or massacre. (In retrospect, it was the *in*action of the military which was most striking.) There had been no open split in the military (whatever General Prabowo might have been planning, he was foiled; by the weekend, he had been relieved of his combat command and dispatched to a distant staff college). This had not been a coup or insurrection, and it could hardly be called a revolution, because only the head of the government had changed. It was hard to call it a triumph of People Power, because the crucial decisions – to stand back from the rioting, to allow the students into parliament, to call the special session of the Consultative Assembly – were not made by the people at all. They were made by the elite, by soldiers and New Order toadies appointed by Suharto himself.

What if the economic crisis or the forest fires had been brought more swiftly under control? What if Suharto had not introduced the price rises? What if he had not gone to Egypt? What if the Trisakti students had not been shot? What if Harmoko's house had not been burned down? What if the Freedom Square demonstration had gone ahead? I stayed in Jakarta for another fortnight, and slipped away for a week in Bali before flying home. At the end of all that time, there were still no clear answers to such *What ifs*.

At some point, between the deaths at Trisakti and the first day of full-scale rioting, Indonesians had simply lost their fear. The pain of economic crisis and the shock of the massacre allowed a numb courage to take hold and Suharto's talisman, the memory of the killings of 1965 and 1966, lost its transfixing power. The students who stood up most prominently against him were of a generation too young to remember them. Everyone else was able to forget for just as long as was necessary. But the fear of Suharto had only gone into hiding. Hardly had he left his palace than it returned.

Within a week, President Habibie had started to release political prisoners. By the summer, newspapers and magazines which had been banned by Suharto began to publish again. In a matter of months, hundreds of new political parties had been established and before the end of the year, the Constitution had been revised: a parliamentary election would be held the following summer, the first free election since the 1950s.

But Indonesia's situation was desperate. All over the country, murderous conflicts were breaking out – political, religious, racial. People made comparisons with Yugoslavia and the Soviet Union. They spoke seriously of the prospect of Indonesia breaking up. For thirty years, conflict had been frozen under the chill of the dictatorship. Now the thaw had come and old rivalries and hatreds were emerging intact and alive from beneath the ice.

I flew back to Indonesia in the spring of 1999. On the island of Ambon, a civil war had broken out between Muslims and Christians. There was guerrilla fighting in Aceh, and militia violence in East Timor. There were mysterious explosions in Jakarta and in East Java hundreds of elderly villagers were being lynched as witches. And there was the killing in Borneo, which I saw for myself. These troubles were separated by thousands of miles. The origins and motives behind them were as diverse as Indonesia. But in every case, people blamed Suharto.

In a church in Ambon a young man told me that Suharto had sent agents to stir up the Muslims against the Christians. A Muslim insisted that Christians had been provoked to take up arms by the same means. A Madurese explained why the Indonesian army had so conspicuously failed to prevent the killing of his people: Suharto had prevailed upon them to hold off deliberately, to permit the situation to spin out of control. A Western diplomat told me of a trip he had made to report on the killings of the East Java witches. In three different towns he had had conversations with three different police chiefs. Each had an elaborate theory about the killings, all were mutually contradictory, and each, at some point or other, made an entirely separate connection with Suharto.

But the basic conviction – that Suharto, in retirement, was actively plotting violence across the country – was shared by everyone. Taxi drivers in Jakarta believed it. Clove farmers in

Ambon believed it. Amien Rais and Abdurrahman Wahid both believed it and said so publicly. But it was an assumption, based on fear; there was no evidence at all. 'One doesn't have any proof,' Dewi Fortuna Anwar, President Habibie's closest adviser admitted. 'But still, by using logic, it seems rather naive to expect that someone who has built up so much power, who has built up this pyramid of patronage, would simply lose all that power in one sweep.'

From time to time, as they approached the ends of their lives, the kings of Old Java would retire to some remote and holy spot where, rather than dying, they would simply disappear. The moment was called *moksa*. 'In this way,' wrote the scholar Soemarsaid Moertono, 'the idea of change was relieved of the banal abruptness of man's work and became coloured with the smooth inevitability of God's predestination'. Suharto, on the day of Christ's Ascension, had done the same.

His life in retirement was a mystery. Occasionally, his presence was reported at a mosque, or at the theme park which his late wife had built on the outskirts of Jakarta. Those who knew him said that he hardly left the house.

He would wake at 4.30 a.m. for the first of the five daily prayers. After that, he performed stretching exercises on a terrace overlooking a small garden. Caged birds were kept there, including mynahs which had been taught to sing the national anthem, and to cry 'Allah is Great!' At home, he wore a sarong and a polo shirt, except when receiving guests, for whom he put on trousers and a batik shirt. At mealtimes, he favoured simple Javanese food – steamed banana, rice crackers, noodles in soy sauce. For several days a week he fasted during the hours of daylight.

Apart from occasional outings, he had all but given up his hobbies of golf and deep-sea fishing. 'He told me, "I feel sad for this country. It's facing difficult times and there's been a lot of bloodshed. I can't bring myself to go fishing,"' one friend said. 'He no longer has state activities, but his religious activities have multiplied. Most of the time he's preoccupied with religion.' The month after his resignation Suharto turned seventy-eight; two years before, he had undergone heart surgery. But despite his age, and despite the tumultuous changes which he had seen in the past year, none of the friends I spoke to had any concerns about his physical or mental health. 'It's amazing, but it's part of his character,' said one of his lawyers. 'He's very calm. Very, very, *super* calm.'

His supporters presented the pious plainness of Suharto's life as something reassuring, a demonstration of his sincerity. But his seeming indifference to his fate, his refusal to be visibly shaken by what had happened to him, was one of the things that scared Indonesians the most.

Suharto saw a lot of his lawyers. It was time well spent. An investigation was in progress into allegations that he had siphoned off billions of dollars of state funds. An American magazine estimated the family's collective wealth at 15 billion dollars. But successive Attorney Generals showed no enthusiasm for pursuing the case. When charges of corruption were eventually laid, his legal team successfully argued that, because of ill-health, the former president was unfit to stand trial. The youngest of the Suharto sons, Tommy, would eventually be sentenced to fifteen years for murdering a judge; his golfing chum, Bob Hasan, got six years for corruption. But Suharto did not even appear in court.

Only once did Suharto dignify his accusers with a response. In a rare interview in a weekly magazine, he denied that he had a fortune, and that he had any part in the continuing violence. He had resigned, not because he had to, but to avoid further confrontation. During three hours of questions, he showed not a trace of self-doubt or regret. 'If I wanted to orchestrate armed disturbance why didn't I do it on 21 May,' he asked, 'since I still had command of the armed forces? Because I did not want to see victims and chaos, I resigned.' At the same time, he had a conspiracy theory about his own fall from power. 'A Zionist plot,' he explained. 'The government of Indonesia is not vigilant enough towards the Zionists' plan which is very well planned and systematic.' An Indonesian who often visited Suharto told me that his private mutterings on the subject were even more fantastical, involving retail bar codes and the number 666.

Habibie's Attorney General, a former army officer named Andi Ghalib, was challenged in parliament about the slow progress of the investigation. 'It's like cutting a big tree deep in the forest,' he said. 'You could not just jump into the forest and cut it down . . . or you'll end up devoured by tigers or big snakes.'

Among more sophisticated Indonesians, the demonisation of Suharto had become a motif of popular culture. You could buy T-shirts depicting him with a huge question mark across his chest; a friend showed me a novelty computer screen saver which had been doing the rounds in Jakarta. It began with a blank screen, upon which appeared the stationary figures of cartoon generals, complete with uniforms and rows of medals. Then – slowly at first, but with increasing speed and frequency – another figure popped up behind them and between them, here, there and everywhere: the grinning, mischievous face of Suharto.

Whatever mysterious forces were at work, it was inconceivable that one man could be behind all Indonesia's troubles. He had become a bogeyman, a ready-made explanation for complicated pain. But Suharto ruled by fear for thirty-two years, and the fear lived on. In the end, it did not matter whether the conspiracies were true or not. What was important was that they were believed.

Suharto's inescapable presence in Indonesia was all the more remarkable for being almost entirely invisible. Even before his resignation, an incurious visitor might pass weeks in Jakarta without ever realising that there was such a man. During three decades in power he eschewed utterly the cult of personality. There were no Suharto Avenues, Suharto Squares or Suharto Mosques; when he resigned there were no statues or public posters to pull down. As a visual icon he survived in only one form – on the 50,000-rupiah note.

During his presidency, every public and private office in Indonesia carried a pair of photographic portraits: the president, twinned with the vice-president of the moment. In the space of a few months, Suharto's image had been removed to leave only that of Habibie. But all over the country, he survived, and in appropriately ghostly form. In companies, schools, government offices, even in some private homes, telltale picture hooks still protruded where Suharto once hung, above unfaded rectangles of fresh-looking paint.

Power, in the ancient Javanese conception, has no moral or ethical component. As Benedict Anderson wrote thirty years ago, it 'antecedes questions of good or evil . . . Power is neither legitimate nor illegitimate. Power is.' And Power can depart as swiftly and mysteriously as it comes. 'The signs of a lessening in the tautness of a ruler's Power,' according to Anderson, 'are seen equally in manifestations of disorders in the natural world – floods, eruptions, and plagues – and in inappropriate modes of social behaviour – theft, greed, and murder.'

By the time the symptoms of declining Power are observed, it is already too late. Power is all or nothing; a king who has to struggle to assert his authority is no king. 'A ruler who has once permitted natural and social disorders to appear finds it partic-ularly difficult to reconstitute his authority,' wrote Anderson. 'Javanese would tend to believe that, if he still had the Power, the disorders would never have arisen.'

The Javanese king was the Nail of the World, the harmoniser of the seen and the unseen. Without him, the kingdom lost its moorings and hurtled off into places unknown. Disasters followed, and fearful supernatural happenings which were both omens of the king's fall and signs that he had already ceased to be the Sustainer of the Universe. The human order was affected as well as the natural one; there was war, violence and unnatural behav-iour between men. The Age of Gold gave way to the Time of Madness. And so the fall of a king became a general catastrophe.

THE SHARK CAGE: EAST TIMOR 1998–1999

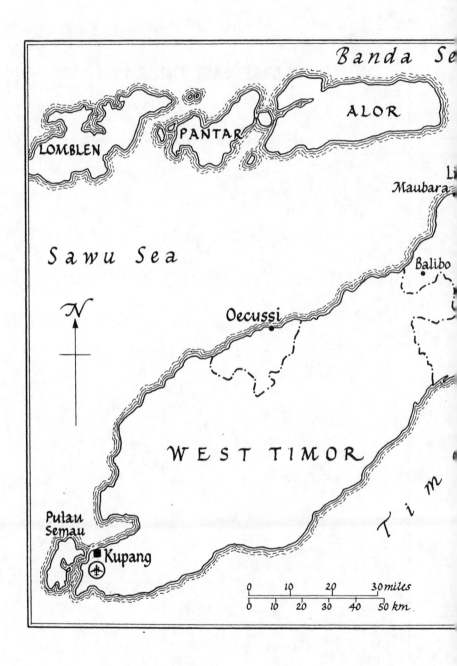

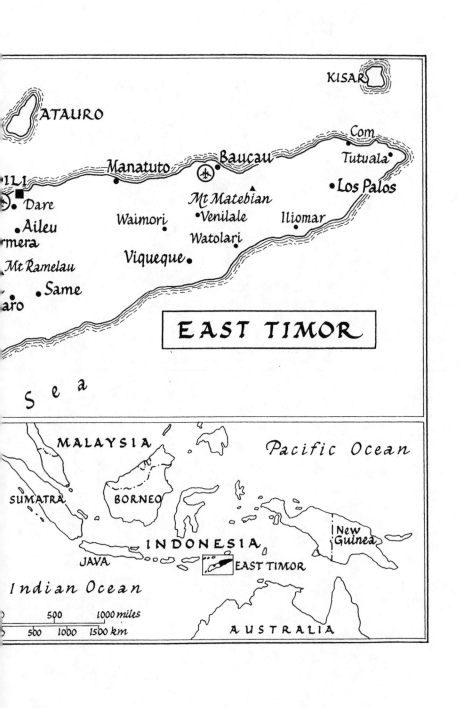

THE CROCODILE

In Dili, a few months after Suharto's fall, I met a young woman named Rosa Soares who worked as a reporter on the local newspaper *Voice of East Timor*. I asked her about Timorese legends, and she told me this story.

Long ago, in this part of the world, there was no Timor and no Timorese, only a tiny isolated island in the middle of the ocean inhabited by two little boys. One day they were playing on the beach when they came across a great crocodile who had been washed ashore. The crocodile was exhausted and close to death; the little boys were afraid of him. But pity overcame their fear. Cautiously, they brought the creature fresh water and fish, and pushed him back into the sea. Soon, he revived; moved by the kindness of his rescuers, he asked what he could do for them in return. The little boys were lonely on their island and had never stepped off it in their lives. 'Let us ride on your back,' they said, 'so that we can see for ourselves this island where we live.'

So the boys climbed onto the crocodile's broad back, and the three of them sailed off. The crocodile swam and swam, and the boys were delighted with everything they saw. Whenever the crocodile was about to pause and rest, they always spied some new attraction and insisted on swimming over to see it. The crocodile began to feel exhausted again; above all, he began to feel hungry. Soon he was very hungry indeed. As the boys laughed and gurgled on his back, he considered what to do.

The boys might be small, but they were tender and juicy: a

flick of his great tail, two gulps, and the crocodile's hunger would be satisfied. But they had saved his life, and he could not bring himself to take theirs. So he continued to swim round and round the tiny island, the burden on his back becoming heavier and heavier, the movement of his tail slower and slower, until he stopped moving for ever.

In death, the crocodile became the island of Timor: his nose was at Kupang in the Indonesian west, his tail was at the eastern town of Tutuala, and his spiny back formed the mountains where Falintil lived. 'So, somehow, the two little boys found two girls,' Rosa said, 'and their children were the first Timorese. The little island where they first lived is Pulau Semau, off Kupang. So that's why Timorese are not afraid of crocodiles, because they protect us.'

A moment or two later, Rosa said, 'Well, that's not strictly true. There's a priest in Dili who has a crocodile as a pet, and once an old man tried to feed it. It bit his arm off above the elbow. So people are afraid, but they're not, if you understand what I mean.'

I asked whether wild crocodiles were often seen.

'Quite often,' said Rosa. 'When they're seen by the shore, it's a sign that something is going to happen, something big.'

'Really? When was the last time?'

'About a week ago. Last Thursday, I think. A few people rang the paper and said that there were crocodiles by the beach, just in front of the Turismo. We sent someone over there to have a look, but by the time he got there they had gone.'

East Timor was in a state of restless uncertainty when I first went there, neither fully at peace, nor properly at war. Suharto had fallen five months ago and, judging from the intermittent news which made it to the outside world, the atmosphere in Dili, the East Timorese capital, had changed dramatically. It was in 1976 that Indonesia had invaded the half-island colony known at the time as Portuguese Timor. At the beginning of 1998, it had still been a country of fear and spies, living in the shadow of the most notorious of East Timor's massacres, when hundreds of young mourners had been murdered by Indonesian soldiers in a Dili cemetery seven years earlier. But by October, Timorese were experiencing more freedom than at any time in twenty-two years. Large-scale demonstrations had been held, warily tolerated by the occupiers. The clandestine groups opposing Indonesian rule had publicly set up shop in an office in the centre of the town. In August, brass bands had played on Dili wharf, as the Indonesians had made a show of withdrawing troops in a seeming effort to reduce tension in the territory. I interviewed the junior foreign minister of a European government who was spending a few days in Jakarta, as many junior ministers were in those days, urging democracy on the new government. 'The ambassador was there a few weeks ago, and he was saying last night that Dili is transformed,' he told me. 'Fish restaurants opening, people staying out in the evening and strolling on the beach. Almost a Mediterranean lifestyle.' The ambassador, who looked like a man who appreciated a nice piece of fish, nodded and smiled.

Even the East Timorese guerrillas, it was said, were spending more and more time in the town, sneaking down from the jungle for meetings, rest and conjugal visits. This information especially interested me for, as long as I had been aware of East Timor, I had been fascinated by the men known by the Portuguese acronym, Falintil – the Forças Armadas de Libertação Nacional de Timor Leste. For twenty-three years they had lived in the jungle, pursued by the Indonesian army, driven high into the mountains, starved, bombed and napalmed, a dwindling force that never quite died out, armed with a few Portuguese rifles and whatever else they could steal from their enemies. As active fighters they seemed to number no more than a few hundred, and the Indonesians insisted that they were spent as a force. Their leader, Xanana Gusmão, was in prison in Jakarta, and it had been almost twenty years since they had won a significant military victory. But somehow they survived, occasionally they mounted an ambush, and on their account some 15,000 Indonesian soldiers were deployed in East Timor. Every few years a foreign journalist would sneak in to see them, and return with stories of hair-raising hikes through the jungle, and with photographs of bearded men in khaki, posing before barbecues of skinned snakes and monkeys. I began to collect books and news clippings about East Timor; I daydreamed about undertaking the same adventure. Falintil were heroes and, as I contemplated an encounter with them, I began to feel a little bit of a hero myself.

But how to bring about such a meeting? I consulted activist groups in Britain and Australia and made discreet enquiries among the small Timorese community in Jakarta. Friends passed me on to friends; after a few days, there was a soft knock at the door of my hotel room. Outside stood three young, dark-skinned men with silver crosses round their necks. They hung back from the door and peered into the corridor before stepping into the room. They sat side by side on the hotel sofa as I explained that I wanted to go to East Timor and to find out for myself the truth of what was happening there. Above all, I wanted to test two of the Indonesians' claims: the first, that they were pulling out troops; and the second, that Falintil was on its last legs. To do this I wanted to travel into the jungle and meet with the guerrillas face to face.

The men listened silently, then spoke quietly to one another in a language which I took to be Tetum, East Timor's lingua franca. A call was made from the telephone by my bed, a long involved conversation in Tetum and Portuguese. All at once, it was agreed. One of the Timorese, a small man with a thin face and creases beneath his eyes, would come with me to Dili. From there, he would make further contact with the fighters; with luck – although there could be no guarantees – he would guide me to them in the forest. He had served under one of the Falintil commanders, and his name was Jose Belo.

After that things began to move quickly. Jose, it was agreed, would travel to Dili first, and I would follow a day later. My cover was that of a tourist. I was to check into a hotel and remain inconspicuous, or as inconspicuous as possible. Then I was simply to wait until I was contacted, although what form this contact would take, and who would make it, was unclear.

The plane from Jakarta flew first to Bali, then Kupang in Indonesian West Timor, and finally to Dili. The journey filled most of a day; I could have travelled to Europe in the time it took to reach East Timor. I lifted the books and folders from my knapsack, pulled down the flimsy plastic table from the back of the seat in front of me, and began to read.

What was East Timor? Until 1975, few people would have been able to find it on a map. The first European traders landed there in the early sixteenth century; two hundred years later, for arbitrary reasons of colonial convenience, the island had been divided into eastern and western zones overseen by the Portuguese and the Dutch. In area, Timor was a little smaller than Belgium, and it had the harshest climate in the archipelago. In the wet season, the rain washed through the jungle and down the rocky hills, carrying away huts, roads and fields; for the rest of the year, there was a penetrating dryness. Timor had none of the mace and nutmeg of the Spice Islands to the north – apart from sandalwood, there was only one significant export. 'Timor provides good-natured slaves for household purposes,' one European traveller noted in 1792. And so, throughout its colonial history, the world at large paid it no attention.

Not that the island was a peaceful or uncomplicated place – beneath the noses of the colonists was a ferment of different languages, races and tribes. Into Timor had come waves of immigrants and interlopers: Belus and Atonis, Malays, Melanesians, Papuans and Makassarese, Arab traders, Chinese merchants, Goan Indians, as well as Dutch administrators, German mercenaries, English sailors, Portuguese friars and their African slaves.

For decades on end, smouldering wars were fought between the colonists, the local chieftains, and a strange kingdom of mestizo bandits known as the Topasses. No white viceroy was able to tame them: time after time, the Portuguese Governor Generals were trounced and humiliated. Low-level warfare was unending and the colonists and missionaries quickly contented themselves with exploiting the coastal region while leaving the interior to look after itself.

A charismatic tribal chief led a long-running uprising which was put down by Portuguese gunboats in 1912. Australian commandos fought the occupying Japanese during the Second World War, and then fled, leaving their Timorese comrades to face vicious reprisals. After the surrender, the Dutch quit and the East Indies became independent Indonesia. But the Portuguese returned to East Timor, and fecklessly took up where they had lackadaisically left off. By the 1970s, as far as the outside world was concerned, nothing of significance had happened there in five hundred years. Then the changes came in a rush.

In April 1974, Portugal's fascist president was deposed by left-wing army officers who quickly set about ridding the country of its colonies. The news caused tumult in East Timor. Within weeks, the territory's tiny middle class – a few civil servants, teachers, journalists, tribal chieftains, seminarians and the handful of students who had been to foreign universities – were feverishly organising and pamphleteering. Soon there was a Labour Party, with ten members who all came from the same family. There was the equally minuscule Popular Association of Monarchists of Timor, later renamed the Sons of the Mountain Warrior-Dogs. There was Apodeti, a small and truculent group of chieftains who supported integration with Indonesia. Only two of these new organisations came close to being authentic political parties: the Timorese Democratic Union and Fretilin, the Revolutionary Front for an Independent East Timor.

The founders of the Democratic Union were conservative civil servants and plantation owners eager to get their hands on the levers of power. Fretilin's activists were young, many of them freshly returned from universities in Lisbon, Macao and Luanda; despite the party's assertive name, their revolutionary zeal didn't go much beyond a passionate yearning for independence. The Portuguese were impatient to get out, and throughout 1974 East Timor appeared to be trundling steadily towards freedom.

The two main parties formed an alliance. By the end of the year, the Portuguese governor had set a timetable for elections. The Fretilin students went out into the villages to set up health and education programmes; the Democratic Union cultivated Catholic priests and conservative local leaders. The pro-Indonesian party was almost completely ignored. There was no doubt – there never had been any doubt – that what most East Timorese wanted was independence.

Then the government of Lisbon, weary of everything to do with colonialism and facing economic troubles, began to have second thoughts. Timorese independence, after all, would not be the end of Portuguese responsibility, but would bring a continuing obligation towards the tiny, neglected state. For Australia, a free East Timor was also a headache – a small, fiddly, unpredictable country just four hundred miles from Darwin. A glance at any map, hanging on the wall of a briefing room in Lisbon or Canberra, presented what seemed like an elegantly obvious solution: Indonesia, the vast, stable, anti-communist state into which East Timor fitted like the missing piece in a jigsaw.

Soon after the coup in Lisbon, a group of Suharto's generals had decided independently that Portuguese Timor must become part of Indonesia. They hatched a plan to bring this about. It was codenamed Operation Komodo, after a small Indonesian island and its most famous inhabitant, the giant carnivorous lizard called the Komodo Dragon.

Our plane stopped for an hour in Bali, then flew east over the shining Sawu Sea and the green and golden brown of the Lesser

Sunda Islands – Lombok, Sumbawa, Flores, Roti. Komodo, too, was down there somewhere. I craned my neck to peer through the porthole, but one island looked as remote and immaculate as the next. I drank from my beaker of warm juice, and read about the dirty tricks campaign known as Komodo.

On government radio stations in Indonesian West Timor, exiled supporters of integration were hired to broadcast bitter propaganda against the 'communist' Fretilin and 'neo-fascist' Democrats. Indonesian spies were spotted taking photographs of East Timorese beaches. Stories were spread about the infiltration of Fretilin; there were tales of Soviet submarines cruising the waters off the coast, and of a secret revolutionary army training with communist-supplied arms. In distant Sumatra, the Indonesian armed forces carried out a large air, sea and land exercise. It began with a naval bombardment, followed by a landing of paratroopers and an amphibious assault on a beach.

In Dili, the propaganda had a corrosive effect on the alliance between Fretilin and the Democratic Union. Both sides suspected the other of planning a coup. Both wanted independence, but the Democrat leaders believed that if Fretilin took power, the Indonesians would invade. In August, the Democrats seized guns from the colonial police and drove Fretilin out of Dili. The Portuguese governor stood by and refused to intervene. The ragged conflict that followed came to be known as the 'civil war'.

It lasted little more than two weeks. By the time it was over, a few hundred people had died, Fretilin had won complete control of the country, and the Democrats had been driven over the border into Indonesia. The defeated refugees were allowed in on condition that they sign a petition appealing for integration with Indonesia.

On 16 October 1975, Operation Komodo was upgraded from a clandestine dirty tricks campaign to a full-scale invasion.

After hours of bombardment from sea and air, Indonesian soldiers, accompanied by a militia of pro-integration Timorese,

drove out the Fretilin defenders and seized a border village called
Balibo. There they encountered five television journalists
employed by Australian television stations. They had come to
film the Indonesian build-up, and they had remained there to film
the invasion. Posthumously, they have become known as the
Balibo Five.

They had painted the Australian flag on the house in which
they were staying. According to several eyewitnesses, they
shouted out 'Australia! Australia!' as the invading forces entered
the town. Accounts of exactly what happened next are contradictory. Were they shot or were they stabbed? Did they die
inside the house or in front of it? During the heat of battle – or
after it was over, executed in cold blood? The Indonesian government insisted that none of its troops was even present in Balibo,
and the governments of the dead men, Britain and Australia and
New Zealand, chose not to challenge this version of events. But
all the evidence suggests that the Balibo Five were killed deliberately by Indonesian soldiers, or by Timorese stooges under
Indonesian command.

Balibo was a turning point for East Timor; the country was
lost there, although it was a long way from being lost on the
ground. As a military force Fretilin was formidable. At its core
were Timorese regulars of the Portuguese army. Many of them
– including their commanders, a pair of brothers named Nicolau
and Rogerio Lobato – had front-line experience in the colonial
wars in Angola and Mozambique. Fretilin's army had mortars,
bazookas, new Nato-issue rifles and 75mm artillery. A light gun
was precariously attached to a patrol boat, and now Fretilin had
a navy. There was even a commandeered Portuguese helicopter
– Fretilin would have had an air force if anybody had known
how to fly it.

Inland, beyond the protective reach of their naval guns, the
Indonesians quickly became bogged down. The local languages
and terrain were unfamiliar to them; as the rainy season set in,
their heavy vehicles were mired in the soggy roads. After their

march through Balibo, it was weeks before they achieved any other significant victories. Fretilin awarded its soldiers a proud new title – the Forças Armadas de Libertação Nacional de Timor Leste, or Falintil. As an army, they were holding up stoutly. But as a nation, East Timor's fate was sealed.

Stubbornness and cunning on the ground could hold the invaders back only for so long and, politically and diplomatically, East Timor was friendless. The Australian government, the American and British governments, and all the governments which mattered, knew exactly what was going on and did nothing to stop it. And when they chose to ignore the killing of their own citizens, it became chillingly clear that East Timor was on its own.

Fretilin made formal appeals to the United Nations, but they were ignored. After a two-week battle, the Indonesians took the biggest town on the road to Dili. That afternoon, in a grim and hastily arranged ceremony, the Fretilin leaders declared their independence as the Democratic Republic of East Timor. The following week, on 7 December 1975, a large Indonesian invasion force assaulted Dili by air and sea, and took control of the city within a few hours.

A taunting message was broadcast the following day from the captured radio transmitter. The Fretilin leaders, the announcer crowed, were 'hiding in the caves, rocks and the bushes'. 'Now you are like a deer, a wild pig, a boa constrictor, hiding in the bush,' he continued. 'Brothers of East Timor, the republic that Fretilin declared is dead. It was alive only for nine days . . . Long live the people of East Timor with the Republic of Indonesia!'

But the abandonment of Dili had been carefully planned. Instead of exposing his army against an overwhelming enemy, Nicolau Lobato pulled back to the mountains, where stores of food and ammunition had been squirrelled away.

Indonesia was not the first invader to underestimate the Timorese. In the seventeenth and eighteenth centuries, the European colonists had abandoned their attempts to pacify the interior, after a series of defeats and humiliations. A Dutch general named Arnold de Vlaming van Oudshoorn wrote of watching his men being massacred by the Topasses 'as though they were helpless sheep'. A Portuguese governor and his entourage spent eighty-five days under siege, surviving on rats, leaves and powdered horse bones.

'The Portuguese of Macao drove a very advantageous trade to Timor for many years,' an English visitor wrote in 1704, 'and ... tried by fair means to get the whole government of the country into the Churches' hands, but could not beguile them that way. Therefore they tried force, and commenced a war, but to their cost they found that the Timoreans would not lose their liberty for fear of the loss of Blood.'

The Indonesians installed integrationist leaders at the head of their own 'Provisional Government'; formal union with Indonesia was declared in June 1976. But a year after the invasion, they controlled only a handful of towns and the areas around them.

Tens of thousands of people had migrated into the mountains and to the east, an area amounting to more than two-thirds of the entire country, where life continued almost as normal under Fretilin. Despite their numbers, the refugees were sheltered and protected. The harvest was successfully brought in, and Fretilin organised jungle factories where medicines were manufactured out of roots and berries. There was an organisation of medical auxiliaries, and a network of children and old people who acted as couriers, relaying messages between the resistance leaders. There was even a radio unit, led by the Fretilin information minister who broadcasted reports of the Indonesian atrocities and appeals for support to a receiver in Northern Australia.

In the forest, the Indonesians and Timorese positions were often so close that they could shout taunts at one another. Falintil were outnumbered, but they knew the country, and their enemy was spooked and demoralised. Accounts of the conflict in those early days describe a strangely lackadaisical war, with long periods of quiet between offensives, and a curiously intimate relationship between invaders and resistance. 'One incident which sticks in my mind was when a friend of mine, Koli, shot an Indonesian officer on a slope of a hill,' wrote one former guerrilla, who was fourteen years old at the time. 'They saw each other and laughed for a while before firing. It was sad. First the Indonesian officer fired at Koli and the bullet cut down a branch of a eucalyptus tree, which fell on him. It was then Koli's turn and, sadly, his bullet took away the life of the poor Indonesian soldier. It is possible that the Indonesian soldier's family is still waiting for him to return to Indonesia.'

The Indonesians were foundering, and as their frustration increased so did their cruelty. It took the form of looting, the burning of villages, mass imprisonment, the torture of suspected Fretilin supporters, the rape of women, the massacre of prisoners. But soon the sheer weight of Indonesian hardware began to have its inevitable effect. There were consistent reports that napalm was being used; the Indonesians also employed the fearful Soviet multiple rocket launcher known as 'Stalin's organ'. Jet bombers emptied the mountain villages. Small units of commandos penetrated the mountains to burn the crops.

Like all their campaigns, the Indonesians christened this one with an expressive codename: Operation Encirclement and Annihilation. Its victims were overwhelmingly civilians. And it was this operation which nearly brought the end of Fretilin.

In September 1977, Fretilin's president, a gentle civil servant named Xavier do Amaral, was arrested by the commander-in-chief of Falintil, Nicolau Lobato. Heartbroken by the suffering being inflicted on ordinary people, Xavier had been openly making moves to negotiate with the enemy. A year later, he was captured by the Indonesians. He ended up in Bali, working as a servant in the home of an Indonesian general.

In December 1978, the information minister defected with four other Fretilin leaders, bringing the Indonesians much valuable intelligence. On New Year's Eve, they caught up with Nicolau Lobato, who was killed after a six-hour battle. Shrewd, handsome Nicolau had become a folk hero, the embodiment of the struggle; to Timorese, the news of his death and the photographs of Indonesian generals crowing over his body were crushing. Within a few weeks, the vice-president and prime minister of Fretilin were also dead, and communication between the remaining leaders broke down. Food was running out and the mountain dwellers began fleeing their bombed homes to live in the forest as scavengers. More and more gave themselves up to the Indonesians to be 'resettled' in strategically placed concentration camps.

The defectors had taken with them Fretilin's radio transmitter. The guerrillas had lost their only link with the outside world. In Darwin, the exiled leaders and their supporters tuned into the old frequencies, but from East Timor they heard only Indonesian voices and the hiss of static.

At Dili airport, children and young women pressed their faces against the wire mesh which separated the passengers in the arrivals lounge from the world beyond. A group of Indonesian officers, who had joined the plane at Bali, strode through the door reserved for VIPs; the rest of us extricated our bags from the untidy heap on the floor and joined a slow-moving queue. In front of me, two elderly men in safari suits, dark-skinned and grey-haired, chuckled together in Portuguese. A Chinese man and his young sons busied themselves with a stack of cardboard boxes containing Japanese televisions. At the front of the queue was a table where a man with the epaulettes of an Indonesian civil servant took down names and passport numbers.

'What is your profession?'

'I'm a teacher.'

'And what is your purpose here?'

'Holiday.'

'How long will you stay here?'

'About two weeks.'

The man with the epaulettes handed back my passport.

Beyond the press of faces, I breathed the exhilaration of arrival. A curly-haired man in plastic sandals carried my bags to a decrepit blue station wagon. Only its front doors were capable of opening. Passengers climbed into the back over the driver's seat, and luggage was passed through the window.

'Do you speak Portuguese?' asked the driver in Portuguese.

'Only English,' I said in Indonesian.

'Where your hotel?' he said in English.

'Hotel Turismo.'

After the humidity of Java, the air was bracingly dry, with the smell of unfamiliar trees. Straight away, the town announced its hybrid nature. The street signs bore names like Alvez Aldeia and Avenida Marechal Carmona; the faces passing by ranged from palely freckled to black. In front of the smarter of the buildings were painted signs bearing the names of Indonesian government organisations and military units; between them were older houses of plaster and tile, or blank new concrete structures with shops on their ground floors. We passed a suburb of prosperous-looking bungalows, then a small park, overgrown with palms and eucalyptus. Then the ocean appeared on the left, and all at once the road became a wide esplanade, with trees and grass alongside the water, and space and light all around.

A quayside was visible through the bars of an iron fence; soldiers stood around a gunmetal naval ship. Two hundred yards on, the porticoes of the governor's residence faced the beach across a breadth of neat lawn. On the beach were sandy metal hulks, the wrecks of Indonesian landing craft from 1975. Far beyond them, the beach rose to cliffs and on top of the highest of them was a titanic statue of Christ gesturing over the sea, a gift to the occupied Roman Catholic Timorese from the Muslim generals of Indonesia.

'Suharto made it,' said the driver, laughing and nodding

towards the statue. 'Suharto made Jesus Christ for the East Timorese.'

Beyond the Red Cross headquarters and the Bishop's House, we pulled into the Hotel Turismo.

In Dili, there were two hotels with pretensions to being of international standard, but the Turismo's advantage, and the reason for its popularity, was its immunity to spies. The Hotel Mahkota, opposite the quayside, was bigger and better located but as dim and dusty as a funeral parlour. In the sepulchral, glass-fronted lobby area, shifty-looking youths with moustaches sat glancing sideways on the vinyl sofas. The restaurant was strip-lit and echoic; whispered conversations hissed off its shiny ceiling and into the ears of solitary men who sat by the window, slumped over glasses of warm Fanta. The Turismo had its spooks too – unidentified locals who sloped in and out, smiling unnecessarily and drawing glares from the waiters. But their work was made difficult by the hotel's garden, where clandestine listeners could never feel at ease and where the real life of the hotel went on.

It was not a beautiful or well-tended garden and the first impression on entering it was as much of cement as of greenery. Ragged umbrellas rose above plastic tables, which were embedded in discs of stained concrete. The vegetation consisted of palms, jackfruit, mango and sandalwood, with the eucalyptus trees that gave away Timor's Austronesian character. Palms and bushy ferns rose like partitions between the stained plastic chairs; the garden divided naturally into zones into which guests and visitors could withdraw as distinct from one another as private rooms. In the evenings, they were filled with the chatter of insects and voices: a pair of military attachés just arrived from Jakarta; a visiting Dutch correspondent, talking to the resident Australian freelancers; a woman from the Red Cross with one of the priests from the Bishop's House.

The Hotel Turismo was the kind of place where you felt nostalgic even before you had left. The author of one of the books I was reading, Jill Jolliffe, lived there during East Timor's last three months of freedom in 1975, between the end of the civil war and the invasion. 'At the Hotel Turismo,' she wrote, 'a Portuguese poet shouted his poems to the night air and Rita the monkey chattered in the splaying branches of the mango tree. Falintil soldiers who looked like black Abbie Hoffmans drank the copious quantities of 'Laurentina' beer bequeathed by the Portuguese and juggled grenades across white linen tablecloths ... Lights from Indonesian warships sometimes winked in Dili harbour at night. After the anxiety engendered by their first appearance they became part of the unreal scenery.'

Two young men were waiting for me in the garden the next morning. Instead of plastic sandals, they wore shoes; compared to the Turismo's drivers and waiters, they were tall and well nourished. They introduced themselves as Felice and Sebastião, and they were students at the University of East Timor. Felice was giggly and skinny, and spoke fluent, jabbering English. Sebastião was calm and athletic, and a member of the pro-independence Students' Solidarity Council. Six months earlier, it would have been unthinkable for anyone associated with the clandestine movement to visit a place as exposed as the Turismo. But something had changed in Dili, even if no one could say exactly what it was.

Just three days before, 30,000 people – students, teachers, civil servants and workers – had marched to demand the resignation of the province's puppet governor. Now the students were preparing for a series of 'dialogues'. Convoys of activists would travel from village to village, organising public meetings where songs would be sung, prayers said, and local people encouraged to talk about their experiences of occupation and their hopes for the time after Suharto. The National Council for Timorese Resistance, a coalition of pro-independence groups including Fretilin, the Democratic Union and even the former integrationists, had just opened an office in town. The new government had already released some East Timorese political prisoners, and there was talk that Xanana Gusmão himself might be next. 'We can speak more freely,' said Sebastião. 'We can walk out in the middle of the night. But there are still soldiers all around us. This country wants its freedom, but the soldiers are still here.'

'They say that they are here to give us security,' said Felice. 'But when there is trouble, do people run to the soldiers for help? No, they run to the Bishop's House, and the bishop doesn't have guns.'

The struggle against Indonesia, they said, was different from the struggle against Suharto. 'The Indonesian students wanted a new government,' said Sebastião. 'But we want our own government. We are human beings, and we have the same rights as other people. If Indonesians have the right to self-determination, why not us?' But the signs were that, far from reducing the troop levels in the territory, the military was bringing in more soldiers.

The ceremony in August, when the brass band saw off the soldiers on Dili Wharf was 'bullshit', according to Sebastião. 'What's the difference if they pull out of one town and bring fresh soldiers into another?' he said. Outside Dili, the tension was rising: at the far eastern tip of the island, members of the clandestine network had reported the landing, by night, of large numbers of troops and even tanks. The Falintil field commander, Taur Matan Ruak, the man whom I hoped to meet, had a narrow escape when Indonesian soldiers pounced on him in a remote village. Among the students, there was a conviction that the Indonesians were acting out an elaborate game for the ultimate purpose of greater control; that, having drawn the clandestine movement into the open, identified its leaders and analysed its structure, they would strike suddenly, with arrests and a military offensive, to extinguish resistance once and for all.

It seemed inconceivable that Indonesia would voluntarily let Timor go, or offer any kind of compromise.

'They have Aceh and Papua to worry about, even Maluku

and Kalimantan,' said Sebastião. 'As soon as Indonesia gives us our freedom, they will also want their freedom. Indonesia is a country made of islands. East Timor could be a small explosion that could lead to bigger explosions.'

Sebastião had been born in 1973. The Portuguese had left before he could walk, and the invasion itself was only the dimmest memory. He had been educated in Indonesian; the Indonesian occupation was a fact of life, as mundane and prosaic, for most of the time, as the existence of motorbikes or telephones. How did it feel, I asked, to live as a twenty-five-year-old in the twenty-fourth year of occupation?

'It feels strange,' he said, 'completely strange. You're in your own home, but you cannot behave freely. You have to be careful what you say. You can't talk to this guy or that guy. You feel isolated. We *are* isolated. It's like darkness behind us.'

For the next few days, there was nothing to do but wait for contact from Jose Belo. I made cautious forays outside the hotel on the back of Felice's motorbike. I visited the *Voice of East Timor*, and talked about crocodiles to Rosa Soares. I called on the National Council for Timorese Resistance or CNRT, which was setting up in a house in the centre of town. The rest of the time I read, and talked to the waiters in the garden of the Turismo, and strolled along the esplanade, watching the sun rise and set. The blue station wagon taxis trundled asthmatically beneath the palms. Motorbikes sputtered past, moving so slowly that it seemed impossible that they remained upright. I had expected Dili to be a cowed, nightmarish place, but it was the prettiest, sleepiest and most charmingly indolent capital city I had ever seen.

Twenty-five babies were christened one afternoon in Dili cathedral. The pews and aisles were full before the service had begun, and an overflow of worshippers peered in through the cathedral door: twenty-five extended families, and twenty-five sets of friends and neighbours, all dressed in their Sunday best.

The men wore creased trousers with ironed shirts, the women wore long flowery dresses, and at least half of the congregation were children. On a plinth above stood a plaster Virgin, wound around with blinking fairy lights.

The doors and windows of the small cathedral were open to the morning air. An organ accompanied the singing of melancholy hymns, sung in Tetum in delicate minor keys. A pregnant woman in a green dress called out the multiple Portuguese names of each of the candidates, and a grey-haired priest daubed the water across their foreheads. Afterwards, the congregation emerged into sunshine and the children shrieked and chased one another through the dust. A column of guffawing boys formed up behind me, until they were chased away by a priest.

'Mister!' the boys shouted. 'Mister! Hello, mister! Hello, mister! Mister, mister!'

At the Turismo, the young man behind the reception desk smiled conspiratorially as he handed me my key. 'You have a visitor,' he said, and sure enough, flickering like a shadow among the palms, was Jose Belo. It was the first time I had seen him since arriving in Dili, and he had news which made my heart thump. The final arrangements had been made. Tomorrow we would travel into the forest.

WITH FALINTIL

In Dili, it seemed that everyone I met was dreaming of the forest. Not only the foreign reporters at the Turismo, but the Timorese as well – students, priests, Rosa Soares and her colleagues at the *Voice of East Timor*. In the smaller villages and towns – where the jungle was close at hand and the line between the Indonesians and Falintil, between peace and war, was vague and shifting – the guerrillas were less of a novelty. But for people in Dili, they were remote, magical and revered, the fount of the struggle, whose waters flowed down from the mountains into the hearts of the city dwellers.

In 1990, an Australian activist had become the first foreigner to reach Falintil in the jungle; his interview with Xanana Gusmão gave the lie to the Indonesian claim that Falintil was broken. The visit became legendary, bringing humiliation on the occupiers, and glory for the Timorese who organised the trip. Escorting foreigners into the jungle became the aspiration of many ambitious young men in Dili – one boy, hardly more than a teenager, became notorious for lurking in the shadows of the Turismo and accosting new arrivals with whispered offers to arrange meetings with the commanders. The journalists would glance nervously at one another, and then invite him into their rooms; for a few days, he would pay them late-night visits, assuring them that matters were in hand, and asking for more time. Nothing ever came of these initiatives, but the fantasy brought excitement and glamour to everyone – to the young man, to the visitors, and to the institution of the Turismo itself.

The idea of the forest, I was beginning to suspect, could be more alluring than the forest itself.

There were eighteen hours until we began our journey. For the first two of them, I felt no more than moderately and constructively nervous. I assembled a small bag of essentials – a torch, a camera, spare film, a short-wave radio, a flask of whisky and many, many cigarettes. It was when I turned to my washbag that doubts began to set in. What toiletries, I asked myself, would be appropriate for a guerrilla hideout in the jungle? Sun cream, certainly, and a toothbrush. Shaving equipment would not be necessary. But what about deodorant? I certainly expected to do a lot of sweating – in fact, it was beginning already. And yet the prospect of the forest made the very notion of deodorant ridiculous. I left it out, and gave over the space to another packet of cigarettes.

After that there wasn't much to do, other than smoke, which I did with vigour and concentration. I didn't much feel like eating, and I was forbidden by Jose to talk to anyone else about my plans. The combination of excessive nicotine, inadequate food and solitude began to make me jumpy in eccentric ways. In the toilet bowl of my room was a long shapely turd which I found myself staring at for a long time. It was a beautiful thing, I remember thinking, as the smoke from my cigarette filled the bathroom: who did it belong to? I had not the faintest memory of leaving it there.

At three o'clock the following afternoon, I walked out of the Turismo in the direction of the governor's residence. In front of the Bishop's House, I hailed a blue station wagon and took it down the road by a dried-up creek, close to where the crocodiles had been seen. After two miles there was a bridge, and here I got out.

I walked slowly across it and past a row of shops on the other side. A baseball cap was pulled down over my eyes; I strained to attract as little attention as possible. But every other passerby seemed to be a young and mischievous child who would pipe, 'Hello, mister!' chuckle and scamper after me for a few hundred yards, before disappearing to summon other little friends who did the same. As inconspicuously as the Pied Piper, I reached the shop at which Jose had promised to wait. To my relief I spotted him at once, hiding under his own red hat, fifty yards ahead and motioning me with a light movement of his down-turned palm. I followed at a distance down a dusty track of palms and cockerels. By now, even adults were greeting me with warmth and familiarity; the whole neighbourhood seemed to have turned out to see me off. Jose walked on, glancing back occasionally. He disappeared round a corner, and by the time I reached it, he had gone.

A young woman stepped out from a stand of palms. 'Are you Richard?' she asked.

'Yes, I am.'

'Please come with me.'

'I . . . who are you?'

'I am a friend of Jose.'

She led me to a bungalow set back among blood- and lemon-coloured blossoms. Inside were four people, who stood as I entered and shook my hand – a nun, two young women in starched white blouses, and a man who introduced himself as Billy. No one spoke more than a few words of English, but it was conveyed to me that Jose had gone out for a while, and I was to wait. The house was a kind of sanatorium. There was a locked glass-fronted cabinet containing syringes and drugs, and in two small rooms at the back, six very old men lay on thin mattresses. 'Tuberculosis,' said Billy. 'They have no families in Dili, no children. Soon they die.'

The nurses brought out tea, and sat me down in the front room where I caught up on my smoking. A feeling of unreality was coming over me. Why was I here? Where was Jose? I had seen him so briefly, and from a distance: was it possible that I had followed someone else? Could it be that this tiny hospice was an Intel trap? An hour passed. Then Billy ran in, and said, 'Mr Richard, you come now.' I stepped outside to see a large white pickup truck race round the corner and stop directly in front of the bungalow. The door of the cab opened, revealing three faces. None of them belonged to Jose. The two passengers jumped out and up into the open back; the driver whispered urgently to me, 'Come, come.' I climbed inside.

For half an hour we drove fast around Dili, in and out of narrow side streets, over and around the same roads and crossings. The driver rarely took his eyes off the rear-view mirror. He looked familiar to me, although I had no idea where I had seen him before. When he was satisfied that we were not being followed, he smiled and offered his hand. 'I am Jacinto,' he said. 'Jose's friend.' We were on a wide road in a residential part of Dili, and the truck was slowing down beside a blue car. Someone got out of the car, the door beside me snapped suddenly open, and Jose clambered in carrying an armful of bulging plastic bags. He smiled and nodded at me, and talked quickly to Jacinto. 'We leave Dili now,' he said to me in English. He scrutinised my face and placed his hand on my shoulder. 'Don't worry.'

The front of the pickup truck seated three people, and I was in the middle. The windows were darkened to cut down the tropical glare; even the windscreen was tinted, apart from a narrow central band of clear glass. From the outside, we were all but invisible. I was instructed to keep my cap pulled down and my hair tucked up inside it.

'Your hair is very light,' Jose said thoughtfully. 'If anyone stops us, you just let me talk.'

'What will you say?'

'If it is the police, I just give them some money. If it is the army, we tell them that you are a tourist, and we take you to see the priests at Los Palos.'

'The priests.'

'But you let me speak to them.'

We climbed the steep cliff road above Dili, and behind us the town lay spread out before the sea. The carrier bags at Jose's feet contained supplies for Falintil, principally cigarettes and Pepsodent toothpaste. Halfway between Dili and Manatuto, we saw a military convoy approaching on the road ahead. In the last truck, the soldiers wore jeans, leather jackets and black bala-clavas instead of camouflage. 'Kopassus,' said Jose. 'The Special Forces. They have just come back from operations in the forest.'

The cliffs rose steeply outside the town; for three hours we drove along the beautiful rocky coastal road which runs east from Dili, then turned towards the south on a route which was regularly blocked by mudslides during the wet season. Rough, tussocky bushes rose up towards the jungly hills; looming above them was Mount Matebian, its summit hidden from view by a single neat cloud, like an abode of the gods. Matebian is the mountain of death, and bristling grey rocks jut out of its flanks. Later I was to hear a Tetum song about it:

> Matebian, Matebian,
> There lie the skulls of Lorosae.
> To the west, behold Mount Ramelau
> But in the east, Matebian.
> So many carried off and killed,
> All for your sake, Matebian.
> Because of you, they're dead and gone –
> The blood flows thick across your stones.
> Why does it flow and never stop?

Matebian was the mythological mountain of death long before the arrival of the Indonesians. But in 1978 it was also the site of some of the worst scenes of Operation Encirclement and Annihilation. On its slopes and in its caves, unknown numbers of Timorese villagers were burned, bombed, shot, or starved to death. 'On one occasion, an incendiary bomb, probably napalm, fell on a group of twenty-seven people, who were instantly incinerated,' one Falintil commander wrote. 'At another time, about a hundred people, many of them women, children and the elderly, who had taken refuge in a cave during an aerial bombardment, were entombed alive when a high-explosive bomb detonated outside and completely blocked the cave mouth. After two weeks, we could no longer hear their groans.'

As Fretilin was routed, and its leaders defected or died, more and more people gave themselves up to the invaders. But the task of feeding all the civilians in the mountains, as well as holding off the Indonesians, had always been an impossible one. Fretilin and its army could no longer claim to be 'governing' East Timor in any meaningful way. Instead, it remade Falintil as a guerrilla movement, highly mobile and organised locally under the command of one of its last surviving founders: Jose Alexandre Gusmão, known as Xanana.

The strategy was to cause maximum disruption with minimal losses. Rather successfully, Falintil began ambushing military convoys and stealing ammunition; there was even a daring attack on Dili itself, in which a television tower was occupied and held for several hours. In response a new Indonesian campaign was launched: Operation Security, known as the 'fence of legs'.

Soldiers would arrive in a village or town and round up all the men and boys between eight and fifty years old. They would be taken into the mountains to become links in two giant human chains, spanning the country from the north coast to the south. One originated near Los Palos and moved west, the other began at the border close to West Timor and walked east. Behind the fence of legs marched Indonesian soldiers. Given the danger of shooting their own people, the idea went, Falintil would either surrender, or slip further and further back into the mountains to be finished off with bombs and napalm. There were numerous massacres, and starvation and disease decimated the press-ganged villagers. But many of them helped the resistance. They led the Indonesian soldiers away from the hideouts; the guerrillas slipped through the fence of legs, and Falintil survived.

For much of the 1980s and 1990s, a force of a thousand guerillas faced an Indonesian army which sometimes outnumbered it fortyfold. But Falintil clung on, and in the larger towns a new generation of Timorese came to maturity, the clandestine movement, or intifada, of which Jose and Jacinto were members. They mounted noisy but peaceful demonstrations in Dili – for the visit of Pope John Paul II in 1989, and the funeral of a murdered student, Sebastião Gomes, at the Santa Cruz Cemetery in 1991. It was there that Indonesian soldiers opened fire and killed hundreds of mourners, an event that was secretly captured on film, and which did incalculable damage to Indonesia's international image. For a while it seemed as if this might be the event which would command the outside world's attention to East Timor. But a year later, in mysterious and probably treacherous circumstances, Xanana Gusmão was captured in a safe house in Dili and taken to Jakarta to be put on trial for his life.

After it had become completely dark, we turned away from the coast and on to another of the rough cross-island routes that cut through the mountains. The road was steep and wet, with an unfenced drop on one side and a rocky slope on the other; every few miles, a fresh dusting of stones and earth lay across the road which the rain had washed down from the mountain above. Jacinto hauled the truck around the bends, and Jose peered uncertainly through the windscreen. The swinging motion of the truck was soothing, and it was alarming to jolt awake a few miles further on and to realise that we were suddenly at rest.

From behind, I could hear the two passengers climbing out of the back; Jacinto jumped out too, and then Jose. Outside, I was aware of low buildings and a gathering of people in the darkness. The jungle noise was loud around us, but otherwise the only voices were whispers and the only light was the glow of cigarette tips. There were no fires, no electric bulbs, no laughter or greetings. Jose came back to the truck, and beckoned me outside. A huddle of men stood in front of thatched bamboo huts; they nodded gravely at me as I climbed down.

'Is anything wrong, Jose?' I said.

'It's OK. It's OK now. There were soldiers here, but they left. But we must go soon.'

I followed him through a gap between the huts and into a small village of similar low dwellings. Jacinto was no longer to be seen, but walking with us were other young men, all carrying bags and backpacks. This, then, was the beginning of our trek through the jungle; it had got underway much quicker than I had expected. Beyond the village a grassy slope led down to a shallow stream with rice paddies on the far side. Beyond these was another downward slope, and after that we were in the forest.

We walked in darkness. The stars and moon were too faint to cast more than a ghostly light. We passed through areas of lushness, but for much of the way the country was dry bush, with rocks underfoot and the silhouettes of spiky plants. Deprived of colour, the landscape resolved itself in simple contrasts of open land and forest, earth and water, darkness and glitter.

There were about ten of us, including Jose and the two boys from the back of the truck, and all were heavily burdened. Several of the boys went barefoot and none had anything sturdier than rubber sandals. I wore thick-soled boots and hiking socks but almost immediately I was falling behind. Up and down we walked, up and down; within a few minutes it already seemed endless. My calves ached with the sudden climbs and brutal descents, and my lungs burned with the cigarettes I had smoked. For half a mile we walked through the waters of a sluggish stream, and the effort of pulling my boots off and then tugging them back on again was excruciating. The knapsack on my back was a curse and, even on level ground, I stumbled constantly over stones and branches. Finally I solved the problem by switching on the tin torch which I had brought for the occasion. Jose appeared alongside me.

'Are you OK?'

'Fine, Jose, fine,' I gurgled through my saliva.

'You're tired? I'll carry your bag.'

'No, really, Jose. Thanks, but it's fine.'

'Better turn off your torch here.'

'Of course, of course,' I wheezed. 'Why?'

He swept an arm towards the hills all around.

A sixth sense seemed to guide my companions. There was little conversation, but they all knew when to quench their cigarettes and torches, and when to pause and huddle down in a clump of palms. Once, on an exposed ridge top, Jose hissed a warning and I dived down, flattening myself against the ground. At other times, we waited as a group while one of the boys scouted ahead, clambering low and deliberately across the slope. I tried not to think too much about the reasons behind this. After half an hour I was beyond noticing how far we had walked or what direction we were travelling in, but I was constantly aware of the sky above, the strange southern stars, and the compelling possibility of eyes, focusing on my stumbling form through binoculars and telescopic night sights, hidden from view beneath the sloping canopy of the jungle.

After an hour, we passed through a thicket of glinting trees and low ferns. Birds or rats riffled in the undergrowth as I stumbled through; the leaves were the shape of swords. Beyond the trees, the undulations came to an end. From here on, it was uphill all the way, a rocky scramble which had me groping with my hands for roots and rocks. The pain in my chest and legs, the sweat in my eyes, were blinding and I knew that there must be many hours of this to go. When the ground levelled out at the top of the climb, I peeled off my knapsack and sank on to the ground, gaping like a beached fish.

When my pulse had calmed down, I became aware that none of my companions was in sight. Then I noticed something that made my stomach lurch – a ring of light a few hundred yards ahead, and standing figures close at hand. I peered towards it, and made out a fire and a circle of people. I stepped closer to the light, and saw Jose talking to a tall man silhouetted by the fire. Jose noticed me and pointed; the other man turned and strode towards me. He was dressed in an Indonesian army uniform, and across his shoulder was a black rifle. He moved closer and half hugged, half caught me as I staggered into the illumination. His arms grasped my shoulders in an embrace, and he kissed me on each cheek, smiling, and declaiming in ringing Portuguese. His voice was deep; he wore a black beard down to his chest and large bifocal spectacles. 'On behalf of Xanana Gusmão, and the Armed Forces for the National Liberation of Timor Leste, and all of the Maubere people,' Jose translated, 'the *comandante* welcomes the *senhor* to his camp and to East Timor.'

What had I been expecting of a guerrilla camp in the jungle? A clearing, I suppose, hacked with machetes out of thick forest, and neatly planted with canvas tents. Sentries would stand guard around it, signalling to one another with imitated bird calls. There would be an open space for drill, and at one end guer-rillas would be cooking a deer which they had shot. It would be many hours', perhaps many days', journey into the forest. Instead, I found myself a few miles from the road, at what looked more than anything like a village festival.

About a hundred people sat on mats and coloured tarpaulins, illuminated by candles and tin lamps. There were small children, holding the hands of older sisters, and women tidying up the remains of a meal. It was cooler up here than on the coast: the men wore long-sleeved shirts as well as jeans and rubber sandals. A few had pocket knives or machetes, but only the guerrillas carried guns. They had dimly glistening automatic rifles, and crisp, faded uniforms bearing the insignia of dead Indonesian soldiers. They were everything that a guerrilla army ought to be, apart from one detail: there were only six of them.

I was installed in the middle of the circle and presented with a small can of warm Singaporean beer and a plate of grilled chicken. The fluttering in my chest was subsiding; after finishing the beer I felt strong enough to smoke again. The *comandante* and Jose talked briskly as I ate, and two more young men, burdened with bags, arrived from the direction we had come. They had news to impart and went into a huddle with the guerrillas.

'Soldiers came back to the village by the road just after we left,' Jose said. 'They saw our car and they were asking questions. But the village people told them nothing. It's OK now.'

The commander settled himself opposite me, cross-legged. The necessity of secrecy led Falintil to take on coded *noms de guerre*, and those chosen by the Falintil leadership were magnificent, in keeping with their status as the guardians of the struggle, the mountain-gods. The commander of the eastern region, Lere, was known as Anak Timur, meaning 'Child of the East'. Beneath his camouflage jacket he wore a dark undershirt, and hanging on strings around his neck were a red plastic whistle and a metal pendant incorporating the photograph of a young man. The people around us became quiet as we began to talk; mothers hushed their children, who stared at us with big eyes.

I said to the commander, 'Is this where you live?'

Through Jose, the commander replied, 'Falintil lives everywhere in the forest.'

'Where did you sleep last night?'

'Far from here,' the commander said.

'And what about these people? Who are they?'

'All of them are with Falintil.'

There was a pause, and I felt a prick of panic. All the way up here, during the long drive and the climb, I had been turning over in my mind the many questions I wanted to ask – but now they had fled my memory. The commander folded his hands across his knees. I noticed how large the hands were. I also noticed that the middle finger of his right hand was missing above the joint.

The commander said, 'Was the *senhor's* journey difficult?'

'It was . . . steep,' I said. I tapped the red packet by my plate.
'Too many cigarettes.'

The commander smiled.

'How old is the *senhor*?'

I added two years to my actual age.

'Oh, you are still young,' he said, and he and Jose exchanged
words in Portuguese which were not translated. Then he said,
'Is the *senhor* afraid?'

I didn't know how to reply.

'If the Indonesian soldiers came now,' the commander said,
'how would you feel?'

I had been afraid: of being stopped at a checkpoint, and
dragged out of the truck and kicked in the testicles at the side
of the road; of skidding over the cliff and breaking my neck as
the truck tumbled on to the rocks below; of ambush in the
jungle, of bullets whipping through the trees and the glint of
Kopassus machetes. For a time I had been afraid of Jose and
Jacinto, and of the commander and his stolen Indonesian
uniform. I had been afraid of the treachery of others, and of my
own hesitation. I had been afraid of coming here, and of being
too scared to come, and on the slope I had simply been afraid
that I wasn't physically strong enough to make it to the top.
But now I felt no fear. The commander's beard was greying
around its edges. One of the guerrillas played with the handle
of his knife. A small thin dog was nosing at the chicken bones
on my plate. I was with Falintil, and Falintil made me feel brave.
But I gave no answer to the commander's question.

'If all of us are killed, then you too will be killed,' he said,
smiling. 'But as long as the *commandante* is alive, the *senhor* too
will live. Please ask your questions.'

I made a tape recording of the conversations which took place
over the next night and day, which I found years later in a dusty
box at the back of a cupboard. On the recording, in the gaps
between my questions, Jose's soft interpretation and the *comandante*'s answers, you can hear the silence of the night, broken

by bird calls, insect notes, the shush of trees and grasses – all the busy noises of the forest.

Xanana Gusmão was arrested in Dili on 20 November 1992. People always seemed unwilling to discuss the circumstances of his capture. It was said that he had been betrayed; there were rumours that he had been taken during a tryst with a lover. Six months later in Jakarta he was sentenced to twenty years in prison for rebellion. His second in command, Ma'Huno, was captured in April 1993, and the next field commander, Nino Konis Santana, was killed in a fall a few years later. After Xanana's arrest, Falintil was more isolated than ever. In his speech to the court, he said, 'I acknowledge military defeat on the ground.' But with its leader's arrest, the resistance became stronger.

After the Santa Cruz massacre and the opprobrium that it brought on Indonesia, Suharto knew that he could not execute Xanana. But in Jakarta's Cipinang prison, under the thumb of his enemy, he became more powerful than ever. Visitors to Cipinang smuggled letters in and out; they even brought in mobile phones on which Xanana spoke to his commanders in Timor. But what Xanana did or said hardly mattered. From the mountain, Xanana the warrior had descended to the dungeon, and there he had become a symbol, an icon, almost a god.

Xanana wrote poetry in Tetum, soft tearful verses of mountains, trees, suffering and loss. The three syllables of his mysterious name were like a cry of liberty, perfect for shouting out loud in defiance or celebration. I once watched a demonstration in which the marchers carried handmade posters of Xanana, which borrowed unconsciously from half a dozen styles and genres. There was Xanana as Che Guevara, the stern, bearded guerrilla leader in bold socialist realist colours. There was Xanana as modern international statesman, photographed in his double-breasted suit shaking hands with Nelson Mandela, that other great icon of struggle, who famously visited him in jail. Some of the younger women had drawn Xanana as romantic hero – a pouting matinée idol with an open-necked shirt and curly hair. And then there was Xanana as Christ, his pencilled face an anguish of compassion and suffering, with a faint but unmistakable radiance around his head.

Xanana was all these things and more. Xanana was whatever you wanted him to be. He didn't have to *do* anything; he only had to *be*. And so it was with Falintil.

All this came to me gradually as I talked with the *comandante*.

Originally, I was to have met Lere's superior, the current field commander, Taur Matan Ruak, but recently he had been hard pressed. Just a fortnight before, he had had a narrow escape when Indonesian commandos came upon the village where he was staying. I had heard about this incident already; as it had been described to me in Dili, there had been a fierce gun battle which Taur had been lucky to survive. But Commander Lere corrected me on this. 'There was no shooting at that time, no combat,' he said. 'The Indonesians knew that they were there, but they could not take them.'

'How did he escape?' I asked.

'The people there warned him that the Indonesians were coming, and he took a secret path.'

'He was lucky.'

Commander Lere did not think that luck had much to do with it. 'This is the situation in East Timor,' he said. 'All the people, guerrillas and civilians, all of them struggle against the Indonesians. They are our eyes and our ears, and the people guard Falintil as Falintil guards the people.

'Always the Indonesians are confused: "Who is guerrilla and who is civilian?"' he said. 'Sometimes the *comandante* and the Falintil wear ordinary clothes and work with the people. We go to the forest gardens, live in houses, work in the rice fields. When combat is what we want, we put on our uniforms, and take guns for the fight.'

In the independence struggle, the *comandante* explained, there were three fronts: the diplomatic, the military and the political. The first was sustained by a few thousand Timorese exiles and their supporters in Australia and Portugal. The second was carried on by the fighters in the forest. The third, the clandestine movement, was carried on in the towns and villages of East Timor. Its most active members were young men like my escorts. But it included old people, married couples, children, nuns and nurses, priests and laymen – everyone.

I nodded at the commander, and said, 'How many guerrillas does Falintil have?' The Indonesians said a few dozen; the Timorese support groups overseas claimed five hundred; a diplomat in Jakarta had told me he thought about 250.

The commander said, 'The numbers depend on the commander. Sometimes ten, sometimes twenty, sometimes eighty. When I need more, I can ask for more.'

'Well, how many guns do you have?'

'You seem to think we worry all the time about guns. But this is a situation that can only be settled through politics, and peacefully. There are certainly things that we need here – communications, money, medicine and food. But we don't need arms, not yet. Because the problem of East Timor cannot be resolved with guns.'

I looked around the pool of light in which we sat, at the mothers and infants, at the children playing, at the wheezy grandfathers and the fit young men, and at the handful of guerrillas who sat among them. The faces and the physiques were indistinguishable; no sense of awe or privilege separated the fighters from the people. The Falintil and the villagers were the same, except that the Falintil carried guns and wore uniforms. But all of them were poor.

On the edge of the mats sat a father with three young children, two little boys and a delicate-faced girl, sitting quietly as the others scampered about. At first I thought they were simply well behaved, but when they stood up to leave, I understood. The three children were crippled by polio. Quietly, they hobbled away from the light and back towards the village, as their father swung the tiniest of them over his shoulders. Their mother, if they had a mother, was not to be seen.

A few miles away were Indonesian soldiers whose greatest glory would have been to capture a man like Lere Anak Timur. What bounty the man with the crippled family could have won by delivering their prize! A new house in a different village; regular visits from an Indonesian army doctor. Surrounding us were a hundred people as poor as he, and dozens of children. A word from one of them was all that would have been needed, and that would quickly have been that – for the commander and his guerrillas, for Jose and the clandestines, and for my adventure in the forest. And yet here in East Timor such a thing was unthinkable, a theoretical possibility only, realistically out of the question.

The commander said, 'For twenty-three years, Falintil has fought against the Indonesians, the biggest army in south-east Asia. Could we have survived so long if the people were not with us? Every Timorese has it in his conscience to fight against Indonesia. If Indonesia wants to kill all of Falintil, they must first kill all of the population of East Timor. If they cannot kill every one of them, then Falintil will still exist.'

People in Dili sometimes referred to Falintil as the *orang utan*, the men of the forest, and although this was a joke, it was a respectful one. The forest was the guerrillas' uniform; it was there that they became Falintil, with Falintil's power and prestige. The village where we met was at the westernmost limits of Commander Lere's territory and, despite the loyalty of the people here, it was a risk to linger too long. As the fires shrunk to embers, the guerrillas gathered up their supplies and I followed them away from the clearing. The route took us down into one of the lush, green areas of jungle, and we stopped at a spot where a large rock formed a natural table beneath the bushes. A square of tarpaulin was quickly suspended from the branches, another one was stretched on the ground with a hurricane lamp placed upon it, and here we settled for the next twenty-four hours. The commander and I talked, with Jose translating; later I slept, and Jose and the commander talked apart. Coffee was brewed and meals of chicken and noodles were cooked on a stove of rocks. The guerrillas dozed, smoked, washed up, combed their long hair and beards, cleaned their rifles, and played with a small white dog belonging to one of the villagers.

Within Falintil, there were only two ranks, commanders and men. Lere carried a Swiss Mauser rifle and wore leather boots, while the others had M-16s and green rubber wellingtons, but there were no other visible distinctions between them. One man wore a bright purple beret, another a black scarf, a third had thick, bushy hair which unfurled to his shoulders. It was hard to imagine any of them in combat, apart from the oldest, a quiet man who seemed entirely indifferent to my presence. He had a thin, unsmiling face, short hair, and instead of camouflage wore a uniform of plain olive green.

'He is a very experienced guerrilla,' Jose said, when I asked. 'His name is Intel.'

'Why do they call him that?'

'Because he likes to kill Intels.'

All the guerrillas were fascinated by gadgets and mechanisms, beginning with their guns which they handled constantly. All but Intel carried little instamatic cameras; my stay with them was punctuated by the illumination of their flashes, and the little mewing sound as the flashes recharged themselves. I was recruited for dozens of pictures: British reporter talking to the commander; British reporter eating noodles; British reporter urinating into the jungle. The films would be taken down to Dili and processed at friendly photo labs, although I knew that this passion for photography had led to tragedy in the past, when the Indonesians had captured prints showing known guerrillas alongside previously unknown members of the resistance. The climax of my anxiety came when each of the guerrillas in turn handed me his M-16 and photographed me posing with it. I imagined how these particular shots could be made to appear: the European mercenary pictured in the act of training the communist terrorists. I held the weighty guns at arm's length and struggled to shape my face into an expression of neutral indifference.

At the centre of his men, the commander sat on his tarpaulin, doing his paperwork. For hours on end he worked, reading letters and newspaper clippings couriered to him from Dili; grubs and beetles dropped on to his lap from the leaves above. He wrote on crisp sheets of printed notepaper, each bearing the name of his district, and the words *Forças Armadas de Libertação Nacional de Timor Leste* in old-fashioned italics. There was a radio, and close to the town the guerrillas used their mobile phones, but among themselves the commanders communicated by letter. I peered over his shoulder and read the beginning of one of them, a long, formal salutation in courtly Portuguese.

I asked the commander how he spent his time in the jungle.

'Reading letters, writing letters, training the Falintil, collecting food, conducting political activities in the villages and military activities in the forest. There is no time for rest.'

'Do you ever get bored?'

'No.'

'Do you often visit Dili?'

'If necessary, I'll go to the town, but usually I will send my emissary. To meet visitors, like you, I come down to this place.'

'What about holidays? Do you celebrate Christmas?'

'We used to celebrate Christmas and New Year,' he said, removing his bifocals, 'but in 1996 the Indonesians mounted a big operation because they realised that Falintil would come down to the villages.'

'What about your men? How do you keep up their spirits?'

'They meet with their families sometimes, their parents. But they are here in the forest because they choose to be, out of their own conscience. They're here to liberate their own people.

Many of our friends have been killed by the Indonesians. Out of that blood, and those bones, we have fashioned a strong spirit.'

'Have you lost many of your own friends?'

He frowned briefly, as if in recollection, then said: 'From the eastern region: *Comandante* Koro Asu, *Comandante* Guba, *Comandante* Falucai, *Comandante* Rank Bian, *Comandante* Letimoko, *Comandante* Mau Bani. From the second region: *Comandante* David Alex. From the third region: *Comandante* Fera Lafaek. From the central military council: *Comandante* Bere Malai Lacan, *Comandante* Mau Nami, *Comandante* Venâncio Ferraz, *Comandante* Mau Caru.'

I wanted to know about the young man in the photograph on the commander's pendant. But direct and personal questions elicited brief and impersonal replies, so instead of asking the commander about his children, I asked him about his wounds. He had been shot in half a dozen places, he said, rolling up his trousers to display a medallion of scarred flesh on the shin.

'The 24th of June 1996 in Iliomar,' he said. 'For a month I couldn't stand. On the 1st of August I could walk again, and they took me down and hid me close to a village where the villagers came and looked after me. The bullet is still in my leg, deep inside. It's still a problem when I run. This one – he pointed to a thin seam of darkened skin on his cheek – 'was in March 1992, also in Iliomar. This one' – he held up the stump of his missing finger – 'was the 4th of March 1984 in the area between Ainaro and Same. Both my legs were injured then too. There was no medicine, and the Indonesians were being very aggressive at the time. So we just used leaves. I spent six months hidden in the jungle. Sometimes, you can't believe that a bullet can pass so close and not penetrate the body.'

'In East Timor, we fight with cockerels,' Jose said. 'They say that a cockerel that has been injured fights more bravely than any.'

The commander had lived in the jungle for more than half his life. He had been twenty-four years old, a student at agricultural college in Los Palos, when the invasion took place, and he lived through the successes of the early war. But then the Indonesians had begun using jet bombers, including, it was said, British-made Hawk fighters; the commander had often seen them in action. 'We shot one down around 1987, but it fell into the sea,' he said. 'We call them scorpions because of the shape as it flies. I didn't see napalm, but I saw the bodies of people who had been killed by it, with all the skin broken and burned.'

As he talked, the pendant around Commander Lere's neck swung and twisted. On the back I made out a name engraved in the metal: Aluk.

'Who is that?' I asked.

'My son,' said the commander.

'How old is he?'

'Twenty.'

'Where is he now?'

'In Jakarta. Before, he lived with a priest in Los Palos.'

'What is he doing over there?'

'He is young. He is just . . . having happy times.' He paused, and then said quietly: 'Aluk.'

The commander's wife was dead, or assumed to be. She disappeared in 1981 after giving birth to a second child, a son, who disappeared himself after being taken away by soldiers a few years ago. The commander's parents were dead too, poisoned, he said, after being interrogated about Lere's activities. 'Out of one hundred people who have died in East Timor,' the commander said, 'you will find five who died naturally. The rest died from the occupation. Ask people, and they will tell you: my mother, my father, my wife, my child were killed by the Indonesians.'

'I acknowledge military defeat on the ground,' Xanana had said in the speech he prepared for his trial. 'I am not ashamed to say so. On the contrary, I am proud of the fact that a small guerrilla army was able to resist a large nation like Indonesia, a regional power which in a cowardly fashion invaded us and sought to dominate us by the law of terror and crime.' The judge stopped Xanana from reading the speech after three pages. 'The Indonesian generals,' he would have gone on to say, 'should be made to realise that they have been defeated politically in East Timor.'

When I asked the *comandante* about his own recent encounters with the Indonesians, he seemed a bit stumped. The previous year, a convoy had been attacked with an unexploded missile which the guerrillas had found and rewired as an enormous grenade. The bomb had destroyed an army truck and killed seventeen soldiers; unfortunately for Falintil, it had also incinerated the precious Indonesian rifles. 'It is easy to attack them,' the commander said. 'But whenever we kill Indonesians, it makes a problem for the civilians.'

By which he meant: rapes, arrests, torture, disappearances. The logic of reprisals had paralysed Falintil as a military force. They were too small, too constrained ever to be more than a nuisance, and terrorism, the only other alternative, had never been the Timorese way. Xanana knew that he could never overcome the Indonesian army. And once he had abandoned that hope, Falintil inherited its full power – symbolic, almost spiritual power, impossible to snuff out by physical means.

Indonesian aggression had given birth to Falintil, and Falintil lived off it, wearing its uniforms, firing its guns and its bullets. Xanana once said, 'We carry the enemy in our bags.' In hunting the guerrillas, the Indonesians were chasing their tail. They could run through the forest for days and never glimpse Falintil, although they were being watched by them, just yards away in the bush. Even with only a handful of guerrillas, without uniforms, living as hungry peasants, their units scattered, their guns and ammunition buried, the movement still lived, the perfect army, without arms and without soldiers. 'To resist is to win,' said Xanana. What was Falintil but an attitude of defiance, a pure expression of resistance?

✳   ✳   ✳

For breakfast the next morning we had sweet coffee, chocolate biscuits and bread baked in Dili the day before. At lunchtime there was rice with tinned sardines, and roast chicken which a group of women brought down from the village. In between chats with the commander, I dozed and finished the last of my cigarettes. I had started them in Dili in a state of anxious excitement, but by now I was smoking out of idleness. The commander was asleep with his head upon a heavy and antique Portuguese dictionary. One of the young guerrillas was picking ants out of his beard, and yellow butterflies fluttered through the bands of shadow and light which penetrated the leaf canopy. I could understand the attraction of the life in the jungle – the gentle glamour of being a guerrilla; exemption from everyday responsibilities and the grind of daily life as a farmer or a member of the urban poor. The days, months and years passed by, none so very different from the one that had preceded it, marked by the wet season and the dry season, an unchanging faith, and life's only care, the distant fear of death.

Jose and I left that evening after dark. Before saying goodbye, the commander presented me with a rich purple weaving from the Timorese enclave of Oecussi, and I wished very much that I had brought something to give to him, apart from Pepsodent toothpaste. The descent to the road was scarcely easier than the journey up; as we approached the village by the road, a boy met us and warned us off because of an army patrol. We hid behind a wall, and soon another messenger came with the all-clear, and we trotted down on to the road and into the white pickup truck.

It was several hours after midnight when we got back to Dili, and the streets were completely deserted. Jacinto dropped me off on the seafront, and I walked to the Turismo, where I sat on my bed, trembling with discharged excitement. Later that day, I checked out of the hotel and took the afternoon flight back to Jakarta.

VAMPIRES

In the garden of the Turismo, eight months after my journey into the jungle, a man named Basilio Araújo invited me to view a dead body in the Hotel Tropicale. Basilio had studied in Manchester on a British government scholarship, and spoke excellent English. He had thick bushy hair, a dense moustache and an indefinably irritating manner, peevish and ingratiating at the same time. He was the chairperson of a pro-Indonesian organisation called the FPDK, or the Forum for Unity, Democracy and Justice. He was the acceptable face of Timorese gangsterism.

'What kind of body is it, Basilio? I mean – whose body?'

'He is a member of Aitarak. The Falintil killed him yesterday, and his body was recovered this morning. He has just been taken to Aitarak headquarters and Eurico has arrived.'

'Eurico is there?' I glanced at the colleague with whom I had travelled from Jakarta, and he looked meaningfully back. We had landed in Dili less than an hour before, and this was a piece of luck.

'Eurico is really there, Basilio?'

'He is there.'

'You can translate for us?'

'I will translate.'

We gathered our notebooks and walked with Basilio out of the hotel and along the seafront.

Eurico Guterres was the leader of Aitarak, the Dili chapter of the militia gangs which were agitating against independence from Indonesia. Aitarak means 'thorn'. Eurico and his men were the unacceptable face of Timorese gangsterism.

There were many fearful stories about what went on in the Hotel Tropicale, and no one could remember a time when it had actually taken paying guests. It was said to have served as an Intel office and torture centre, and now it was Eurico's headquarters. Short, well-built Timorese in black shirts and jeans greeted Basilio as we entered. At the back of an untidy yard was a dim hall containing oddments of furniture and a board bearing a large map of the island of Timor. On a low table, the body had been laid out.

It was a man in his twenties, dressed in sodden khaki trousers and a T-shirt. He had been fished out of the harbour that morning, and the night's immersion had washed away the blood from his clothes and skin. His face was crushed and blackened, and gaping knife wounds were visible on his neck and shoulders. The torn edges of the skin had turned white, like toes which have been in the bath for too long.

An Australian cameraman was panning his camera slowly across the table. At the end of it stood Eurico, booming grandiloquently, with a scowl on his face. He had heavy, fleshy features, and shoulder-length hair which flowed from beneath a white baseball cap. He gestured towards us as we entered, and Basilio immediately began translating.

'He is saying, "We have the journalists here already. We have the police of the Republic of Indonesia. But where is the United Nations representative, come to offer condolences? They are not here, they are not interested. Because it is their friends who have done this, their murdering friends in the pro-independence. They come to our country promising to be neutral, but they support and . . ."' – Basilio paused, groping through his impressive vocabulary – '". . . exculpate only the one side. We reject their partisanship and their bias, and we warn that the United Nations is pushing the East Timorese people into a sea of blood and flames."'

There was sweat on Eurico's cheeks; his eyes were shiny and distant as if he was on some kind of drug. He was very angry indeed, but I suspected that Basilio's translation was a good deal more polished than the Indonesian original. The black shirts standing around gave gruff cheers and grunts, and flashes went off as a couple of Australian photographers arrived. The crowd inside the room was growing, and it shifted and rearranged itself respectfully as a group of Indonesian policemen stepped forward.

The senior among them was a short, sleek moustachioed man with a shiny revolver and a sharpened pencil sticking out of his breast pocket. He and Eurico greeted one another with an embrace, and went into a confidential huddle.

'Basilio,' I said. 'Who is the . . . deceased?'

'He is an Aitarak member. His name is Muhammed Ali.'

'Muhammed Ali?'

'He has eleven wounds in his body. You can only see five of them.'

'Was he an important member of Aitarak?'

'All members of Aitarak are important.'

More reporters were arriving, and Eurico had stepped out into the courtyard so that the cameramen could get the benefit of the light. The police colonel, whose name badge identified him as J. J. Sitompul, was particularly keen to appear on camera, gently steering Eurico to one side to make room for himself in the shot.

People were calling out questions which Basilio translated.

'Will this incident have any effect on the independence referendum?' asked an Australian.

'The pro-independence are looking for trouble,' said Eurico. 'They're trying to get a reaction from us. But I have given my commitment. We are not going to retaliate.'

'But how do you know that Falintil are behind this?'

Colonel Sitompul said, 'If you see the method of killing, you will know that it was done by the pro-independence. He was stabbed with a knife and his face was crushed with stones.'

'But why does that mean it must have been the pro-independence?'

The colonel frowned. 'The police know these things,' he said, after a moment.

'Falintil are saying that this guy was a gambler, and that he got into a fight over a gambling debt,' said one of the resident freelancers. 'They say that your men killed him.'

Eurico looked pained. 'He was one of Aitarak,' he said. 'Why would we kill the member of our own group?'

There were a few more questions. Basilio was taken to one side by one of the junior policemen. By the time he resumed his translation, Eurico and the colonel were in their stride.

Eurico said, 'East Timor will become like Kosovo and Angola.'

'The United Nations and that spokesman of theirs must remain neutral,' said the colonel.

Eurico said, 'When has the UN ever handled a situation like East Timor well? All over the world, in every case like this, they have failed.'

Even then, there was clear evidence that Eurico Guterres was a murderer, or at the least that he had ordered the murders of several dozen people. The Indonesian police claimed to be investigating these cases – but here Eurico stood, side by side with Colonel Sitompul. The journalists began peeling off and going inside to look at the body again, but the two of them continued their double act, prompting one another and completing one another's sentences, so rapidly that it was difficult for Basilio to keep up. When they had said everything that they wanted to say, the Indonesian colonel put his hand on Eurico's shoulder, gave it a firm shake and looked directly into the cameras. Even Basilio looked a bit embarrassed. 'My friend,' said the colonel, 'my brother – Commander Eurico Guterres.'

It was June 1999 when I returned to East Timor, and in the time that I had been away something dramatic had happened to Dili.

At the airport, there was an air of bustle and urgency among the luggage handlers and the taxi drivers. Even after dark, there were young men and children on the streets, and new stalls had sprung up selling cigarettes and noodles and chewing gum. But the biggest and most obvious sign of change was on the roads. Power-steering their way around every corner, parked in front of every official building, were the emblem of the United Nations in the Third World: white Toyota Land Cruisers.

Radio aerials curved from their potent bonnets. Along the promenade and on the roundabout in front of the market, they glided through the rabble of bicycles and station wagons like diesel-powered swans among ducklings. A white helicopter, stencilled with the UN's blue symbol, buzzed to and fro. Children waved and cheered as it passed overhead.

'Unamet!' they shouted. 'Hooray for Unamet!'

It had all happened so quickly.

Soon after my visit to the forest in 1998, the atmosphere in East Timor had deteriorated badly. After a Falintil attack in the south-west, the Indonesians had carried out unusually violent reprisals, burning houses and killing fifty villagers. Military documents were leaked which proved beyond doubt that troop levels had been increased, and that the army was organising local thugs into anti-independence militias. In Indonesia, there was a new president – B. J. Habibie – and plans for new elections. Political prisoners had been released and magazines and news-papers were starting up all the time. But East Timor remained under the heel of the army.

In New York, the Portuguese and Indonesian governments continued to hold desultory meetings on East Timor, as they had fruitlessly done for years. The latest talk was of something called an 'autonomy package', which would give the province control over a few of its internal affairs. Then the European Union declared for the first time that the East Timorese should be given the right to self-determination. A month later, Australia, the only country to have officially recognised the Indonesian annexation, said the same thing. Such diplomatic utterances were significant in their way, but there was little sense of urgency. So nobody was prepared for President Habibie's sudden announcement that, if its people rejected the autonomy proposal, East Timor could have its independence.

The Indonesian foreign minister, Ali Alatas, who had spent a lifetime ruling out the slightest possibility of such a thing, was completely taken by surprise. Even Xanana Gusmão was not asking for independence right away. East Timorese were sceptical and suspicious. Some almost regarded it as a threat. What did it mean, this sudden reversal, after twenty-three years of stubbornness and bloodshed?

But the president had said it, and the UN took the matter up with Portugal and Indonesia in New York. In Jakarta, as a token of Habibie's goodwill, Xanana was released from prison into house arrest. But in East Timor itself, life became more and more frightening.

Militiamen attacked pro-independence villages. There were massacres, and thousands of poor farmers fled for refuge to the towns. Indonesian doctors and teachers began packing up and leaving. And the talks in New York went nowhere.

Habibie had promised unambiguously to give East Timor a choice between autonomy and independence. But Ali Alatas refused to agree to a mechanism through which the choice could be presented. Finally, a solution was reached. Instead of a referendum, the UN would supervise something called a 'popular consultation'. This would involve a period of political campaigning, a choice between two options (autonomy under Indonesian rule or independence) and a popular vote. It sounded just like a referendum, but it was not to be *called* a referendum, and with this Indonesian pride was salvaged.

In April, the police and anti-independence militias fired tear gas into a church where 1,500 refugees were sheltering, and shot and stabbed dozens of them as they fled outside. They attacked the house of an independence leader in Dili and killed thirty more people. They told their victims that this was what they could expect for supporting independence and that if they were stupid enough to vote for it, there would be worse to come. Reports of organised intimidation were coming from all over the country, but mostly from the west, close to the border with Indonesia. One element was common to all of them – the involvement in the violence of the Indonesian army and the Indonesian police.

There were stories that Indonesian government officials, who under the UN agreement were barred from any part in the referendum, were already running pro-Indonesia campaigns in the mountain villages. There were rumours that the militias were planning a 'sweeping' operation in which thousands of them would descend on Dili to kill and drive out all the supporters of independence. The referendum – or rather 'consultation' – was due to be held on 8 August, although whether it could realistically be held then was seriously in question. Diplomats from Indonesia, Portugal and Australia descended on Dili, along with human rights activists, electoral monitors, volunteer doctors, spies and journalists. And, shortly before I arrived that day at the Turismo, the United Nations landed in Dili, and the UN Mission in East Timor – Unamet – was born.

Unamet based itself in the campus of Dili's former teacher-training college. I went there that same afternoon, after taking my leave of Eurico, Basilio and the dead Mr Ali. 'The compound', as everyone called it, consisted of a walled rectangle, a few hundred yards along each side, wedged up at the rear against a steep hill. The offices were in whitewashed classrooms, overshadowed by billowing green trees, and every vacant space was allotted to a Toyota Land Cruiser. It is a place that I will always remember; my heart fills as I think of it. But on my first visit it made little impression.

The Unamet press office was responsible both for relations with the media and for the public information campaign which would precede the referendum. In charge was the man whom

Colonel Sitompul had referred to as 'that spokesman', a dry, schoolmasterly Canadian named David Wimhurst. Every weekday, he gave a press conference, although at this early stage there was often nothing to say. On such mornings, the game was to ask questions anyway, in the knowledge that sooner or later he would make the inevitable mistake.

'Unamet just doesn't have the authority,' Wimhurst would say tetchily, after another question about why the UN wasn't doing more to thwart the militias. 'The Indonesian police are entirely responsible for security matters up to, during, and after the referendum.'

'Er, you just said "referendum", David,' someone would point out.

'Popular consultation,' Wimhurst would say quickly. 'You're quite right. It's not a referendum, it's a popular consultation. And the Indonesian police are responsible for its security.'

This, it was becoming more and more clear, was the profound flaw. The UN knew what it was doing when it came to elections. In the weeks leading up to the vote, it would create an electoral register, and conduct an information campaign by radio, television, newspaper, pamphlet, and through public meetings across the country. It would distribute ballot boxes, ballot papers and electoral lists, supervise the voting, transport the ballots back to Dili and count them. For all these tasks, it had adequate numbers of experienced personnel. But it had fewer than three hundred civilian policemen – or 'CivPols' – and just fifty military liaison officers, or MLOs. They were a picturesque force. Each wore his national uniform while on duty – the police sergeants from Japan, and the army men from Uruguay. The chief of the MLOs, a Bangladeshi brigadier, went about in dark glasses brandishing a little cane which quivered as he walked. His swagger stick was the heaviest weapon which Unamet had at its disposal. For these were not 'peacekeepers'. Under the terms of the agreement in New York, they were nothing more than 'advisers' to the Indonesian police. And the Indonesian police, along with the Indonesian army, were not just a part of the problem. They were at its root.

As I had seen for myself at the Hotel Tropicale, the police made no effort to disguise their enthusiasm for the anti-independence cause. During the massacre in the church two months before, survivors had reported seeing Indonesian infantrymen and members of the police mobile brigades – the BriMob – looking on as the killings were carried out. Three days after I arrived, a UN convoy was driving back towards Dili when it came across a group of soldiers and militiamen burning down a village and beating up its inhabitants. The most flagrant insult to the UN was the appointment of a new head of a local body of volunteer constables. The man chosen by the Dili police was Eurico Guterres.

On the first day I looked in, there wasn't much going on in the compound. The desks had been delivered, but few of the computers worked, and the roof was leaking water on those that did. So I sat outside with an Australian UN man, who told me about the blood-drinking ceremonies organised by the anti-independence groups ('For solidarity. Everyone puts a drop in the cup; everyone takes a sip out'), and the appointment of Eurico as Dili constable ('like putting the fox in charge of the chickens') and the difficulties of recruiting Timorese local staff.

'They're scared,' he said. 'They want to help us, but they're scared. The message has successfully been put about now that if you associate with us, you're in danger. And maybe it's true. We're not the police. We can't secure the voters. We can only secure the vote.'

I asked about the police and the army, and the absurdity of entrusting security to the institution which had undermined it for so long. The Australian nodded and drew on his cigarette, and then said, 'But at least we're here.'

'What do you mean?'

'We're here. The UN is in East Timor: don't forget how

remarkable that is. Look, no one forced the Indonesians into talking about independence. It was all Habibie's idea; nobody saw it coming. So then they came to New York and eventually, after all the farting around, they agreed to hold a referendum. We couldn't force them to do that either, but they did – and imagine how much that must have upset the generals. So then the Indonesians say, "We'll look after the security." Well, they're a UN member state, a respected member of the Non-Aligned Movement, and they're offering to look after security in a territory which they control. The UN could have said no, and the whole thing would have been called off, and for the next twenty-four years we'd've had chunks ripped out of our hides for the great opportunity that we'd thrown up. But we didn't, and we're here. The system's not perfect, in fact it's terrible, and God knows what's going to happen before this is over. But it will get done, and whatever happens the world will see it.'

A bit later, he said, 'We're asking for one last act of bravery from the people of East Timor.'

After it was all over, when there was much bitter talk about Unamet and its responsibilities, I sometimes repeated what that UN man told me to Timorese who had lived through the violence. Some of them had lost a great deal. Some of them had lost everything. But not one of them said that it wasn't worth it, and that it would have been better if Unamet had never come to East Timor.

During the same conversation, my Australian friend had said, 'I've yet to meet a sane, educated East Timorese who is against independence.' Basilio Araújo was sane and educated; unfortunately, he was also pompous and ridiculous. I went to see him the next day at a lovely pale blue villa set in its own garden on the quietest part of Dili's seafront. A maid appeared with tea and dainty biscuits, and I asked Basilio about his student days in Britain. He was guarded, as if they had not been a time of undiluted bliss. I suspected that this was because members of the Manchester student body found Basilio as irritating as I did, and gave him a miserable time.

He worked at a mid-ranking post in the East Timor Investment Co-ordination Board, which had the task of attracting foreign business to one of South-East Asia's most notorious war zones. The Forum for Unity, Democracy and Justice had been founded five months earlier. 'Our mission is to create unity, democracy and justice,' Basilio explained. 'These are the three main qualities we lack.' Its members, from what I could tell, were men much like him: young pro-Indonesian civil servants, local leaders and businessmen – men who would never personally fire an M-16 into a church but who shared the goals of those who did, and were vague about the means.

Basilio was full of grievance and a wounded sense of justice. He had spent his life outside majority opinion and took a petulant pleasure in the slights and injuries which his position brought him. He was thirty-five and had been born in Aileu, a strongly pro-Falintil area – although his own family was deeply involved with Apodeti, the integrationist party. He was prone to reciting lists of indignities and outrages, suffered by himself and those close to him, enumerated in pedantic detail.

'My house was attacked by thirty people in December last year,' Basilio said as he poured the tea.

'What happened?'

'They gathered outside, they shouted insults and independence slogans, they banged on the door and windows. Some of them were my neighbours.'

'That must have been very frightening.'

'Yes. Fortunately, I wasn't there at the time.'

And, a few minutes later: 'On the 28th of May this year, I was attacked again at a conference in Jakarta. They attacked me physically.'

'Did they hurt you?'

'They pushed me and tried to grab my shirt. One of them

kicked me on the leg. And not just Timorese do this. Once I got an international telephone call threatening to attack me. He said they'll kill me, destroy my balls. He was Australian. I could tell. I was attacked by Australian independence supporters in Canberra too.'

'Physically attacked?'

'Yes, almost.'

There were 'many arguments' against independence, Basilio said. 'Number one,' he said. 'Try to be realistic. Try to follow the global trend. Look at East Germany, Hong Kong, Macao. Countries are uniting, not dividing. People are talking about regional associations – APEC, ASEAN, the EU. Even Portugal is a member of the EU. Soon Europe will be just one country. Why should East Timor go in the wrong direction?

'Secondly,' Basilio continued, 'it is just not practical to be creating borders, when other countries are eliminating them. Thirdly, our consumer products. We depend for our consumer products on other parts of Indonesia. We have hardly any manufacturers here. Are we to expend all our capital importing from Indonesia, from Australia? We have only one product of our own. Can a country rely entirely on coffee? I don't think it's enough.

'What I'm trying to say is that these people don't have any notion about how to go about building a country. You can't just *think* yourself independent. When you are independent, you have to feed your people. They think: "We can eat stones when we are independent. Other countries will help us!"' (For this part – his version of the thinking of the ignorant mass – Basilio adopted a vacant, comically imbecilic voice. He seemed rather pleased with it, but it made me want to throw my tea in his face.) 'But we have to know our weaknesses,' he went on. 'We are not prepared to lead our people over the edge.'

I asked about the Indonesian human rights record in East Timor; I mentioned the Santa Cruz massacre where the army had opened fire on the student mourners.

Basilio said, 'Mistakes are normal everywhere.' Then he said, 'Nineteen ninety-one, Santa Cruz – that can happen anywhere in the world.'

I picked a sugary dainty off the plate and weighed it in my fingers. Then I asked, 'How many people in East Timor support integration, would you say?'

'It's difficult to say. There is so much propaganda. I would say there is a floating mass of 60 to 70 per cent, people who don't know anything about politics. Farmers, illiterates. These people don't know enough. It's up to intellectuals to lead them. If you force them to make a choice, you're leading them over the edge. That's where we reject the Western way of thinking about democracy.'

'But you understand democracy, Basilio. How can you be so sure that other people don't?'

For a moment he looked a little wounded. 'It's different,' he said. 'I'm in the same . . . family.' Then the peevishness reasserted itself. 'Why should we accept the outcome of a ballot just because it's democracy? We don't want to accept it. If people are realistic, they will say no to independence.'

'What's the relationship between your organisation and the militias?'

'We are independent, but we have the same goals. Aitarak and the other militias are for ordinary people, the angry people who are against independence. FPDK members are civil servants, intellectuals.'

'And what about the Indonesian armed forces and the police?'

'We fight for the same government. We both want to maintain East Timor as part of Indonesia. Sometimes we help each other. Sometimes they need me to act as their interpreter.'

'What about these killings and attacks on villages. The UN says –'

Basilio interrupted. 'Falintil burned down those houses.'

'But the UN says that the militias –'

'Don't blame the militias – they don't know the rules! They

have misbehaved themselves? OK, they should be reported to the police, and the police will do their job to clear it up.'

I drained my teacup and took my leave. The garden of the villa was very beautiful and I wondered idly how a mid-ranking civil servant could afford such a place. But it turned out that the house was not Basilio's. It belonged to the regent of Dili, president and benefactor of the Forum for Unity, Democracy and Justice.

Across East Timor, one third of the population was under the power of the militias. More than 40,000 people had been forced from their houses and villages. Outside Dili, the UN hadn't yet established a single branch office and its corps of civilian police was still in Australia, under training. The UN helicopter skimmed across the territory, and convoys were sent out from time to time on reconnaissance missions. But at night, when the Land Cruisers had returned to Dili, the rest of East Timor was as dark and fearful as it had been at any time since the invasion.

One day I hired a car and went out into the militia country. It was hard to find an interpreter (because Unamet was hiring them all) and a driver (because they were scared). Eventually, Felice's friend Fernão took time off work and persuaded the friend of a cousin to take us there in his jeep. We drove towards Liquisa, twenty miles west of Dili, on the road which led to the border and Indonesian West Timor. A dense margin of mangrove ran between the road and the sea. We drove past a salt lake, and along the top of spectacular, teetering cliffs. In the villages we saw almost nobody, except a middle-aged man without a shirt who lay slumped asleep in an open-sided hut. Beside it flapped a large Indonesian flag at the top of a tall pole. Above it was a sign bearing Indonesian words painted in blood red.

'Besi Merah Putih,' Fernão read. This was the Liquisa equivalent of Dili's Aitarak militia; its name meant Red and White Iron. 'Now we cross from Dili regency into Liquisa regency,' said Fernão. 'Here the BMP have the power.'

A few minutes later we passed a row of burned-out huts. Fernão inhaled sharply and shook his head; Fernão's cousin's friend, who had not wanted to come, speeded up and tightened his grip on the wheel. Soon we reached the town of Liquisa, where everyone was afraid.

Lisquisa was a delicately pretty town, and it was made prettier still by the presence of the refugees. Most of the homes were palm and bamboo, and the bigger houses and public buildings were picturesquely decaying Portuguese brick and plaster. Livid blossoms grew in front of them and along the road, and there were more children than I had seen even in Dili. The bushes and fences were draped with what I took, at first, to be decorative bunting. But it was washing – the shorts and T-shirts of thousands of people.

Liquisa was full of small tokens like that – normality ever so slightly twisted, warped and made sinister by slight differences, invisible to the casual eye. The refugee children were laughing and energetic, but then you noticed the swollen bellies and the silvery patches of rough skin on their legs and necks. 'Do you see the flags?' said Fernão. 'Each of the houses has an Indonesian flag. When do you ever see houses in Dili with a flag like that?'

By now the driver was thoroughly scared. When we persuaded him to slow down, the group of men to whom Fernão whispered through the window were scared too. We stopped at a little canteen on the corner, but they were afraid to serve us, so we turned right towards the church where the massacre had taken place. The day was passing; the sun was already in decline. The driver looked anxiously at the clock on the dashboard; it had been his firm condition that we should not be caught on the roads after sunset. At night, the town changed. Darkness was what people here feared most of all.

Liquisa was a town of vampires.

'Do you really want to go into the church, Richard?'

'Do you, Fernão?'

After a few minutes of peering up and down the road, we stole into the church's back entrance. The floor was freshly scrubbed and the walls were whitewashed, but you could still make out the scars of bullets and grenade fragments in the stone and plaster. Suddenly, a voice filled the church. 'Please,' it said. 'What are you doing here?' A middle-aged nun had entered, and was talking to me in English. 'Please, you must not stay. If we talk to you here, then, after you have left, they will come and ask why, and they will give us trouble.'

'Who will come, sister?'

'There are spies here, even inside. They can have me sent away, and if I am sent away from here and the refugees are left alone it will be your fault.'

'Forgive us . . .'

'Go! It will be dark soon. You must go back to Dili.'

We climbed back into the car and drove away from the church and towards the west. Within five minutes Liquisa was behind us, and we were back on the empty road in the landscape of scrubby grass and open-sided huts.

'No one will talk,' said Fernão. 'The driver wants to go back.'

Then a man became visible on the road in front of us, silhouetted against the afternoon sky. He was walking towards Liquisa with the sun behind him, and a large and awkwardly shaped branch was balanced across his shoulders. He walked very slowly towards us and, as he passed the car, Fernão spoke to him through the open window. He looked ahead and behind him, but the road was empty. Carefully, he laid down his branch and climbed into the car.

'He will speak to us,' said Fernão. 'Ask your questions.'

He was from a village called Hatoguesi in the hills above Liquisa, and he had been here for two months with his wife, his five children and all his neighbours. The militia had arrived in Hatoguesi one day and ordered them to leave. They burned down a few houses, shot several cattle and buffaloes, and lamed a horse. There wasn't much of an argument. 'They told us if you don't go, you're bad and we'll kill you,' he said. 'We wanted to take our coffee in first, but they wouldn't let us.'

It was the harvest time for coffee, so this was serious. An entire year's income was hanging from the trees, ripening and overripening, prey to thieves and vermin. Once a week, the man slipped back to the village to gather some fruit and check on the coffee. In Liquisa, there was no food.

'What did you eat yesterday?'

'Yesterday, I ate nothing.'

'What about the day before.'

'Cassava.'

'Where are the militias now?'

'In Liquisa? Everywhere. They are everywhere.'

The vampires haunting Liquisa came out at night, and held indoctrination sessions in the grounds of the military outpost. All the refugees were required to attend and to wear red-and-white headbands. The militia threatened and screamed at them. Standing beside them were Indonesian soldiers. 'Every night, there is intimidation,' the coffee farmer said. 'If we don't go to their meetings, they will beat us. They tell us that we must choose to stay with Indonesia, and that if we don't, they will come and find us and kill us. They say, "If you vote for independence then, when the Western people go back to their countries, we will come and finish you off." They say the Western people are only staying for two months, and when they are gone, we will be finished.'

'And what do you want? Independence or autonomy?'

'Independence,' he said. 'We all do.'

After the indoctrination meetings, the militias held 'parties'. They prepared for them by visiting the houses of local people. At some houses, they would ask for a goat, and when the family had no goat, they took money instead. But sometimes they invited the unmarried girls of the house to attend the parties. 'They come round at ten, eleven, twelve o'clock at night. They come in big cars and trucks, and they say, "Come to our party and dance." So the girls go to their parents, and if the permission is not given, then the father is beaten.'

'What happens at the parties.'

'They drink. They dance with the girls.'

'Are the girls OK?'

'No.'

'Do they harm the girls?'

'Sometimes the girls are . . . dishonoured.'

I asked, 'Who helps the refugees here?'

'No one,' he answered. 'The sisters and the priests try to help. But they don't have enough food. And they are afraid.' The UN was no good because the UN was in Dili and Dili was half a day's walk away. Unamet was supposed to have opened a branch office here by now, but the date had been repeatedly put back.

'How will the people here vote?' I asked.

'When the militias ask us, we say, "Autonomy, autonomy." But when August comes we will choose our independence.'

'Can you manage for two months?'

'Two months is not long.' His eyes were darting outside. It was getting late and the sun was setting. Fernão mouthed to me: *We must go.*

I said to the man, 'Why do you support independence?'

Fernão translated, and the answer came immediately back. 'He says, "Yes, I support independence."'

'Yes, but why does he support independence?'

Fernao put the question again, more elaborately.

'He says that all the people in his village support Falintil and support independence.'

'But *why*?'

Fernão began speaking again, a lengthy patient explanation. The man nodded, but he was frowning and he kept interrupting, as if what Fernão was saying made no sense. Soon the interview had turned into a conversation, and the two were first smiling, then chuckling and finally laughing out loud. For the question was absurd. Why independence? There was no answer. It was like questioning a natural drive: why breathe, why eat, why marry? Without independence, Timorese were like men without air or rice or women. They had been that way for twenty-four years, but now there were just two months to wait.

The man looked carefully up and down the street, then climbed out of the car and shook hands with us through the open window. He picked up his firewood and walked back down the road.

Apologetically, Fernão said, 'It was hard to explain the question. He just . . . wants independence.'

'I know, Fernão. It's OK.'

When enough time had passed we drove back through Liquisa in the thickening light. The washing had disappeared from the bushes. The flags were stirring on the poles. All the people had vanished.

EAGLE OF LIBERTY

Why did B. J. Habibie suddenly hold out to East Timor the promise of its independence when so many of his ministers, his generals and his soldiers on the ground viscerally opposed it? Not even his closest advisers seemed to know. Habibie was a peculiar and eccentric man. He was the protégé of a dictator. No one had elected him, and he had not, like Suharto, hoisted himself to power through his own will and cunning. The best explanation was that he was weary of hearing about East Timor and the shame which it brought on Indonesia, and that, personally, he was quite happy to let the place go. He consulted no one, persuaded no one, and once he made his historic utterance, he ceased to concern himself with putting it into action. 'I will prove that I can make a major contribution to world peace as mandated by our Constitution,' he told his advisers. 'It will roll like a snowball, and no one can stop it.'

After my afternoon in Liquisa, I left Asia for more than a month. The violence, I knew, was continuing; the referendum was postponed not once, but twice, to 30 August. I flew back to Jakarta with ten days to go, amid a gathering sense of occasion. In the shopping centre where I bought sun cream and malaria pills, I ran into newly arrived colleagues from America and Holland. Early the next morning, there were more of them on the plane to Dili. I passed the flight reading a book about East Timor by James Dunn, Australia's former consul in Dili who had been evacuated just before the invasion. At Bali, passengers from Sydney joined the plane and there among them was

James Dunn himself, a talkative old gentleman in shirtsleeves and sunhat, returning to Timor for the first time since 1975.

There was a happy and excited atmosphere on the Dili plane. Old friends greeted one another in the narrow aisles; the overhead luggage bins were crammed with TV cameras and sound equipment. Just as we reboarded at Bali I saw another familiar face travelling a few rows ahead of me in economy class. The baseball cap was new, but the long voluminous hair, the plump features and the shiny-eyed look were just as I remembered from the Hotel Tropicale.

'Eurico! Mr Guterres! Who's going to win the referendum?'

Eurico shot me a glassy look and manoeuvred himself into his seat without replying.

At Dili airport, the atmosphere of festivity was even more marked. Colleagues turned out to meet arriving colleagues. There was a whole jeep full of nuns waiting for James Dunn. Only Eurico disappeared quickly and quietly with his small entourage, as if he had places to go and tasks quickly to be undertaken. On the slip road from the airport, someone had put up a poster with a message in large stencilled letters: 'If you love East Timor, love both the Pro-Integrationist and the Pro-Independence.'

Dili was overflowing with election observers, democracy activists, government officials and United Nations volunteers. There were Filipina nuns, Irish judges and Canadian diplomats. There were Portuguese MPs, Ghanaian policemen and Australian producers of independent documentaries. The Turismo was bulging. People were doubling and tripling up, and most of the journalists had to stay at the dreary Mahkota, or at the Dili Hotel, an assembly of mosquito-blighted cubicles down the promenade. Rates were quadrupling and quintupling, and competition for somewhere to sleep became bitter. A contingent of European policemen were gazumped at the last minute by a team of high-spending American diplomats. The British Embassy had forgotten to make a booking altogether, and its ambassador ended up sharing a billet with one of the senior CivPols.

There was a terrible shortage of everything – vehicles, petrol, cassettes, even notebooks and Biros. The mobile telephone network was being stretched to its limits; it often took twenty attempts to get through to a number half a mile away. But the landlines were even worse, and outside Dili the only means of communication were satellite phones and field radios. The journalists fell naturally into small teams, and shared what resources were available. At any one point during the day, there was always someone out driving around town, and news – of street scuffles, demos and official announcements – quickly got back to the garden of the Turismo.

The days had a certain loose routine. First thing in the morning was David Wimhurst's Unamet press conference. Basilio and the FPDK often called in journalists just before lunch. Afternoons were for interviews, and for driving around Dili to the obvious sources of information – the hospital, the UN compound, the Hotel Tropicale, and the poorer suburbs where the militias would turn up in ugly groups to bait and goad the independence supporters. Dili was seething; there was a knifing or shooting or a punch-up every day. And the news from outside the capital – from Liquisa, Los Palos, Maliana and Suai – was even worse.

I was one of the privileged; I had booked early. My room overlooked the garden from the first floor of the Turismo. I could sit at my desk at the end of the day, and the day's gossip would float up to me from the greenery below.

The referendum was to be held on a Monday. The week before a group of us squeezed into a jeep with Felice and drove to talk to the UN in the town of Maliana, three and a half hours' journey by road to the west, close to the Indonesian border. There were militia posts in every village along the road. Indonesian flags flew from bamboo poles, and the people in the streets wore new baseball caps and T-shirts bearing the red and white colours and the word *Otonomi*. Our driver, whose name was John, had a baseball cap of his own, in grubby brown. But whenever we approached a town or a militia checkpoint he would take it off and turn it inside out, exposing the red and white colours inside. When we had passed, he would stop the car and reverse his hat once again.

'Those village people in the autonomy T-shirts and the hats,' said Felice, 'they are just pretending for the sake of the militias. In their hearts, they feel the same as John.'

The centre of Maliana was dominated by a big open green of tussocky grass. Felice had been there the year before and during the drive he had described the lively scene: the farmers from the outlying villages who walked for miles into town to sell a few peppers or onions, the market stalls, and the impromptu football games. It was lunchtime when we arrived, but the green was almost empty. On the far side, an overflow of parked Land Cruisers announced the presence of Unamet. The Maliana regional headquarters had a metal gate, painted in UN blue, and deeply marked by powerful dents.

In the front office of the Unamet headquarters, embedded in the far wall, was a heavy grey stone the size of a mango.

It had established itself there two months earlier. A group of the local militia, Besi Merah Putih, had materialised in front of the gate one day and begun hurling obscenities and stones. This one had been thrown with enough force to sail over the gate, through the glass of the office window, across the room and into the plaster.

The mood among the UN staff in Maliana was quite different from that of their colleagues in the capital. The MLOs and CivPols in Dili were wary of journalists, but here they were jumpy and strung out, and their isolation made them eager to talk. They talked about the militia leader João Tavares, and about Lieutenant Colonel Siagian, the local military commander who made no effort to disguise his closeness to the militias and his contempt for Unamet. Militiamen could be seen around town, openly carrying army rifles and squat blunderbusses made out of metal piping, and charged with weedkiller and nails. There were rumours of nasty things being plotted against UN staff: one Australian MLO had to be sent back to Dili because the death threats against him had become so detailed and consistent.

A week before, the head of Unamet, Ian Martin, had come to Maliana with Jamsheed Marker, the Pakistani diplomat who was the personal representative of the Secretary-General. 'There was shooting going on in the background all the time that they were here,' said a British colonel who was one of the remaining MLOs. 'The Besi Merah Putih were walking round carrying M-16s. Siagian saw it: he didn't do anything. They were walking across the green. He just sat there by that little stall, eating peanuts.'

That day two young independence activists were pulled off a bus by the BMP. One of them managed to run away, but the other boy, Agusto Martins, was taken away by the militiamen. His body was found that night, with a cut throat and the marks of torture. On the same afternoon a team from Unamet's voter-education programme had found itself surrounded by a mob of militiamen in one of the small villages. They were chanting, 'We want war!'

Three thousand people, Indonesia supporters and their families, had left the area in the last week for West Timor. 'Some of the trucks went past here,' said the colonel. 'They were piled high, those trucks – beds, mattresses, goats, wardrobes. They weren't leaving anything behind. João Tavares has sent his family out. Why? What are they expecting to happen? Well, I think I can guess, and I've packed my bags. I'm ready for evacuation.'

The Australian who ran Unamet's Maliana office felt that his bosses in Dili were not taking his concerns seriously. He showed us a report he had recently sent, based on 'intelligence sources' tapped over the last few days. The violence, he believed, was not random and opportunistic, but part of a carefully laid plan which would climax in an attack by the militias on the UN and on known independence supporters. It would take place either on Friday, the last day of campaigning, or on Monday, the evening after the referendum itself. Automatic rifles would be distributed among the militia. The electricity supply would be cut to the entire town.

'And then?'

'Then they can do whatever they like,' said the regional head. 'The students, Agusto Martins' friends, they're living next door. They've been attacked three times already and they've only got the police guarding them, so they'll be the first to go. Then they'll probably go for the priests, and then they'll try it on here, but with something a bit stronger than rocks. So they'll be out there with their guns, and we'll be in here, unarmed, trying to get out.'

Including the local staff, there were a hundred Unamet employees in Maliana, too many to evacuate by helicopter. So the plan was to leave by road, a journey through the most vampire-haunted regions of Timor, which even in daylight had taken us three and a half hours.

The British colonel's name was Alan. He had a square chin and gentle blue eyes. The Australian head of mission affected a weary irritability when he spoke of the danger in Maliana, but Colonel Alan was the first foreigner I had met in Timor who was badly spooked, and didn't mind admitting it. 'I wouldn't relish that drive by night,' he said. 'No, I don't fancy that at all.'

Colonel Alan made us tea in his little office. When we left, he walked out with us and shook hands as we climbed into the jeep. 'Come again,' he said cheerily. 'I'll ring you if anything happens here. Roll on Monday, anyway. After that I'll see you in Dili.'

The pros and the antis had their allotted days for campaigning, and on Wednesday it was the turn of the independence movement, the CNRT or National Council for Maubere Resistance.

The CNRT was an umbrella organisation for various groups campaigning for independence, but the differences between them seemed to mean very little. When the supporters of independence turned out, they rallied not for a party and an ideology, but for a face and a name: Xanana Gusmão.

Xanana remained under house arrest in Jakarta and the fighters of Falintil were nowhere to be seen. They had refused to disarm, but agreed instead to withdraw with their guns to three cantonments, remote sites in the mountains where Unamet could visit them, but from which they could quickly withdraw and scatter if the Indonesians were to move against them. The guerrillas were scrupulous in observing the letter of the UN agreement. It would have been a simple thing for them to take on the militias but, even after the worst of the massacres, they had remained in the cantonments and resisted the urge to revenge.

Impeccable conduct was the independence movement's campaign strategy. From the beginning, the Indonesians had always claimed that the East Timorese were hopelessly fractious and divided, that without the firm hand of Jakarta the place was doomed to civil war and anarchy. Within Timor itself, that argument had been lost decades ago. But to foreign governments, who neither understood the country nor really cared, it had a tempting plausibility. The CNRT did not have to persuade or mobilise: there was simply no doubt that, given a free choice, most East Timorese would choose their independence. All that was necessary was to ensure that the choice remained free by mitigating the effects of the Indonesian intimidation, keeping up morale and rejecting the repeated invitations to violence.

The independence rally that day was immaculate. People began gathering along the promenade and in front of the governor's residence shortly after dawn and they kept on arriving all morning – from Bacau and Los Palos in the east, and from Aileu and Ermera to the south. They were well organised: each group had a leader who supervised the painting of the posters and the raising of the banners, and made sure that everyone was embarked upon the right truck. There must have been two hundred of these vehicles, and new ones were joining the parade all the time – rackety flatbeds which had spent most of the year bouncing over potholes, laden with coffee and planks and sacks of cement. All morning the demonstrators drove up and down the centre of Dili in a slow convoy, honking horns, waving and cheering. People shouted Xanana's name. They shouted, '*Viva Timor Leste!*' and '*Viva independencia!*' It was hard to estimate numbers on the convoy, but they were fewer than I had expected.

It took courage to join this rally: there were strong and well-founded fears that the militiamen were massing and would ride into town to attack the independence supporters head on. So most of the people on the trucks were young, and many of them were experienced activists. For them it was a rapturous day – the first public celebration of the clandestine movement which had operated perilously in secret for so long, the largest independence demonstration which Timor had ever seen. And for every Timorese riding in the trucks, there was someone else, waving from the side of the road – old people, and men of working age, mothers and babies, children. They waved and clapped, some of them cheered, but most simply stared, unable to take in this sudden display of freedom and impunity. They smiled shy smiles, and glanced at one another, as if they might have liked to have been up there on the trucks too, but couldn't quite bring themselves to dare, wouldn't yet commit to believing that this could happen, and continue happening, and yet no harm come of it.

But none did. Just before noon, the trucks discharged their passengers who gathered along the promenade, dancing and singing while the CNRT leaders gave speeches. They were more like Unamet public information broadcasts than the propaganda of an independence movement. Vote for whomever you like; do not be intimidated; your vote is secret; the UN will stay here after the referendum – they even referred to it as the 'popular consultation'. There was a certain amount of technical explanation – the CNRT was worried, for example, that voters would misunderstand the question on the ballot paper and vote 'yes' for autonomy in the belief they were saying yes to independence. But the speeches didn't amount to much. The arguments had been won and lost years ago. Nobody needed to be persuaded, so what was there to say?

Trucks full of BriMobs stood on the street corners, with riot shields and body armour. Standing beside them, the demonstrators' vehicles looked even more puny and ramshackle. The police were watchful and unsmiling. They made no eye contact with the Timorese; there was no banter or barracking. The demonstrators passed by, cheering and holding their banners aloft, and paid the police no heed at all. Not a look, not a word was exchanged between them. It was as if the Indonesians were not there, and never had been.

The following day, Thursday, was the turn of the pro-Indonesia campaign; in Dili, this meant Eurico and Aitarak. It was a ragged, bloody day of scattered rumours, frights, and long, looping drives around the city.

The rally was gathering in front of the Hotel Tropicale, and when I arrived Eurico was already there, mustering the troops. There was little doubt that Eurico was a thug and a killer, but I was never able to take him seriously. Like most militiamen, he was frightening only from a distance. Close-up, the swagger and the menace became camp and pantomimic. Today he wore the full battle uniform of a militia *panglima*: camouflage jacket, camouflage trousers, military boots and a black baseball cap bearing the official *otonomi* symbol, a map of Timor in a blue sea, with a red-and-white flag planted in the middle.

Eurico's goons were assembled on the street, making as much noise as possible on a small fleet of motorbikes. They were very crappy motorbikes, with an engine note closer to a wheeze than a roar, but overall the effect was impressive enough. Behind them, the main body of the convoy was assembling; I walked down the line, peering into the trucks. The thugs snarled or gave sinister smiles; ordinary people looked away. The comparison with yesterday was interesting, for there were obvious and striking physical differences between the supporters and opponents of independence.

I don't like to generalise. I hesitate to say it. But the autonomy supporters were repellently ugly. The true believers, the Aitarak corps men who led the procession, were the worst – no casting director could have come up with a more cartoonish array of slavering degenerates. Most were deeply pock-marked. All had blackened, broken or gold-filled teeth. One of the bikers was cursed with a jaw several sizes too large for the rest of his body. It bobbed beneath his face, and his mouth hung permanently ajar even when he was chewing betel. The chewing made him salivate constantly, and a string of weighty drool extended itself down his chin and on to his smeared denim shirt.

The militiamen wore a jumble of garments, but the image which they projected was consistent. They were tropical, Third World Hell's Angels; they called to mind the covers of 1970s heavy metal albums. Hair was long and oily, forearms were bare and ringed with mysterious tattoos. The staple was the black T-shirt, bearing the *otonomi* symbol or the word *Aitarak*, in jagged, Gothic lettering like the titles of a cheap horror film.

They wore denim and khaki jackets, with the sleeves cropped to expose lumpy shoulders. They wore heavy rings and large mirrored sunglasses; multiple medallions and crucifixes jangled round their necks. One of the senior goons sported a bandolier threaded with greasy bullets. Knives and machetes were visible, although, at this stage of the rally, there were no guns. Several of the bikers had Eurico's glassy expression – people said that this was a result of low-grade amphetamines known as 'mad dog pills'. They were grubby, tawdry and smelly, but they were not ragged, and they were getting plenty of money from somewhere.

An oily head stuck itself out of the cabin of a pickup truck. 'Australia? Are you Australia?'

A few weeks earlier, Eurico had promised to 'kill all Australians', in a notorious declaration which had been only incompletely retracted.

'No, from Britain.'

'*Inggris?*'

'*Inggris.*'

'Go home, *Inggris!*'

He gave a theatrical snarl; I smiled apologetically and walked further down the line. I still couldn't take these people seriously.

Towards the middle and back of the procession, the nature of the ralliers changed. They too were disfigured, but by extreme poverty rather than poor taste. Their ages ranged widely. There were entire families of thin, sullen people – a pair of wizened grandparents, a haggard mother and father, and a brood of children, from consumptive teenagers to mucus-nosed toddlers. Many lacked shoes. Their dun, shapeless clothes were home-made. They must have been from the countryside; even the poorest Dili people looked slick and metropolitan beside them.

'From where?' I said in Indonesian to one group. 'From Ermera? Maliana?'

The people in the truck muttered and looked away.

A concerned-looking thug wandered over and said, 'Yes. From Maliana.'

But Felice, who had been watching from a safe distance, laughed. 'You can see from their faces,' he said. 'They are from West Timor. They are Indonesians, not East Timorese. The Aitarak bring them in from across the border. For a day Eurico will drive them round Dili to make it look as if he has many supporters and then he will send them home. They have no vote in this referendum. They don't even speak our language. They are only here because they are afraid.'

The pro-autonomy convoy finally growled into motion, led by Eurico's Land Rover. After a few circuits of central Dili, they gathered at the football stadium for songs and speeches, including one by Eurico in which he predicted that a victory for the independence movement would turn Timor into 'a sea of flame'. The rental crowd from West Timor was served boxes of rice and chicken; afterwards, the goons and the bikers broke up into smaller groups and took to the streets again. This was the time of danger, as campaigning degenerated into marauding. Ordinary people had disappeared inside and the shops were shuttered, although it was still mid-afternoon. The BriMobs were visible here and there, glaring impassively from their big trucks, but doing nothing to intervene. There was bound to be trouble, and it came soon enough.

At Kuluhun, one of the poorest and most vehemently pro-Falintil suburbs of Dili, a posse of Eurico's men turned up, accompanied by a truck of BriMobs. Young men came out of their houses to see off the militias. There was stone throwing, and the home-made guns were fired. On the pretext of keeping order, the police acted as a shield for Aitarak. The militia hurled stones and bottles over their heads, but when the independence supporters tried to retaliate the BriMobs raised their rifles. Rage emboldened the Kuluhun men; they got too close. It was all caught on film by an American photographer: a young man running up to the police line, turning to run back, and being shot dead through the back of the neck by a BriMob at a range of a few yards.

There was only the weekend to get through before the referendum, and an unnatural quiet fell over the town. Most of the shops in Dili did not reopen. In areas like Kuluhun and Becora, the young men took turns standing guard all night, but women and children stayed inside. Unamet issued furious statements, denouncing the militia attacks, and icy representations were made to the Indonesian police and military. The CNRT's office had also been sacked by the Aitarak, and its leaders went back into hiding, moving from house to house, by day as well as night. It became difficult to pin them down and to keep track of their plans, and the unity of the leadership was said to be strained by the violence.

The Falintil field commander, Taur Matan Ruak, was under intense pressure to retaliate on behalf of the persecuted population; but Xanana, who was still under house arrest in Jakarta, insisted that there must be no reaction. A Falintil offensive was just what the Indonesian's wanted; it would give them the only excuse they needed to attack the cantonments and force the abandonment of the referendum. 'Falintil is a national army,' a CNRT member told me, when I was finally granted an appointment, in a safe house in Becora. 'They are disciplined. They won't just act without orders. It's the general population we're worried about. There is a sense of desperation. Finally, after all this time, the international community has come here – and yet they still allow the killing to go on. Well, everything has its limits and then it cracks. If there is a popular uprising, then there will be an absolute bloodbath.'

Early every Sunday morning, Carlos Ximenes Belo, Bishop of Dili and winner of the 1996 Nobel Peace Prize, would give a mass in the garden of his residence; the day before the referendum, I went there hoping to hear him preach. The dawn mass was always a time of gentle dignity, with prayers and singing beneath the flowering trees and the kind morning light. Today there were more people than usual in the garden, although Belo himself was attending a mass on the south coast. A priest read out a message on the bishop's behalf. 'Brothers and sisters, many people here in this time are very afraid,' it said. 'Do not be afraid. Be brave, and choose the future of East Timor. This is the generation that will create history, and one day people all over the world will speak of us, of the warrior people and the bravehearted.'

All afternoon, cars and jeeps drove out of Dili as the visiting members of parliament, the diplomats, activists and journalists dispersed across East Timor for voting day. My colleague Alex and I left that afternoon with Felice and John the driver. The road to Maliana was thicker than ever with the militias. Three times we passed through bamboo roadblocks, operated by young men carrying swords and spears. Three times, John reversed and unreversed his baseball cap. The closer one got to Maliana, the more alarming the picture became. Half an hour out we saw a mixed group of machete-wielding militia and rifle-carrying soldiers; a few miles further on was another militia group, carrying M-16s of its own.

In Maliana, we were put up by a group of nuns who laid out beds in their front room. We sipped whisky from the cap of the bottle and sat up very late.

Before dawn we dressed and walked down towards the polling centre, a grubby sports hall which faced the town green. Felice gasped as we turned the corner.

There was an hour to go until the polls opened, but already the green was filling up with thousands of people. They were streaming in from all directions, in groups large and small, carrying bundles of food, infants and even rolls of bedding. They were dressed as the congregation at Bishop Belo's house had been dressed twenty-four hours before. The older men and women wore batik headdresses, the younger ones wore cleanly pressed jeans and rubber sandals. They pressed close against the wide, barnlike doors of the sports hall.

Colonel Alan stood in front of them, frantically attempting to make a gap: the wooden doors were beginning to buckle under the pressure of the crowd. But there was no shoving and shouting, no obvious excitement, not even very much smiling. People were there for a reason – to vote, and then to get away as quickly as possible. Each gripped a white printed document with handwritten particulars, the official registration form without which nobody was allowed inside.

On the outer fringes of the crowd, people were squatting down on the grass and unwrapping small breakfast parcels of rice and vegetables. A group of militiamen, seemingly unarmed, stood beneath a large sandalwood tree. An invisible force field surrounded them: despite the surging volume of the crowd no one approached within ten yards of their tree.

Eventually, Colonel Alan created a narrow corridor through the crowd and we squeezed into the hall.

Inside, final preparations were being made before the doors were opened. A line of tables had been set up where each voter received his or her ballot paper. On each table were pens, pencils, a box for the registration forms, and a plastic bottle of ink for marking the fingers of those who had voted. Outside, Colonel Alan had marshalled the crowd into a rough queue. At exactly 6.30 a.m., the first voters were allowed in.

First inside was the regent of Bobonaro, a notorious sponsor of the Besi Merah Putih militia, plump and sleek in shiny batik. 'Of course, we're not supposed to give preferential treatment to anyone,' said the UN volunteer at my side. 'It's a compromise – but look how happy he is.' The next to be admitted were the elderly and the infirm.

Among them was a middle-aged man supported by two broken sticks. His legs were bent permanently beneath him by accident or disease, and it took him five minutes to cross the room, collect his ballot and shuffle into the booth in front of me. It was painful to watch; as he edged forward I became aware that my heart was racing. Finally – finally – the referendum really was under way. What would happen next? Could Eurico and Basilio have more support than I had assumed? How could the violence of the last seven months fail to have an effect? I should have looked away, but I watched, and saw the man on sticks painstakingly mark his cross in the lower of the two boxes, the one rejecting continuing association with Indonesia. Then he folded the paper, turned his legs around, and began walking slowly towards the ballot box.

Maliana lay in the middle of a broad and fertile plain. After leaving the sports hall, we drove out of the town and towards the hills that rose along the horizon. It was a clear, dry, hot day. On the road, the hides of cows and goats had been laid out to be seasoned by the sun and the tyres of the passing cars.

In every village, it was the same. People had walked all night to get to the polling stations at the moment that they opened.

At a tiny place called Odomao Atas, the referendum was held inside the miniature white church. The voters here were the 'hill people', the euphemism which the UN used for Falintil families, who lived and moved through the jungle with the guerrillas. The church was built on a great rock which jutted out above a bend in the narrow road, and the way was completely blocked by people, all wearing their Sunday best and clutching their registration documents which flapped in the breeze. There were children on the shoulders of their older brothers, and boys clinging to the branches of the wiry trees. They looked as if they had walked a long way through the forest. Most of them were barefoot, and many of them had cuts and scratches on their feet.

The inside of the church was bare, apart from framed paintings of the Stations of the Cross. The polling booths were directly in front of the altar. A plump American volunteer named Jean Feilmoser told me about the difficulties of registering the hill people – the secret meetings with Falintil, mediated by local priests; the two-hour walk down from the mountains, escorted by the CivPols and MLOs, under the gaze of the Indonesian police and army. 'These are people the Indonesians have been chasing for years,' said Jean. 'They were risking everything by coming down here.' Almost none of the mountain people were literate; they didn't even speak Tetum. But the two local priests had worked for days, writing out the affidavits necessary to identify each voter. Then the voter-education teams and their interpreters had set about explaining the mechanics of the poll, translating from English into Indonesian, from Indonesian into Kemak or Bunak, and translating all the questions back again.

When she wasn't working as a UN volunteer, Jean was a travel agent in Florida. She was tough and wise-cracking and sentimental. She said, 'In one of the villages where we went for voter education, they gave me a bag of eggs and two chickens. I named them Independencia and Otonomi. Tomorrow one of them goes in the pot.' All through the registration period, Jean's Timorese workers had received threats; two of them had failed to turn up this morning. A tear rolled down her nose when she talked about leaving in two days' time. 'I'm afraid for them after the election,' she said. 'I'm afraid for Timor and I'm afraid for my local staff.'

Just before we left, Jean said, 'You know what else? Falintil is here. They're not armed, but they're keeping an eye on things. Can you spot them?' I peered among the hill people, and thought that perhaps I could: an older man with an air of authority; a young man with a vigilant look about him, moving from group to group, appearing to direct and advise the other voters. I couldn't be sure. But that was Falintil, after all: never wholly present nor completely absent, a sense of reassurance rather than a physical force: something watching over you.

Whatever other mistakes Unamet made, as an electoral exercise the referendum was a staggering success. By lunchtime, across East Timor, four out of five of those registered had already cast their votes. The final turnout was 98.6 per cent. Within East Timor, there were only 6,000 people who had failed to vote out of an electorate of 438,000. Had any free election anywhere in the world ever secured such a remarkable turnout?

That night, the Unamet helicopter flew around the polling centres, collecting the ballots and bringing them back to Dili. In Ermera, a handful of votes were lost when a ballot box split open as militiamen fired on the staff who were loading it on to the chopper. In Atsabe, a Timorese who was working for the UN was stabbed through the lung and died two hours later. But overall the day had gone more smoothly than anyone had dared hope.

The predicted attack on Maliana, which had not come on the

last day of the campaign, did not come that night either. There were no reports of significant intimidation. Jamsheed Marker, the grandiloquent UN special envoy, spent the day flying from town to town, and the experience stirred his poetic soul. 'I returned with vivid impressions of the awesome majesty which is manifest in the power of the people,' he told a press conference in Dili late in the evening.

'Many who went to the polling stations today did so under conditions of considerable hardship. They defied poverty, distance, climate, terrain and, in some cases, dark intimidation in order to exercise their God-given right to vote in freedom . . . It is yet too early to assess the result of the polls. But whatever the outcome, the eagle of liberty has spread its proud wings over the people of East Timor and nothing, by God's grace, will ever take it away.'

Ambassador Marker was not slow to identify the agency responsible for this heartening outcome: the Indonesian police. Their conduct, he said, had been 'of the highest order'. The leadership of their commanding officer, Colonel Timbul Silaien, had been 'superb'.

FLAT OF THE BLADE

After the calm of referendum day, the violence quickly returned. The following day, the black-shirted Aitarak men were out in force along the Dili waterfront and in front of the airport. They were stopping boats from leaving, and forcibly preventing Timorese travellers from boarding the Jakarta plane. From all over East Timor, there were reports of road-blocks – not the feeble bamboo poles which we had encountered, but big assemblies of branches, girders and oil drums manned by aggressive militiamen who would send cars back where they had come from, and slap and threaten the Timorese inside them.

South of Dili, the militia burned the houses of independence supporters in the town of Ermera and took potshots at local people working for Unamet. At least two more UN local workers were killed. The Ermera police were doing nothing, and the decision was made to evacuate the Unamet office. Its complement of 150 – including the surviving Timorese staff, always the people in the greatest peril – climbed into their Land Cruisers. But the militia blocked the way.

Hours passed. The UN helicopter flew in to negotiate and eventually the convoy was allowed to drive back to Dili.

Throughout the campaign, one message had been repeated over and over – on Radio Unamet, in the printed pamphlets and bulletins, and at all the voter-education meetings. It was repeated in Tetum, Portuguese, Indonesian and English. It was repeated by Kofi Annan in his message two days before the referendum: 'Unamet will still be here after you vote.'

But in Ermera, that was no longer true.

The ballot papers were taken to the old Dili museum; the count was expected to take an entire week. Two days after the referendum, Aitarak turned out in force for the funeral of one of its militiamen, a middle-ranking goon who had been stabbed to death by a Falintil member. (Falintil admitted it; they had already tracked down the suspect themselves and handed him over to the police.) The service was held on a patch of open ground near the airport. Three hundred militiamen were lined up in ranks; there was even an attempt to perform a ragged drill. Eurico gave a relatively unincendiary speech and there were penitent and conciliatory words from a Falintil representative. It began and ended with the usual motorbike-led convoy through Dili.

'Australian?' a biker called out to me as I watched them leave.

'No. *Inggris.*'

'Journalist?'

'Yes.'

'You must write the truth. If you don't write the truth, all of us will die here. You too.'

This was just the kind of corniness that prevented me from taking the militias seriously.

In the afternoon I went to see my contact in the CNRT. Security had not been relaxed for the leadership, who were still living in hiding, and surrounded by bodyguards. But my CNRT friend was highly excited. He was already anticipating victory. He talked about the need for a government of national unity, about education and health programmes, and about the reintegration of the guerrillas into society. Towards the end of our conversation, my mobile phone gave one of its rare and unreliable chirrups. It was my friend, Alex, who was out in the jeep with John and Felice. They had heard about some kind of trouble at the Unamet compound.

'Where are you?' said Alex. 'We'll pick you up.'

Ten minutes later, John was nosing the jeep up the road which ran past Unamet. These days, he wore his hat with the militia colours turned permanently out. He was unhappy about being here, and did not want us to get out of the car.

'Don't worry, John,' Alex said, through Felice. 'We'll be careful. You wait here. We'll be back in ten minutes.'

The compound itself was five hundred yards away, invisible to us beyond a curve in the road. This was the centre of residential Dili, a district of wooden and plaster houses set among palms and eucalyptus; none of their inhabitants were to be seen. We walked fast; other journalists were climbing out of their cars and moving in the same direction. Suddenly, there was a loud crack up ahead, and three skinny young men in T-shirts pelted around the curve.

We jumped awkwardly for cover behind trees and walls. Two of the boys ignored us, as they sprinted straight down the road. The third, a gaunt teenager with a skull-like face, jumped behind the wall where Felice and I were sheltering and began talking rapidly in Tetum.

'They are pro-independence,' said Felice. 'Up ahead are Aitarak. They came to one of the houses to attack it. There was a fight. He says that Aitarak are killing people up there.'

Whoever had been pursuing the three boys had not followed them. We walked on cautiously along the verge, close to the drooping palm trees and the houses.

The road leading to the Unamet compound came into view a hundred yards away, and in front of it a ragged street battle was taking place. More young men in T-shirts appeared, running forward to hurl stones at the enemy before retreating. Then their antagonists ran forward, wearing the Aitarak colours, red and white and black.

'*Milisi, milisi!*' said the young independence supporter, who was following us back up the road.

Two of the militia carried guns and all had machetes. A camera crew – I couldn't quite tell which one – was filming from quite close up. 'Do you want to go up there?' said Felice uncertainly, but neither Alex nor I did. 'Maybe we should go back to John,' I said. After that, everything happened very fast.

There was a great commotion behind us, more young independence boys were running and shouting, and following them more red-and-white-and black-clad goons. They were Aitarak; they had crept round the back to come up on us from the rear. Suddenly, we were trapped: militiamen in front as well as behind. One of the newly-arrived Aitarak had a machete which he was swinging over his head like a war sword. I watched a fat man with a great frizzy head of hair stop as he ran towards us, and raise the home-made gun in his hand. Was he thirty yards away, or was it more like thirty feet? His blunderbuss was squat and very dirty; I could make out the abrasions around the barrel where the metal cutter had bitten into the pipe. I ran without much conscious thought away from the road and through whatever looked like open space, and found myself panting in thick rough grass between two houses. There was a swampy patch where my boots sank deep into mud. I climbed over a fence of barbed wire and found myself looking at a five-foot-tall grey wall over which people were scrambling. To my relief, I recognised friends whom I had seen on the road. Felice and Alex were there too. We helped one another over the wall, and found ourselves at the back of a large low building with desks and computers visible inside. We were inside the Unamet compound.

From the direction of the road came a loud flat pop, perhaps the gun which the man with the frizzy hair had been priming as I fled. We picked our way among outhouses and dustbins to the centre of the compound, where the Land Cruisers were parked. Many of the UN staff were standing around hesitantly, and a dozen journalists had gathered, having scrambled like us over gates, doorways and walls. One of the television correspondents was describing how he had taken shelter in a pigsty after being chased by a man with a machete. He was worried about Jonathan, who had been separated from the others when the militiamen had made their surprise attack from the rear. One man, an independence supporter, was certainly dead. He had been running away when he fell and was set on with machetes.

Towards the rear of the compound was the hall where press conferences were held. It was now entirely filled with fearful Timorese, two or three hundred of them, sitting on chairs, tables and on the floor. Most of them were women and young children, and many of them were crying. A teenage girl was leading prayers and hymns through the public address system. They were refugees who had been sheltering in the school next door to the compound, and they had scrambled over the walls when the popguns had started going off.

Now there was a new noise, close at hand: a burst of automatic rifle fire, followed by a series of single shots. David Wimhurst was standing on the steps of the hall. Somebody said, 'David, what kind of rifle was that?'

'I don't know,' said Wimhurst.

'Was it, like, an AK?'

'I don't know,' said Wimhurst.

'Or some kind of sub-machine gun?'

'I DON'T FUCKING KNOW, DO I?' said Wimhurst.

There was a silence.

'That was an M-16,' said the Australian army officer beside me.

'Thank you,' said Wimhurst and, to the original questioner: 'IT WAS AN M-16.'

'In this country, there are only two groups of people who carry M-16s,' said the officer. 'The Indonesian army, and the people that the Indonesian army give their guns to.'

A voice came over the public address system: 'We have authentic gunfire outside the compound. Please move inside. Repeat, will everyone please move inside? This is not a request.'

We crowded into the already crowded hall. There was more irregular firing. Every time it was heard a little shiver of distress went through the refugees. Then it stopped. At the front of the compound Indonesian policemen were visible, talking to the CivPols. Soon, the voice of the announcer came over the tannoy again: 'Ladies and gentlemen, thank you for your cooperation. The police have now restored order, and all UN staff are requested to return to their offices.'

From the time of the first shots, it had taken the police more than an hour to appear on the scene. But now they had 'restored order'. They even provided trucks to ferry the journalists back to their hotels. As we were waiting, Alex said, 'What happened to Jonathan? I hope he's all right.' I remembered my short-wave radio and tuned into his station. And out of it came the voice of Jonathan. He was speaking live into his mobile phone; he couldn't have been more than a few hundred yards from the spot where we stood, listening to him. He was safe.

He was describing what had happened to him. It had been caught on film by one of the cameramen, and we would all watch it later that evening. It showed Jonathan, cut off from the escape route into the compound, being chased by a militiaman, perhaps the same one whom I had seen waving a machete over his head. It showed him slipping and falling, and the sickening moment as the man stood above him and struck him with the butt of his automatic rifle. Jonathan held his arms up to protect himself, just like the Timorese who had been cut to death a few moments before. He thought that he was going to die. But an Indonesian man, an Intel working with the militias, trotted up and pulled the militiaman away. Nearby, the correspondent from the *Washington Post* was actually struck by a machete. But his assailant turned it as he brought it down, so that he was struck by the flat of the blade and not by its cutting edge.

More than anything else, this was what persuaded many of the journalists to leave Dili over the next few days: the film of Jonathan, lying on the ground beneath the descending rifle. There were those who pointed out how careful the militia had been *not* to kill a foreigner, when it would have been so easy for them to do so. But for many people, it was too close, too imaginable – the proximity of the Intel, the angle of a blade, marking the difference between life and death. People gathered around the monitors in editing suites which the TV teams had set up, and watched the sequence over and over.

The following day, Maliana finally fell. As Colonel Alan had predicted, the UN building was surrounded while the militias roamed around the town firing their M-16s and burning the houses of those associated with the independence movement. Four people were killed, including two Timorese Unamet drivers, and six others were missing. More than twenty houses were burned down. The firing went on for most of the night.

The Maliana Unamet team arrived in Dili on Friday morning, many of them in shock and in tears. The next day the Unamet radio broadcasts stopped because the technicians were afraid to come to work. Many of the television crews were leaving; most of the election observers had already gone. Suddenly, hotel rooms were plentiful and cheap. But drivers and interpreters were scarcer than ever. Felice turned up at the hotel one morning and quietly explained that his family was worried about him, and that he would not be able to work for us any more. But John the driver stayed with us. After the fright at the compound, he had driven round for hours looking for us. He convinced himself that we had been snatched by the militias, and that it had been his fault for not waiting with the jeep. Late that night, he had appeared at my room, shaking with relief.

On the day of the withdrawal from Maliana, we discovered a new UN euphemism. Instead of being evacuated to Dili, we were told that the Unamet operation had been 'relocated'.

'We're worried that they'll ask for a territorial division,' said Joaquim Fonseca. 'They'll try to break off Bobonaro, Ermera, Liquisa and the rest of the western regencies, and attach them to West Timor. That's where the militias are strongest. It's a large part of the country, and it contains most of the natural resources. The coffee, the sandalwood. And maybe there'll be politicians in Jakarta who'll want that. And if those politicians make enough noise, then countries in the UN, those countries who supported Indonesia for all these years, they'll begin to think that's reasonable. That's the scenario that worries us.'

Joaquim ran a local human rights organisation, and he had been recommended to me as a militia expert. I wanted to learn more, to overcome my inability to take Eurico and his men seriously. But everything I heard made them seem more ridiculous.

There were so many different pro-Indonesia groups; every day I learned of a new one. There fell into two categories: the militias, and the Abbreviations. The second group consisted of various semi-official organisations and united fronts, known by elaborate acronyms such as UNIF, BRTT, PPI and FPDK. The militias favoured catchier and more evocative names, the creepier the better. In Dili, there was Eurico's Aitarak and the Besi Merah Putih. Ainaro regency had Mahidi, a complicated acronymic rendering of the Indonesian phrase, Life or Death for Integration. Viqueque had Makikit, which meant Bat, and the enclave of Oecussi had Sakunar, which meant Scorpion. The militia names were in keeping with the militia clothes, the militia motorbikes and the militia smell. They were swaggering, adolescent and camp, suggestive of long hair, studded leather and heavy metal. Their leaders were an assortment of Indonesian-appointed administrators, Timorese tribal chiefs and gangsters. Eurico, not yet even thirty, was the youngest and most interesting of them.

As a teenager, he had been active in the clandestine movement. His parents, it was said, had been killed by the Indonesians and he had been captured by Kopassus. Under torture, something in him had changed. He was put in charge of a 'casino' in Dili, little more than two pool tables and a room for playing cards. A few years later he became involved in a paramilitary group called Team Sepulo. 'It was a kind of hit squad,' said Joaquim. 'They drove around town, intimidating people, kidnapping them for a few days.' Soon after the referendum announcement, Team Sepulo was reborn as Aitarak, with Eurico in command.

Joaquim hated the militias but part of him pitied them too. 'Many of them have been threatened or coerced,' he said. 'A few of them have come to me and told me they felt trapped and asked me what they should do. Once someone has joined the militia, he doesn't have choices. He could walk out, but then his family would be at risk. The hard core, the leaders, have been cooperating with the Indonesian military for years and they know so many of their secrets that it's very dangerous for them to leave the militia. They could be killed easily.'

The new recruit was often subjected to an initiation. He would be required to assault someone, or stab someone to death, or infiltrate the clandestine movement and bring back its secrets. Having succeeded he would be paid 50,000 rupiahs; more importantly, he would find himself bound to the group through their knowledge of his crime or betrayal. 'Many of them don't have a logical motivation,' said Joaquim. 'They could be killed at any time. What do they get out of it? Often they're not really aware what they're doing, with the drugs and the drink. You must have noticed it. Look in their eyes and you can tell.'

How many militiamen were there? I asked a diplomat I knew in one of the big embassies in Jakarta. 'You're talking at most a few hundred dyed-in-the-wool believers, a few hundred to a thousand at most,' he said. 'A lot of the rank and file are freaks – I mean, you've seen them. They get drunk, they take drugs, they don't know what they're fighting for. As for the leaders, the ones who know what they're doing, the numbers are insignificant. There's fifty, maybe just twenty people, and if you took them out, you'd solve the problem.'

The Indonesian police looked away when the militias went on their rampages, but the army actively helped. Indonesian soldiers and their agents supplied them with drugs and with money. More than once Unamet staff on convoy in the countryside had passed by villages where soldiers were practising drill with units of the militia or leading them as they drove people out of their homes. It was more than a rumour or an assumption:

it had been witnessed time and again. Unamet complained, 'assurances' were given. Nothing changed.

The Indonesians armed the militias, although they did this carefully. 'Put aside the home-made weapons, and they've got maybe a couple of hundred real guns between them,' said the diplomat. 'The army hands them out, lets them play with them and wave them around for a while, and then takes them back before it gets too obvious. There's a guy named Domingos Soares who has an Uzi he's very proud of. Hermínio had a couple of sophisticated weapons. We haven't seen any really large displays of guns. But in a place like this, with the population unarmed and the guerrillas stuck up in the mountains, how many guns do you need?'

Alex and I paid a call on the militia commander named Hermínio – Hermínio da Silva da Costa, 'chief of staff' of the PPI, the Armed Forces of the Integration Struggle for East Timor. The pro-independence leaders might be in hiding, but making an appointment with Hermínio was easy. We met in one of the whitewashed Portuguese villas along the seafront and sat on carved teak thrones in front of a coffee table laid with an elaborate lace doily. The sea breeze floated in through the open door. As we talked, Hermínio slowly ate sweets from a heavy glass bowl. He was in his fifties, pot-bellied, with small shrewd eyes which he fixed upon you as he spoke. When he was not speaking, he smiled, nodding gently as the questions were translated for him. He wasn't a clown like Basilio or a crazy like Eurico. He made me think of a crocodile – a patient, pot-bellied crocodile with sophisticated weapons.

Hermínio had been in the Portuguese army, and was a founder member of the integrationist party. Now he was leader of the PPI, one of the pre-eminent Abbreviations. He explained his present role by comparing the Armed Forces of the Integration Struggle for East Timor to the North Atlantic Treaty Organisation. 'Every region has its own militia group and I am like the roof above all of them,' he said. 'If one group from this region asks for help, for example, they don't ask directly. They come to me first. I'm like the Secretary-General of Nato. But if I'm captured or killed, my forces still go on.'

From the beginning, Hermínio's account of himself was dismally confused. It was a sign, I later realised, of how completely he was under the control and protection of the Indonesians – he didn't even feel the need to lie effectively. He lost his thread, blundered into conversational traps, and contradicted himself between one sentence and the next. When it was pointed out to him, he just smiled. He was in the happy position of not needing to be consistent. He could just be sinister instead.

As an interview, though, it seemed like a waste of time. We asked about Hermínio's relationship with the Indonesian army, and he said that it had all changed. Formerly, the army 'supported' the militias with weapons, but nowadays they had to protect both sides, and the 'donations' had dried up. 'But if there is a conflict,' Hermínio said, 'they will support us one hundred per cent. There has been no promise of this, but I know.'

We asked him how he could be so sure. Hermínio said, 'The Indonesian military will not favour one side or another. If a conflict comes, they will stand in the middle.'

'But didn't you just say that the Indonesians would support you one hundred per cent?' Alex asked.

Hermínio smiled.

We asked how many guns he had at his disposal. He shrugged and popped another sweet in his mouth. 'We used to have 10,000 weapons. Now in the thirteen regencies of East Timor, there are only about a thousand left.' The other 9,000 had been 'given back' to the Indonesians 'on condition that they look after them'. But soon he was insisting that the militias had never received *any* guns from their friends. 'The only real arms we have had are captured from Falintil,' he said almost indignantly. 'Of course, we hand them over to the police.'

It was becoming rather boring, but we asked him anyway how many men were in the PPI. Hermínio said, 'About 10,000 to 15,000 in total. The women also are eager to get involved. If the situation is an emergency, if we have war, we can mobilise 150,000 people.'

One hundred and fifty thousand was a quarter of the adult population. I thought to myself: this isn't going anywhere. Some of it might be true, much of it was lies, but all of it was designed to bamboozle. A telephone began ringing on the teak sideboard. 'Excuse me,' said Hermínio, and stood up to answer it. The telephone, I noticed, was also clad in a lace doily, similar to the one on the table. Hermínio spoke briefly, and returned to us with apologies.

We asked him what result he expected from the referendum and he smiled lazily, as if it was hardly a matter to which he had given much thought. 'Of course autonomy will win,' he said. 'Ninety-five per cent is certain, if they count fairly. Maybe 80 per cent if Unamet cheat. The worst we'll get is 60 per cent.'

We asked Hermínio to imagine a situation – hypothetical to the point of absurdity – in which the pro-Indonesia movement actually lost the vote.

He said, 'I will reject the result. If they announce that result, it's clearly cheating. And it's Unamet's work, because the ballot is the responsibility of Unamet. My plan is to bring the problem to the United Nations Security Council in New York and ask Kofi Annan to hold another ballot, but organised by Indonesia, not by Unamet.'

(I formed a mental picture of Hermínio striding indignantly through the streets of New York, and confronting Kofi Annan, one Secretary-General to another.)

We put to Hermínio an even more fantastic scenario in which this proposal was turned down.

Hermínio said, 'If the UN really claim that independence has won, I promise it will be civil war again. If the UN say that, then the independence forces don't deserve to live any more,

266

because it is not fair. I would rather go to war to slaughter all the independence people.'

At the last minute, he had become rather heated. He wasn't smiling any more. We thanked Hermínio, and took our leave.

Walking back to the hotel along the seafront, I found myself in a dilemma. On the one hand, it was obviously rubbish. The militias didn't have 15,000 men, they didn't carry a thousand guns of any type, and they weren't going to carry out a general slaughter. On the other hand, he had said it and it was, as the expression goes, good copy. I wrote the interview up, omitting Hermínio's more egregious lies and keeping as neutral a tone as possible. It appeared under the headline IF POLL IS LOST THE SLAUGHTER WILL BEGIN, and I felt the mingled embarrassment and pride that comes from filing a misleading story which is prominently displayed.

When I had finished – and after the nightly struggle with the Turismo's clogged phone lines and antique fax machine – I sat out in the garden smoking a cigarette. The hotel was pleasantly empty; another planeload of its guests had left that afternoon. Service in the restaurant had improved greatly; I ordered a grilled fish and several bottles of iced beer. One of the young waiters sat down and smoked with me. He was as relieved as anyone that the crowds of guests had thinned out. But he was worried about the future, above all about what would happen when the militias and the Indonesians realised that they had lost. He wanted to know if it was true what he had heard, that the result was going to be announced the next day.

It was true: the counting had taken less time than expected. In a few hours, it would be over. What would happen after that? I didn't know. But Hermínio da Silva da Costa knew.

He had told us exactly what he was going to do. Later, it came out that Unamet and the foreign embassies had been receiving similar reports for weeks. The militias made no secret of what was being planned.

Unamet passed the information to New York, the embassies

passed it to their capitals. It was there in my newspaper the next morning.

But none of us believed it.

THE COMPOUND

The result was announced at nine o'clock on Saturday morning in the ballroom of the Hotel Mahkota. It had not been expected for another three days, but the count had gone quickly. It must have seemed an obvious thing to get the news out as soon as possible, and to catch unprepared the plotters and their puppets. But later people cursed Unamet for this. Ordinary Timorese, too, were making their plans – plans to leave the towns for the mountains, to send into hiding children in the independence movement, or simply to gather in supplies in preparation for weeks of danger and isolation. By Saturday, few of these plans had been completed. Later, much later, Felice said to me, 'People died, I think, because they announced the result early.'

The ballroom was packed. The head of Unamet, Ian Martin, walked briskly to the front and read out the results. He was a thin, bespectacled man with a patient, bureaucratic manner which tended to enfeeble his angrier and more forceful statements. When the announcement came, it was almost an anticlimax. Strict instructions had been issued to the UN staff to display no reaction to the result, and among the journalists this had also been agreed. 'In fulfilment of the task entrusted to me,' said Ian Martin, 'I hereby announce that the result of the vote is 94,388 or 21.5 per cent in favour and 344,580 or 78.5 per cent against the proposed special autonomy.'

Four out of five East Timorese had voted for independence.

Martin began reading out a statement from Kofi Annan, but, even before he had finished speaking, people were standing up

and walking out of the room. A murmuring crowd was gathering in the hotel's dingy lobby. Friends smiled thinly at one
another, and congratulated the few Timorese who were standing
around. John the driver ran forward and embraced me speech-
lessly. Tears were on his cheeks. He looked terrified.

On the steps of the hotel, people were milling uncertainly.
There were no cheering crowds, no jubilation. Apart from a
single vendor, the street was empty. Whatever else happened, it
seemed important to buy a lot of cigarettes. As I was stuffing
the packets into my bag, a pair of Aitarak men drove slowly by
on motorbikes, expressionlessly eyeing the front of the hotel.

It was fifteen minutes on foot from the Mahkota to the
Turismo. But this morning nobody wanted to walk and John's
jeep quickly filled up with people who needed rides. At the
quayside a crowd of families sprawled in front of a large barge,
among mattresses, refrigerators, motorbikes and furniture.

Along the road we passed small groups of women and children, all of them converging on Bishop Belo's house. They had
been arriving there since the previous night; in the bishop's
garden hundreds of people were sheltering from the sun beneath
sheets suspended from the trees. An open-backed BriMob truck
went by, carrying young men in jeans and T-shirts. Some of
them looked like plain-clothes policemen, but most had the oily
Aitarak look about them.

There was little talking on the drive to the hotel. Back in our
rooms, we each instinctively went to our short-wave radios and
computers to check the headlines. Here we were, at the epicentre
of this remarkable news, and yet for the moment what we had
witnessed ourselves was less important than the rest of the
world's reaction to it. People called out the headlines as they
came up. Xanana Gusmão, speaking from house arrest in Jakarta,
said: 'This day will be eternally remembered as the day of
national liberation.' The East Timorese foreign minister in exile,
Jose Ramos Horta, had words for the defeated supporters of
Indonesia: 'They have not lost – they have won a country.' There

was even a reaction from Eurico Guterres. 'We are defeated diplomatically,' he was quoted as saying. 'But we will not give up.'
Eurico was no longer in Dili, it seemed. He had left on the morning
flight to Jakarta, and it was difficult to tell whether this was a
good sign or a bad one. 'Either he's throwing in the towel,' said
Alex, 'or he knows that something very nasty's going to happen.'

Alex, John and I went for a drive around Dili. Within an hour
of the announcement, we heard the first distant pops of the blunderbusses. There were no signs of euphoria or celebration. The
cameramen and photographers were beside themselves because
the visual image which the story demanded, of locals joyously
celebrating, was nowhere to be had. There was some creative
improvisation; groups of Timorese were accosted on the street
and encouraged to whoop for the cameras. But the doors and
windows of the straw and bamboo houses were shuttered, and
the streets were almost empty. The only people to be seen were
family groups hurrying anxiously along the pavements, with
cloth-wrapped bundles of possessions on their heads. Hundreds
of them had converged on the Unamet compound. On being
turned away, they went next door to an abandoned school used
as a UN car park. As we drove back towards the hotel, the
passengers on the quayside were loading their belongings on to
the barge, and the police were placing roadblocks in front of the
Hotel Mahkota, big spindles of timber wrapped around with
barbed wire, supported by hulking green trucks.

Back at the Turismo, the residents were enjoying lunch in the
garden. The man from the *Sydney Morning Herald* handed me
a printed letter headed 'Rising Security Costs'.

'Dear Guests,' it began.

In line with rising concerns over safety and security in the
city of Dili, the Hotel Turismo has been forced to increase
its security measures. We have incurred additional costs in
protecting and safeguarding the hotel. Guests will be asked

to contribute to the arrangement, which involves a 24-hour police guard, consisting of officers from the special mobile police brigade and intelligence units.

The Hotel is seeking contributions of Rp. 15 000 per day to be included in the hotel bill. Naturally we regret having to take these steps but feel they are necessary given the emergency conditions

Receipts can be provided.

In other words: we were paying the BriMobs to protect us from militiamen whom the BriMobs were sponsoring in the first place.

Shooting could be heard all afternoon, and people stopped going out. Reluctantly, John was persuaded to go home. He had a wife and a small baby, but at some point he had decided that our safety was his personal responsibility. After dark, the shooting became less sporadic and more regular, and could be heard from much closer to the hotel. The journalists deserted the garden, and drank and smoked in their rooms and on the balconies. The most frightening news of that day came quite late. The Unamet mission in Liquisa had come under fire as it was being evacuated, and an American CivPol had been gravely injured when his Land Cruiser was fired upon. The bullets were from an M-16; they had been fired by the BriMobs.

Four planes full of journalists left the next day, and the population of the hotel dwindled to its dregs. Those who had decided to stay gathered in the garden and began to organise. There were fewer than twenty of us – Alex and I, a handful of other newspaper correspondents, several stringers, a couple of documentary-makers and a single photographer. The Turismo's staff had gone; we had the place completely to ourselves. We began by drawing up a list of our names. Someone volunteered to gather supplies of food and to look after the cooking. Someone else took responsibility for establishing escape routes from the hotel, in case it should be attacked. We had all the time we needed for our meeting; no one very much wanted to go outside. *Pop, pop* went the blunderbusses in the distance. *Thucka-thucka-thucka* went the AK-47s and the M-16s. Then they fell quiet for an hour or more. John reappeared at the front of the hotel. I was so preoccupied with how unafraid I was that I scarcely noticed him. Members of the Food Committee sat around the garden, discussing that night's dinner. I began to think about what I would write.

In the late afternoon I dozed in my room, and when I awoke everything had changed. People were trotting urgently across the garden carrying bags and equipment. A captain in the marines was at the front of the hotel talking to the few journalists who understood Indonesian. Two dozen armed men stood by him. They carried automatic rifles and long combat knives and wore flak jackets. But they had bad news. A 'warning' had been received that Aitarak was planning an attack on the hotel – Aitarak, with its leather jackets, rusty machetes and popguns. And regretfully, the Indonesian Marine Corps, together with the Indonesian Police Mobile Brigade, were 'unable to guarantee security'.

'But why not?' one of the Indonesian speakers asked, pointing to the captain's rifle. 'You have this. You are strong. Make the Aitarak go away.'

The captain smiled and shrugged and spread the palms of his hands wide.

'"Cannot guarantee security,"' someone else repeated. '"Cannot guarantee security." Well, that's enough for me. I know a death threat when I hear it.'

Open-backed police trucks were already pulling up in front of the hotel. I hurried back to my room, shouldered my knapsack, and hesitated over my suitcase before deciding to leave it behind. I locked the door behind me.

The chairman of the Escape Committee had elected to stay

on with a handful of others, but everyone else was moving to Unamet. I had no hesitation in leaving the Turismo because it was becoming impossible to work there. The phones were increasingly unreliable: as long as we were unable to come and go safely, it was impossible to know what was going on beyond the road in front of the hotel. In a few days we would return here when everything had calmed down; for now, Unamet was the centre of information and communications, and the only place to find out what was happening in the rest of the country. But once we were embarked in the big truck I began to feel angry. The BriMobs laughed as they hauled us over the wooden sides of the trucks. J. J. Sitompul, the police colonel who had been so friendly with Eurico, oversaw the operation. He held a swagger stick under his arm, and barked at us as we heaved up boxes and bags and bottles of water. We were so obviously doing exactly what he wanted.

The trucks started off with deliberate abruptness, and the BriMobs guffawed as the jolt sent us sprawling. I pulled myself off the man from the *Sydney Morning Herald* and looked back towards the hotel to see a militiaman run out from a side street. Soldiers and police watched him with amusement from just feet away. He raised his blunderbuss, and we all cringed into the corners of the truck as it went off. He was a hundred yards away and had no chance of hitting us; it was more of a two-fingered salute than a genuine attempt on our lives. The policemen riding with us snickered once again.

At the UN compound, nobody was surprised to see us. The Portuguese government delegation had turned up a few hours before; just after us, a convoy of fifty-five Unamet staff arrived from the town of Suai. The Dili staff had all abandoned their lodging houses and hotels and were sleeping in the compound. During the short drive from the hotel, the sun had set and lights were going on inside the offices. Inside, people were setting up lamps and camp beds alongside their desks. We climbed out of the police trucks, and stood around feeling lost.

Alex arrived separately in John's jeep. I ran over as it pulled up outside the compound. But the sky was darkening and the CivPols at the gate were urging us to come inside. Alex was pleading with John, who was shaking his head.

'I'm telling him to come inside the compound,' Alex said. 'But he wants to go back to his family, and he's worried about the car.'

'John, where will you go? Bring your family here.'

'Please, John, come inside.'

He shook his head. He looked as scared as ever, but I was beginning to understand that the more scared John felt, the more determined he became. There was a silence. The CivPol at the gate told us to hurry up.

Alex and I stared at one another. Then Alex said, 'Well, we should pay him.'

'What do we owe him?' I said. 'How much money do you have?'

The CivPol at the gate was shouting at us.

'How many days has it been?' asked Alex.

We made a crude calculation and counted out a mixture of dollars and rupiahs. I felt ashamed to be saying goodbye to John like this, handing over a bundle of creased notes and sending him off into the darkness.

Alex said, 'The militia know he's been working with us. He'll never make it back.'

'Please, please come inside, John,' I said.

Alex said, 'But for God's sake, he does have a home. He has a wife and child.'

'Well, we should have thought of that.'

'We can't even talk to him in his own language.'

'Gentlemen,' said the CivPol, 'we are now closing the fucking gate.'

'John! Thank you. *Obrigado*. Be careful.'

He reached out across the mess of money on the passenger seat, and squeezed each of our hands, then pulled the door shut, gripped the wheel and turned the car round. A big house was burning half a mile away and sending up smoke into the dusk. As John drove away, he turned round and waved, and forced a smile onto his face, as if it was he who owed us courage.

The UN staff were busy turning their offices into sleeping quarters; the floor space was quickly filling up with folded camp beds and boxes of food. But here in the press room there were at least computers and power sockets and satellite phones. On the tops of the cluttered desks Unamet walkie-talkies sat in their cradles, crackling out conversations between the CivPols and MLOs who stood watch around the perimeter. In normal times, journalists were not allowed in here, but the press officers seemed glad to see us. I found myself a camp table, an electrical socket and an ashtray, and sat down to write.

The worst thing happened about an hour later.

It began with a new kind of shooting, not popguns or automatics, but the long ratcheting bursts of a machine gun, very close, from the other side of the compound. We hurried outside, and now there was a new noise – the screaming of women, close at hand, but muffled, coming in waves from over the wall.

It was the wall which divided the compound from the abandoned school; in the last few hours it had completely filled with refugees, cooking, eating and sleeping on the floors of the classrooms. And now somebody was firing a machine gun over their heads. The rounds were purely for effect. They harmed no one directly, but they didn't need to. There were more than a thousand people in the school, most of them women and children, and now they were all rushing, terrified, for the single door which connected the school to Unamet. A similar panic had taken hold the previous week, and someone in the UN had taken a decision: not only had the door been locked, but the top of the wall had been festooned with ribbons of bright new razor wire.

The door quickly burst open, and people oozed through it,

winded and crushed against the narrow wooden frame. The wall was only seven feet high and refugees were attempting to climb over the wire. They tried to use clothes and bedding to pad its sharp teeth. Parents behind were pushing their children over the top. The children were being forced on to the barbs. Bundles of possessions were being thrown over and becoming entangled. There were Indonesian policemen in the school, bellowing at the refugees and trying to pull them back. The CivPols in the compound were carrying megaphones and booming uselessly through them in English. The machine-gun fire stopped, and then another volley was heard again, followed by a new wave of screaming.

I stood in front of the gate and thought: what is the best thing to do? I didn't know. No one knew. So I shouted out to the CivPol with the megaphone, 'They can't understand you! They don't speak English.' Then I just stood and listened to the screaming, staggered by the terror on the far side of the wall. I could feel it almost physically, like a wind. How strong is the fear that makes a mother lift her baby up over her head and push him on to razor wire?

Eventually the refugees calmed down. The shooting had stopped, but it was obvious that it could start again at any time. So the door was opened and the refugees came through one by one, calmly now, with sobs instead of cries, some of them gashed and bleeding where they had been bitten by the barbs. That night the man from the UN High Commission for Refugees told me that there were 150,000 people displaced all across East Timor. Fifteen hundred of them were here with us now, inside the compound.

The gunfire continued all evening, sometimes close by, sometimes distant, but by now it was little more than background noise. At 10.37, there was an intense and prolonged burst. Ten minutes later came a loud, proximate boom which shook the windows, followed by the shriller sound of more automatic fire.

'Down!' someone shouted. 'Off with lights.' Everyone in the press room jumped to the floor, and crawled up against the walls and beneath tables.

'What was that?'

'It sounded like a rocket.'

'It was bloody close.'

There was silence. Someone sniggered mirthlessly. A match flared, and soon the only light in the room was a dozen orange cigarette tips. I remembered the head of the Escape Committee and the small band who had remained in the Turismo, and wondered how they fared.

The walkie-talkies on the tables had been left on, and crackling out of them came conversations between the CivPols, as they peered out into the darkness.

There's the glow of a fire on the horizon. Crackle, crackle.

We have a group of men, possibly military, possibly militia, moving away from the west wall of the compound. Crackle, silence.

The weapon has been identified. A grenade, a military issue grenade.

Ten minutes later, the alarm was over and the lights were back on.

Who threw that grenade? It hardly mattered. Between the militias and the Indonesian security forces the only difference was the uniform. I carried a trestle table outside and finished writing in the open air. I called London on my mobile phone and dictated the story, reading it out word by word. Afterwards, I drank whisky with my friends, nibbled at the UN's unappetising packets of military-style rations, and smoked and smoked. When it was very late, we helped one another erect the clumsy camp beds. I placed my bed outside, under the eaves of an old classroom.

When was the last time I had slept outside beneath the stars? It had been that night in Bali, when I had had my first dreams of Indonesia. Three years ago: so much had happened since then;

so many bad dreams had come true. Then I had been alone, and peaceful, and the strange dreams had been breathed over me by the jungle. Now I was surrounded by people, highly excited, and hemmed in by a small desperate city, on another island of the same great archipelago. Two moments, linked by the sensation of air on my skin and the sight of the southern stars.

I thought back to the brutal raid on the democratic party in Jakarta and the fiery riots which followed it. Something had been born in that moment, a creature of violence which had grown in Borneo, gathered strength during the forest fires, and the ruin of the economy, and reached its maturity during Suharto's strange fall. By chance, I had been there at its birth, and followed it, and now I was here again at what felt like the end of something, although the end of what it was impossible to say.

I arrived at the UN compound at dusk on Sunday; I would leave on Tuesday afternoon. I was thirty years old at the time, but I doubt that in one lifetime I will experience another forty-eight hours so rich, so fearful and intense. In Borneo and Jakarta, I had seen violence and cruelty. But I had watched them on my own terms. The life of the world had always been there in the background; at any point I could have stepped back from the edge to enjoy food, company and a peaceful bed.

In Dili, all of these were gone. Law, reason, pity, civilisation had shrunk to the breadth of the UN compound, to the few thousand square yards between the walls of the old teacher-training college. When I slept on my camp bed outside the press room, I didn't only dream conventional nightmares of violence and pursuit. I dreamed of being a small child: of going to church with my grandparents, of walking across a wide lawn holding the hands of my mother and father. I dreamed of all the certainties that had gone from Timor: the child's trust in his parents, the parents' promise that everything will be all right. They were the saddest dreams possible in such a place, and I woke with tears in my eyes.

I dreamed, too, of the shark cage, and of myself as a diver

inside it. The water all around was murky and cold, and there was a rushing noise in my ears. Without warning giant shapes emerged out of the dimness: sharks. They swam around the cage with terrible speed and their noses clanged against the bars, which bent and snapped and fell away. Soon there were no bars at all, just me suspended alone in the current with the sharks swimming around me, brushing my diving suit, circling me over and again. I could feel tugs on the tube which connected me to the surface and I knew that it was a message in a code which I had once understood but which had become meaningless.

I woke as the sun rose. I felt dirty and sweaty and I had a metallic taste in my mouth. People were already up, setting tins of beans and stew on the paraffin burners which came with the ration packs. I began to see faces I recognised, and this too was dream-like, the incongruous coming together of people whom I had never expected to see in one place. There was a UN political officer whom I had once met in Macedonia, there was a British policeman from Liquisa, and the gentle Colonel Alan from Maliana. We greeted one another like long-lost friends.

After lunch, the remaining journalists arrived from the Turismo. Soldiers had forced them to leave. Much more alarming, the Red Cross next door had been overrun, along with the house of Bishop Belo. Three or four thousand refugees had been sheltering in the two compounds, and our friends had watched from the windows of the Turismo as the soldiers and militiamen had entered together, firing automatics into the air and kicking the women as they scrambled to gather up their children.

It was too dangerous to step more than a few yards beyond the front gate, impossible to do anything all day but wander up and down, buttonholing the CivPols and MLOs as they returned from cautious sorties. Most had nothing new to tell – fires, smoke, streets deserted except for the militia. The political officers and the senior CivPols, who must have had access to the upper levels of intelligence, were brisk and unforthcoming.

Once again, I was conscious of the paradox of the compound: that here, at the heart of the unfolding events, we could catch no more than a glimpse of them. Fires were burning all over Dili; the smell was in our nostrils from the moment we woke up, and occasionally we could see columns of smoke. But the flames themselves, and the faces of the fire starters, were invisible. At the computers in the Unamet press room, we waited in turn to log on to the news websites and learn what was happening to us.

On Monday evening, my second in the compound, I set up my laptop in the press room and began trying once again to write. Outside, people were heating up tins of lumpy peaches and chicken stew, but smoking and tension had killed my appetite. On the desk at which I sat was a Unamet walkie-talkie; the conversations of the CivPols crackled out of it as they patrolled the compound. For most of the day, these exchanges had been technical and uninteresting – reports on the movement of troops, the direction of gunfire, and the movement of staff. By evening, though, their character changed and as I reviewed the events of the day, turning over in my mind what had happened and what might be to come, the little black radio began to give me the spooks.

Repeated gunfire on the way to the airport, drawled the radio.

Numerous militias on street and streets are impassable without armed escort, came another crackly message.

Smoke rising from the second floor of the electoral commission building. Houses of the Portuguese mission burning.

It was at this point that I noticed Alex, who was sitting at a table close to mine, staring into space, dead pale.

'Are you all right?'

'No. I'm starting to feel bad.'

I was feeling quite peculiar myself.

Alex rose from the table and lay down on the floor. The shooting started up again outside. The phones were ringing constantly with requests from foreign news organisations for interviews. I did an Austrian news agency and the BBC, and the act of articulating the situation to an interviewer thousands of miles away made it appear far worse than I had previously imagined. The thrust of the questions seemed to be: do you expect to be killed tonight? Just then one of the UN staff came in and announced that Ian Martin, the head of Unamet, was ready to receive the press.

We had been pushing for this all day: within the sealed community of the compound, Ian Martin's intentions were the subject of as much speculation and rumour as those of President Habibie and General Wiranto. There were two opposite and increasingly indignant theories. The most common assumption, among the political staff and the CivPols, was that Unamet was on its last legs, that it was preparing to abandon East Timor to its fate, and that its chief was now searching for a face-saving means of accomplishing this betrayal. But another faction believed that Unamet should pull out completely as soon as possible, and that Ian Martin was spinelessly irresponsible in failing to order an immediate evacuation. The members of this faction were in the minority; some of them were administrative staff who had never imagined this situation, and were frankly scared. But they also included a number of Military Liaison Officers: for men trained in arms, the sensation of gun nakedness, of being taunted by bullets and deprived of their own weapons, was unbearably frustrating.

Ian Martin found himself in the middle. He was a distant personality, with few confidants among the Unamet staff and, justly or not, his low-key, bespectacled manner gave the impression of indecisiveness.

'What's the atmosphere like up there?' someone asked our Unamet escort, as we were led towards his office.

'Martin is jelly-bellying,' came the answer.

It was a strange interview, more of an inquisition than a press conference, and when I listen to my tape recording of the occasion parts of it make me squirm. All of us were tired, dirty and hungry. We were conscious that, in having stayed for this long, we were unusual. But each of us, every minute, was secretly asking ourselves the question: am I afraid yet? And so our doubt was converted into aggression, and Unamet itself became our object. There was finger-pointing and petulance, and Ian Martin was thrown on the defensive. Instead of breathing moral outrage and authority, he sounded weedy and nit-picking and querulous.

He told no lies; he answered every question as honestly as he felt able. But it was a dismal performance. The meeting lasted about forty minutes, but there were really only two questions, asked over and again in different forms: was Unamet going to evacuate and, if it did, what would happen to the refugees in the compound? Martin didn't help himself by referring to them as 'internally displaced persons'. He didn't help by saying, 'What we've done so far is in Unamet terms not an evacuation.' He acknowledged that 'what Unamet can do is extremely limited' but insisted that this 'doesn't make our presence here useless or even merely symbolic'.

'We do have the capacity to continue to bring to the attention of those who are responsible for the security forces, whether it's the police or the Indonesian army, elements of what is going on,' he said. 'And there are people inside those two institutions that wish to act properly in certain circumstances.'

John Martinkus of the Associated Press said, 'Is there any indication they have any serious intention to stop this violence?'

'I think you can expect some announcement from Jakarta following the special cabinet meeting that's taken place today,' said Ian Martin.

'What sort of announcement?' said Lindsay Murdoch of the *Sydney Morning Herald*.

'I can't tell you.'

'I mean, is it good news or bad news?'

'It depends how it turns out.'

'I mean,' – and Lindsay, a formidable character, was off – 'it's an absolute disgrace what's going on out there. Isn't it time for heads to roll? Something's got to happen, I mean, people are getting killed, we don't know how many. People are – it's one of the worst, the biggest disgraces this century. Isn't somebody going to, you know . . . whose head's going to roll?'

On my tape there is a hissing silence. Then Ian Martin says, 'I mean, you know, that's not a particularly helpful question for me to try to answer, not least because you don't know who within the government or security apparatus are in fact the ones who are prepared to take the necessary action and who are not. I mean, obviously I agree with the premise that the situation is indeed appalling.'

Bullets were passing through the air a few feet away, explosions were going on a few yards away, within a mile of where we sat armed soldiers were killing unarmed civilians. And here, at the centre of it all, the Special Representative of the Secretary-General of the United Nations was urging us to look for the good in the Indonesian army. From now on few of Martin's answers were heard through to the end. We were unwashed and underfed, we did not know whether we were courageous or afraid, and it was easier to talk than to listen. And so it went on – more questions, plenty of indignant speechifying, and Ian Martin's meticulous, bloodless answers.

What we wanted was simple: not fury or denunciation, but an echo, just a faint reverberation, of our own nausea and disgust. But Martin gave no echo at all. Interviewing him was like dropping stones into a well only to have them pop out again, scrubbed, disinfected and carefully wrapped in transparent plastic.

Eventually, I realised what it was that I really wanted to know.

'Do you feel physically safe staying here tonight?'

Ian Martin gave a thin laugh.

'Do *you*?' he said.

'Well, I'm asking you. You're the boss.'

284

'Again, I don't want to answer that on the record because it's sort of – you know – whichever way I answer, it's an unhelpful thing to say publicly. I mean, I think we are reasonably safe because we do have quite strong protection out there from people whom I believe have been genuinely ordered to maintain protection of this compound by those who understand the consequences if it were attacked. But, I mean, I can't give you an assurance that that will hold.'

I said, 'Supposing the militia were to directly attack this compound tonight, what's your personal plan of escape?'

'I don't have a personal plan of escape.'

'So if people started coming over the walls firing automatic weapons at people, what would happen?'

There was a pause. Then Ian Martin said, 'I think that's obvious.'

And after an even longer pause, Lindsay Murdoch said quietly, 'We'd die?'

'Yes. I mean . . . you know . . . what . . .' And he fell silent, and there was another long pause.

There was a large flowering tree outside Ian Martin's office, and as I stood beneath it a deep tropical heaviness overcame me. I could remember almost nothing of what had just been said, and the effort of going through my scrawled notes or listening once again to the tape recording seemed insupportable. Unamet was crumbling and sinking, like an iron ship with rusty bulkheads, holed below the waterline. MLOs and political officers were gathering in huddles around the compound and wild rumours were circulating. The militia and Kopassus were going to come over the walls tonight. They were being given 'mad dog pills', the amphetamines which deadened fear and intensified aggression. The CivPols, meanwhile, were handing out radios to their Timorese staff and telling them to escape over the hill while they still could. More than a few of the MLOs came from the British and Australian special forces; these men, it was said, had found a way to get hold of guns. With each one of these rumours another rusty flake fell from the bulging hull.

Finally, I was discovering my fear. It had been stalking me these last few days, watching invisibly from the jungle with green eyes. But now it was out in the open, padding slowly towards me. I could see its saliva and its whiskers, and soon I would be able to smell its breath.

It was hard to face the Timorese whose numbers seemed to be increasing all the time. Jose Belo and Sebastião were here. 'Richard!' a voice called out to me, as I walked back in a daze to the press room – and it was Felice. He had about him the delirious air of one who feels lucky to be alive. We embraced, but I was so preoccupied that I didn't even ask him how he had found his way to the compound. I opened my knapsack and gave him my unopened ration tins. Grandly and self-consciously, Felice – who didn't smoke – lit up one of my cigarettes, before disappearing to find his relatives. He said, 'Tomorrow we go back to the Turismo, yes?' and I found it hard to look him in the eye. Then he said, 'What's wrong with Alex?' Alex was lying on his mattress, shivering beneath a film of sweat.

Among the more suspicious or astute of the Timorese, there was an overwhelming sense that something awful was going to happen. 'Physically the United Nations are still here,' said Jose Belo, looking me in the eye. 'But mentally they have already gone. And when they go, the militia will come in, and the army will come in, and they will kill us.'

That night, at quarter to four in the morning, a child was born in the small clinic at the back of the compound. The mother was a refugee named Joanna Rodriguez; the child, a boy, was baptised immediately by a member of the mission who was a Jesuit priest. He was christened Pedro Rodriguez, and his middle name was given as Unamet. Later, I would hear this described as a gesture of 'gratitude' to the United Nations for 'protecting' Joanna Rodriguez and her family. But I liked to think of it as something more ambiguous and ironic – a reproach, as well as a plea; a challenge to Unamet; a direct look into Ian Martin's eyes.

It was quiet compared to other nights: one burst of concentrated automatic fire at midnight, and a second one a few hours later. Two hours after that the cockerels started crowing and with them came another distinctive sound, the low, whispering bustle of the waking refugees. There were two thousand of them now, but their presence in the compound could not have been more discreet or unobtrusive. Without fuss or supervision, they had filled the space between the buildings with coloured blankets and faded sheets. After dark, they sat together in family groups, whispering to one another or singing prayers and hymns. As the sun rose they washed and prepared tiny, ingenious meals on stoves made out of twigs and tin cans.

As I walked through the spaces which the refugees occupied, people bowed and nodded. Mothers shooed their children to clear a path, and the children smiled and said hello. In the two days I spent among them I saw no fights and no fits of temper, no thievery or truculence. Even the babies hardly cried, and despite the uncertainty, the rumours, and the shooting all around, there was no pleading or begging, no ranting or ill temper or threats. I began to dread the sight of the refugees for I was becoming tormented by a single question: whether to stay, or to run away?

The Australian air force was carrying out evacuation flights today, although no one could say whether there would be any tomorrow. At home, the people I loved most were gravely worried about me. In London, my editor was suggesting that I should leave. Overnight, my friend Alex had become seriously ill, sweating and groaning in what seemed to be a malarial fever. But the decision was mine, and I felt it as a constriction around my heart from the moment I woke up.

A list was being drawn up of those intending to evacuate. I marked my name down, then took it off, and then put it down again.

I paced around the compound, seeking out corners of it which I had not seen before, as if its physical structure, the condition of the paths and roofs, could provide an answer to my dilemma. I took many photographs; I felt an urgent need to fix in my mind the appearance of the compound – this mundane, remarkable place. The outer walls were crumbling cement. At the very back was a gap in the wall beneath the steep slope which led up and away to the hills behind Dili. After dark, many of the refugees were slipping through here to spend the night on the summit, rather than in the snare of the compound.

At 8.20 a.m. there was a burst of machine-gun fire across the slopes of the hill.

It was about this time that a tiny, practical crisis unfolded within the larger one: simultaneously, it seemed, the entire compound was running out of cigarettes. I was down to my last, my very last, packet and the prospect of being without tobacco made me feel weak. I found a camp chair and smoked three cigarettes in a row, beneath a wide, cool tree on the edge of the yard. Soon, my head was beating with exhaustion and nicotine and lack of food. In front of me was a CivPol Land Cruiser which had been shot up the previous day on a foray into Dili. Its rear window was a mess of jagged glass pebbles.

I felt the weight of the ocean pressing in on the rusty sides of the old iron ship.

I slipped into a fractional sleep, and in the second or two before being awoken by the slump of my neck, three dream images flashed through my mind: the edge of a well, a buffalo, a heavy stick.

I tried to identify what exactly I was afraid of. What was the worst thing that could happen here? More images leaped to mind. Rocket-propelled grenades arching over the walls, clattering and exploding through the thin roofs of the classrooms. Screaming refugees, the sight of people with severed legs or hands, bone jutting through skin. And then the figures in khaki bobbing over the wall, scuttling from one doorway to another, the *thucka-*

thucka-thucka of the automatics, running on frozen legs, a rifle raised, friends stopped by bullets, lying in the dust with blood running from their mouths.

A massacre.

It was unlikely: if they had wanted to kill us they could have done it days ago. But it was imaginable. And I had never been in a place where such a thing was imaginable.

My fear needed reasons, and it found them in the idea of evacuation. It seemed inevitable that at some point there would be a general withdrawal to the airport. Whether the Timorese were flown out, or left to their fate, it could not but be a moment of dread and chaos. I imagined the mutinous disgust among the younger Unamet staff when the order came through, the angry fear of the Timorese. Would the CivPols follow Ian Martin's orders? Or would they make their retreat up the hill? I imagined being squeezed into a Land Cruiser for the procession through the streets, the snarling of the Aitarak motorbikes, the waving of the blunderbusses. A scared, flustered driver taking a wrong turn, the way blocked by militia, BriMobs turning a blind eye, mad dog pills and the squeeze of a trigger . . .

The gates of the compound opened and an Indonesian army truck began to back its way in, the truck which would carry the day's evacuees to the airport. A line of people had already assembled, and began heaving up bags and boxes. A New Zealand MLO clambered in and took charge of the loading operation. 'All aboard, ladies and gentlemen,' he chirped. 'Bags on the outside, bodies on the inside.'

I stood up and walked towards the truck.

Colonel Alan was standing to one side watching.

'Are you going, Richard?'

'I don't know. I don't know.'

'You don't want to stay with us, see this through?'

'I don't know.'

There was a rattle of automatic fire, and with it a new sound, a migraine whistling which accompanied each report.

'Now *that*,' said Colonel Alan, 'was close. When they fire into the air you just hear the crack. But when you hear the bullet singing, that means it's directly overhead.'

Alex was being helped groggily into the truck. Two Australian radio reporters ran up dressed in helmets and flak jackets, and began loading their bags into the back.

The tailgate was being raised and the colonel was saying goodbye to those on board. I stood there with my bags in my hands, waiting for somebody to stop me going, to make me stay.

'Goodbye, Richard. Good luck!' said Colonel Alan. 'Don't worry about it. I'll see you in Darwin.'

I was in the back of the truck.

From inside the truck, the compound suddenly seemed a very safe place. It sides were made of wooden slats, with inch-wide gaps between them. The briefcases, suitcases, boxes and backpacks of those who were evacuating were stacked up against them to form an unstable wall. A tremendous fusillade of automatic fire burst out from close by as we passed the Unamet gates.

'Heads down, ladies and gentleman,' said the cheerful Kiwi. There were about a dozen of us in the back, and eleven Indonesian soldiers. I had no flak jacket; instead I had a portable computer in a leather bag. I braced it vertically between my head and the wooden sides, and wondered exactly what effect the interposition of a Toshiba laptop would have upon an M-16 round. I looked up at the Indonesian soldiers who stood above us with smirking expressions. They felt no need to cower in the bottom – our guards, here to protect us against an attack by their own comrades.

Through the slats in the truck, Dili could be glimpsed, utterly transformed. It felt like a scene from a science-fiction film, a journey through a town overtaken by body-snatchers. During the fifteen-minute journey to the airport, I saw not a single ordinary person. The shops were boarded and shut, the houses still.

In front of them, milling singly and in groups, were hundreds of soldiers and the black-shirted militia.

The streets teemed with them. I felt a wave of nausea, like the shock of opening a neglected cupboard to find it seething with rats or maggots. I saw one Aitarak man with an AK-47; the rest carried spears or machetes and the soldiers towering above us waved and smiled at them. Behind us passed a stolen UN Land Cruiser, driven by a grinning militiaman, although which were genuine Timorese and which were Indonesian soldiers in bandannas it was difficult to tell. The shooting resumed again in the middle distance. Thick smoke from newly-set fires rose close to the road. I had been in the compound for forty-eight hours and the sudden sensation of being outside and in motion generated a rush of euphoria.

The airport was as ghostly as the town. Papery litter drifted across the tiled floor. Someone had removed all the bulbs from the overhead lights. At passport control was an unexpected sight: a dozen young Australian soldiers, several of them women. Very formally and politely, in a parody of airport procedure, they checked our bags and passports and explained the operation of the seat belts. 'Just a few quick health questions, sir,' said a soldier with a red cross on her armband. 'This may sound a bit strange, but have you been scuba-diving at any time in the last week?'

The engines of the Hercules could be heard, roaring and whining on the tarmac. We ran out towards its stubby shape, cringing in the noise and heat. The adrenalin was ebbing now, and I began to feel deep weariness, and inklings of dread, as if I had done something terrible and was only now beginning to remember what it was. Inside the plane's belly, we strapped ourselves to the green webbing. One of the soldiers wrapped an aviator's jacket around Alex, who was barely conscious and convulsed with shakes. The engines pulsed and surged; the wheels rumbled below us and then came that moment of sudden lightness and lift, and we were in the air.

The hold of the plane was dark and windowless, but the

cockpit was flooded with light. Spread out below in greens and browns, almost close enough to touch, was Dili. It terrified me to see it still there. I could make out the familiar landmarks: the white church and the cathedral, Bishop Belo's house and even the Turismo, still unburned. But the rest of the town was all fires.

Even from this height, I could see the licking shapes of individual flames in the town centre. Whole districts were invisible beneath a generalised haze of smoke, and half a dozen big fires sent black billows hundreds of feet into the air. Two large Indonesian naval ships lay at anchor offshore. But the details of the scene were dissolving in the simple and staggering knowledge that I was no longer down there. I had become afraid and run away. I had jumped. I had fled because I was afraid of being killed or, more precisely, of dying in fear.

I still find it difficult to accept. Before me, as I write, are notes from that time – buckled exercise books and fragments of paper. I long to turn them over and to discover that, after all, I stayed.

Every man hopes that he is brave, and few have the opportunity to find out. But I found out. I know exactly how brave I am, and no more. I thought of George Orwell, shot through the throat at Huesca, and Kapuscinski, doused in benzene at the burning roadblocks – but I was not one of them. The town grew smaller and more distant as the plane rose higher, but I felt myself to be the one who was far below, as if I was looking up at Dili from the bottom of a deep and narrow well.

IN THE WELL

What drove the violence in East Timor? Even now, I cannot say that I understand it. In all the obvious ways, it was nonsensical. No one had forced the referendum on Indonesia, after all: President Habibie himself had suggested it. The Indonesian government had freely signed the agreement with Portugal and the United Nations which had brought Unamet into being. And then there was the quality of the violence – so messy, indecisive and ugly. Burned houses, terrified mothers and children, frightened UN workers – they seemed almost calculated to make the worst possible impression on international opinion.

By the time it was underway, most people agreed, the role of Habibie himself was marginal. 'He is impotent,' a first secretary in Jakarta had told me. 'He's just not capable. We are all desperately trying to get a grip on what the military is doing and who is in charge.' Crucial to understanding the situation was the role of commander of the armed forces, General Wiranto. Was he the puppet master, planning and directing the violence? Or had he, like Habibie, lost his authority? My diplomat friend explained a third view: that Wiranto *could* have called off the militias if he had wanted to, but chose not to because he would have forfeited the loyalty of subordinate generals. Was he, then, responsible for the violence or not?

Among army and police officers in Timor and their immediate superiors in the regional command, there was a remarkable degree of planning, coordination and control. Like all war zones, East Timor occupied an emotional place in the military psyche. Plenty of senior officers had served their time there, and for many of them it had been the formative experience of their lives. They had killed there, and seen their friends killed; for the first time, they had been afraid. East Timor was a proving ground and a symbol of the proud unity of the Indonesian state. Now the bug-eyed lick-spittle Habibie was giving it away.

Habibie's announcement had appalled and affronted the armed forces and the violence and intimidation had several goals. The most obvious was to reduce the number of ballots cast for independence by terrifying voters into supporting the other side, or by driving people out of their villages so that they couldn't register and vote. The terror also served as a goad to Falintil – if the guerrillas could be provoked to fight back, then the army would have just the excuse it needed to call off the ballot and resume its operations.

But why go to such trouble after the referendum? The battle was lost; the cause was plainly hopeless. And it was not as if this was an instinctive, berserk reaction. How remarkable, for example, that, despite the close shaves, none of the 'internationals' – no UN worker or journalist or observer – had so far been killed. It had been carefully, minutely planned. The intention was to terrify but always, at the last moment, to turn the flat of the blade. Five months after the referendum, at the end of January 2000, I was to revisit East Timor, and see the plans for myself.

Joaquim Fonseca and his human rights group had discovered them in an abandoned military building on the main port road. The rooms had been stripped of furniture, and were carpeted in a thick litter of hundreds of thousands of papers. The activists gathered up as many as they could, and slowly began to sift through them. It was weeks before they realised the importance of what they had found.

Many of the documents confirmed what had long been obvious: that the army, as a matter of official policy, had done its best to help the pro-Indonesia side and victimise the opposition.

There was, for example, a request for a naval ship to be sent with a cargo of rice to buy off voters. There was a logbook from the city of Viqueque recording the guns distributed to the local militia. The most important document dated from the day that the referendum was born.

It was sent out on 5 May 1999, a few hours before the foreign ministers of Indonesia and Portugal signed the agreement at the United Nations in New York. It was a telegram from the Indonesian army's chief of staff, signed on his behalf by his deputy and addressed to the military commander in Dili and the high command in Jakarta. The crucial order read: 'Prepare a security plan to prevent civil war that includes preventive action (create conditions), policing measures, repressive/coercive measures and a plan to move to the rear/evacuate if the second option [independence] is chosen.'

'Preventing civil war', of course, is exactly what the Indonesian army claimed to have been doing since 1975, so preparing a 'security plan' for this purpose could only mean a return to a military campaign. 'Preventive action' meant making sure that the independence movement lost the referendum; 'policing measures' meant operations against civilians as well as the guerrillas in the hills. But no decoding was required for the expression 'repressive/coercive measures'. In Jakarta, I showed copies of these documents to a diplomat I knew; he brought with him a colleague who, I suspect, was a spy. 'That is very strong language,' said the spooky diplomat when he read this telegram. 'Even in their most honest, private discussions, generals don't often own up to that kind of thinking.'

The 'plan to move to the rear/evacuate' was contained in another document found in the abandoned office. At first glance, it appeared unpromising, a report from the Dili police traffic department entitled 'Operation Remember Lorosae II'. But its contents were staggering – a meticulous scheme for forcing hundreds of thousands of people out of their homes and transporting them to West Timor.

There were maps indicating the condition of every road and bridge in the territory. There were charts containing the precise population figures for each of the regencies. Ports and airports were catalogued with their precise capacity for planes and ships. The victims of this plan had been driven out of their homes within hours of the announcement of the referendum result. Most were taken by road; others were forced on to passenger ferries – in at least one case, young men were separated from their families when the ship was at sea and thrown over the side to drown. But, from the far side of the Indonesian army looking glass, these were not unwilling deportees. These, in the minds of the military bureaucrats, were the 'supporters' of Indonesia. They were being transported to Indonesia to 'maintain public order'. It was a 'preventive action' to 'prevent civil war'. There it all was, soberly set out by the traffic department in Operation Remember Lorosae II.

One theory had it that the violence was not principally aimed at the Timorese, but at other rebellious provinces of Indonesia – at Aceh and at West Papua. 'You want independence?' the army was asking. 'This is what you will get.' Before the referendum there was also the idea that, having been cheated of their rightful victory, the pro-Indonesian forces would retreat to West Timor and take with them the four westernmost regencies, which would remain Indonesian. But the plan came to nothing. It was an absurd notion, a fantasy – indeed, beneath the violence, there was an adolescent quality to the whole undertaking: the oily alienated youths in their fighting fantasy militia uniforms, the drugs and the motorbikes, the toy blunderbusses. What made it unbearably frightening was the presence of efficient and grown-up killers in army uniforms, egging them on, giving them guns and bullets, and joining in themselves.

There may indeed have been an order from the top, but when the time came nothing so direct as an order would have been necessary. Everything had been laid so carefully in place, responsibility had already been dispersed across so many different departments, commands and individuals, that no words were necessary. Jakarta's silence was the command. In Timor, the army knew what to do and once the thing had started it gathered speed and power and continued until it had exhausted itself. This was the strangest and most fearful aspect of the violence in East Timor: that it could be so meticulous and methodical, and at the same time so completely out of control.

People were being deported as I flew towards Darwin on the Australian Hercules. They were also being killed. It was happening as I paced around the compound, although we could only guess about it at the time.

From the report of the Indonesian Commission for Human Rights Violations in East Timor, January 2000 (the initials TNI stand for Tentara Nasional Indonesia, the Indonesian National Army; POLRI is the national police):

On September 6 at around 14.30, the Laksaur Merah Putih and Mahidi militias and members of the TNI and POLRI attacked refugees staying in the Suai Church complex. The attack was directly led by the Regent of Covalima, Herman Sediono, and the Suai subdistrict military commander, 1st Lieutenant Sugito . . . At the time there were approximately 100 refugees staying in the church complex and an unknown number of refugees outside the complex. Father Hilario was shot once in the chest and Igidio Manek, a Laksaur militia member, stepped on the priest's body. Father Fransisco was stabbed and sliced by Americo, also a member of the Laksaur militia. Another witness, Domingos dos Santos, saw Father Dewanto killed in the old church. At the time of the attack, the Police, the Loro Sae Mobile Brigade Contingent and members of the TNI were outside of the fence shooting refugees who tried to flee outside the church complex. It is thought that at least 50 people were murdered in this incident.

From the report of the UN International Commission of Inquiry on East Timor, January 2000:

On 8 September 1999, over 100 militia entered the police station in Maliana, where about 6,000 people had sought shelter against the attacks of the military and militia. The police station was entirely surrounded with concentric rings: militia, the Mobile Police Unit and TNI. The people inside the police station were first attacked with machetes. When they fell down, they were hacked into pieces. This was done in front of the people, who were forced to watch. The witness identified by name members of the militia and TNI who were responsible for this massacre.

From 'Crimes Against Humanity in East Timor, January to October 1999: Their Nature and Causes', prepared for the UN Transitional Authority in East Timor by James Dunn, February 2001.

On Wednesday 8 September a force, including about 200 troops, attacked the villages of Tumin, Kiobiselo, Nonkikan and Nibin, and killed about 14 men. The next day at Imbate about 70 young men, who were said to have been selected on the basis of their educational ability, were separated from the rest of the people gathered there. They were bound in pairs and were marched to Passabe. At 1 a.m. on 10 September, following a pre-arranged signal, a mass slaughter of these young men was carried out, the victims being shot or hacked to death. According to the investigators, the main instigators of the massacre included the Police Chief of Passabe, Gabriel Colo, and Laurentino Soares, aka Moko, but it is also recorded that the massacre was controlled by a small number of men who were both TNI soldiers and members of the militia. The total number of victims is estimated at more than 70 . . .

I passed two weeks in Darwin. It was a sad, disembodied time. The crisis was drawing in people from all over the world and the small city was already overcrowded with evacuees from Dili, human rights activists, Australian military officers, and edgy teams of journalists who had underestimated the news potential of the referendum and were anxiously trying to recreate the drama at long-distance. The hotels were full and I had to move from one to another every two or three days. But there was little to carry, because my suitcase was still in the Turismo. For days the only clothes I had were those I wore.

My memories are of air-conditioned hotel rooms, and of hours spent watching the televised news conferences in Jakarta and New York. There was nothing to do in Darwin: it was just the place closest to the crisis, or rather the place closest to the crisis where you could stay in a hotel, make a telephone call and walk outside without fear of being killed. I wrote until the early hours, slept dreamlessly and woke with a jerk at six every morning. Once or twice, I joined disconsolate groups of fellow evacuees and trailed around Darwin's attractions: Shenanigans Irish Pub, Bar-Café Rourke's Drift and the Petty Sessions nightclub, whose sign announced that collarless shirts were not permitted after 7 p.m.

It was still possible to telephone people in the compound in Dili; once I got through to the satellite phone of the Falintil commander, Taur Matan Ruak, at his cantonment in the central mountains. The violence continued in Timor, but beyond my reach, intermittently heard but not seen. I felt detached from everything around me, as if I was the one who had been abandoned. I felt like a thin uprooted tree.

Operation Remember Lorosae II was underway, and tens of thousands of Timorese were being transported to West Timor,

to Bali, and as far away as Papua. Atrocity stories began to filter
out: the murder of the priests in Suai Church; the young men
thrown off ferries in the open sea. Hundreds of thousands of
refugees had fled into the hills – a multitude had converged on
the Falintil cantonment, and within a few days the youngest children there had started to die of diarrhoea and fever. Entire towns
were reported to have been burned down; in all of East Timor,
almost no one was safe and in his home.

I went to Darwin airport almost every day. I felt happier
there; my shame was quenched by the boom of the planes, the
tannoy announcements and the bustle of arrival and departure. Evacuation flights from Dili were coming in all the time.
Nurses and psychiatric counsellors were there to meet them.
An ambulance had been waiting on the runway when our plane
had landed and Alex had been stretchered into it. Sometime
before our evacuation, it turned out, his appendix had burst;
another few hours and he would certainly have died. Within
a few days, Bishop Belo had flown in from Baucau with the
local Unamet mission, its local staff and their families.
Indonesian soldiers had tried to stop the Timorese from getting
on the planes, and Belo and the UN workers had stood on
the tarmac between the guns and the refugees, and refused to
leave without them.

In the compound, Ian Martin announced a full evacuation. It
was just as everyone had feared: the Timorese staff would be
allowed to come to Darwin, but not the refugees. Indonesian
soldiers began gathering around the perimeters of the compound,
snickering, fondling hand grenades and leering at the women
inside. One hundred Unamet staff signed a petition of protest
and, to everyone's surprise, the evacuation was postponed. When
it finally took place, three days later, all of the Timorese were
included. The Hercules shuttled to and fro, bringing political
officers, CivPols, MLOs and the remaining journalists. And
everyone who landed in Darwin became immediately obsessed
with returning.

Some flew to Jakarta where flights to Dili were being organised, only to be aborted at the last moment. A few went to Kupang
in West Timor where the mass of the refugees was ending up.
But it was a town ruled by the militias and the road into the East
was impenetrably dangerous. In Darwin, the former head of the
escape committee and I hatched a plot to take a fishing boat
across the Timor Sea, and meet up with a Falintil detachment on
the south coast. It came to nothing, of course. It was just an
absorbing fantasy, a way of passing the time. We had fled, and
the bolts of the gate had clanged shut behind us. It was no more
possible to return to Dili than to travel back into childhood.

But it was only my frame of mind and the atmosphere of
sleepy Darwin which made it seem as if everything was standing
still. Indonesia itself was seething. Xanana Gusmão had been
released from house arrest in Jakarta and had taken refuge in the
British Embassy. The Secretary-General of the United Nations
and the President of the United States demanded that Indonesia
accept armed peacekeepers in East Timor. Habibie's power had
never been at a lower ebb. A *coup d'état* seemed imminent –
indeed, it was entirely possible that the president had been
deposed in all but name several days before, without anybody
noticing. But then, on 12 September, he appeared on television,
flanked by his cabinet, and announced Indonesia's unconditional
readiness to receive peacekeepers.

Suddenly, the bolts were grating open again. Soldiers –
Australian, British, Filipino and Thai – were arriving in Darwin
all the time, and every journalist in the city was pleading and
hustling for a seat on the plane with the first of the peacekeepers.
I found myself on the list, and then off it, and then back on
again. One day I was summoned to an Australian army base and
presented with a kitbag, water bottles, a helmet and a laminated
press card. Early on Monday 20 September, the International
Force East Timor – Interfet – took off from Darwin and two
hours later I was back in Dili.

✳   ✳   ✳

On the first night I slept on the perimeter of the airport, and worked at a table in the abandoned departure lounge. A house was burning a few hundred yards away; it had been set alight that evening and from the runway you could smell the smoke and see the flames. The floor tiles of the departure lounge were coated with dried human excrement. It was thinly and evenly distributed; it looked as if it had been applied with palette knives by a team of decorators. But it had been spread by human feet, the bare feet of the thousands of frightened deportees who had been trucked here and made to wait before being airfreighted out to God knew where.

I waved down a puttering motorbike on the road outside the airport the next morning. Much too late, I noticed that the driver was wearing a scrap of red-and-white cloth around his arm – but when he saw me he smiled, untied it and tossed it away. I climbed on and the motorbike laboured up the familiar road. There were few fires by now, but a lot of smoke. Scarcely one building out of three was unburned. How boring it must have been to set fire to all of those little houses, each one identical to the next. We passed gutted shops, gutted offices, the burned-out shell of a canteen. A convoy of Australian jeeps overtook us, with machine guns mounted at their rear. An office telephone lay on the road, with its cable trailing around it, and further on the crushed carcass of a dog.

For the first two miles we saw almost no one. Then the sea appeared on the left and beside it thousands of people in family groups, crowding the quayside and the road along the beach, sitting among mattresses, wardrobes, bicycles and sacks of food. On the wharf, Indonesian soldiers were shepherding them on to a pair of grey ships; on the road, they were climbing obediently into a long convoy of trucks. The trucks rumbled west towards Indonesia; on the way they passed the Australian jeeps motoring from the airport in the opposite direction. It was strange and sinister that people should be leaving now, with international salvation at hand. It was stranger still that Interfet should be doing nothing to stop them.

'They are not leaving because they want to,' a priest told me in the garden of Bishop Belo's burned-out house. 'They are being made to leave, by the army and the militias.'

Of the militias, I caught the merest glimpse – Aitarak T-shirts whipping by on motorbikes, or disappearing into side streets. But the Indonesian soldiers and police were everywhere – at the wharf, at the airport, guarding their barracks and headquarters. There had been keen apprehension about the kind of reception that Interfet would meet in Dili; the first of the peacekeepers had half expected to fight their way in. But on the ground they were greeted with nothing more than friendly indifference. The Interfet commander, Major-General Peter Cosgrove, met the Dili commander, Major-General Kiki Syahnakri, on the afternoon of the first day. Cosgrove reported that Interfet had been 'benignly and cordially' received by the Indonesian army. He sounded almost grateful.

On the second day, I moved to the Turismo which had been commandeered by the Australians as an official press centre. I felt tearfully happy to see it again. The Mahkota Hotel and Bishop Belo's house had been burned, but apart from the loss of its electricity the Turismo had suffered little damage. In my pocket I still had the key to my room – room 47, overlooking the garden on the first floor. But the door had been kicked in, and flapped on the splintered frame. Inside, everything movable had been stripped from the room – bed, desk, drawers, television, refrigerator, as well as my suitcase and all its contents. In the bath, I found my tube of brown shoe polish. The floor of this room too was coated in a fine glaze of shit.

More and more journalists were arriving in Dili, and a system of apartheid was in operation. The official Interfet 'pool', of which I was a member, was billeted in the Turismo, where we were provided with Australian army rations and briefings by the Australian officers. Everyone else had to make do, squeezing in where they could, cadging food, electricity, even water. The dishes of satellite phones bloomed along the balconies and in the garden. At night, the journalists squeezed around tables stacked with torches and candles, and jostled for the few plugs which sprouted from the army's emergency generator. At eleven, the generator was switched off and the darkness which covered the rest of East Timor rolled over the Hotel Turismo.

The next morning I travelled with an armoured convoy out to the seminary of Dare, high in the hills above Dili. Dare was East Timor's Oxford or its Sorbonne, a famous Jesuit institution where many of Timor's leaders had studied. During the fort-night of anarchy and isolation, some of the most disturbing stories had come from there. Tens of thousands of refugees had fled to Dare from the towns. In the face of such numbers, the protection provided by the fathers was entirely symbolic but, because it was a relatively easy journey from Dili, there was a higher than usual proportion of the old and very young, the sickly and the pregnant. A couple of the priests had mobile phones and early on, before the batteries died away, they put through desperate calls to Australia describing night-time attacks by the Indonesian army, old people scrambling through the jungle to escape bullets, encirclement operations, imminent star-vation. Food had been air-dropped, a few parcels of biscuits launched into a jungle. Now the UN aid agencies had returned, and Interfet was to escort them to Dare.

It was the first sortie outside Dili, and the convoy was accompanied by soldiers in jeeps mounted with machine guns. They were a mysterious kind of soldier, who became familiar after a few days with Interfet. They wore no marks indicating their regiment or even their rank, and their accents suggested a mixture of nationalities – Australian, American, Scottish. The strangest thing about them was their means of communica-tion – rather than speaking to one another, they preferred to use hand signals, and when they did use words one in three was an oath. Most things about civilians appeared to irritate them; above all, they were explosively hostile to any kind of publicity.

'OK to take a picture?' a photographer asked one of them as we boarded the convoy.

'No, not OK,' came the reply. 'Not fucking OK at all.'

'Um, I hope you don't mind me asking,' I said, 'but are you the special forces?'

'You fucking print that, and you're in big fucking trouble,' said the man from the special forces.

Four of the mysterious guards sat in the front and back of the Land Cruiser in which we travelled. Their rifles were pointed out of the windows, and they had miniature radio receivers in their ears.

The road to Dare rose through hairpin bends with dry, scrubby jungle on either side. There were rumours of army and militia roadblocks along the way, and no one knew exactly what to expect. Our guards signalled esoterically to one another and muttered into their radios. Then after half an hour a sound could be heard from the bush, growing louder and closer with every yard – a mixture of cheering, chanting and clapping, like nothing so much as the noise of a football crowd. The convoy slowed almost to a crawl, the road bent sharply again, and suddenly we were among them – thousands of men, young and old, all cheering and singing. The Land Cruisers were surrounded; clasping hands passed through the open windows.

'*Viva Timor Leste!*' people shouted. '*Viva independencia! Viva Xanana Gusmão!*' A sheet was being held aloft, bearing the words 'Welcome to the New Nation – you are saving a people from destruction'. These were the lost people of Dare, about whom so many terrible things had been heard and, for now at least, every one of them had a smile upon his face.

Those who had come down to greet Interfet were a fraction of the total: a multitude – 40,000, it was said – were still hiding in the jungle beyond. There they slept; during the daytime, the men made the perilous descent to scavenge for food in the ruins of Dili. I kept seeing faces I recognised and people I knew, and strangers came up all the time, just to shake hands.

The crowd was almost out of control; the truculent commandos whispered feverishly into their radios and attempted, with ill grace, to clear a space around their machine guns. At one point I found myself squeezed between a jeep and an emaciated young man whose face was turned away from me. A group of Timorese in front of him were shouting and embracing, but he was silent and his body felt almost limp as it was pressed against mine. When the crowd eased, he turned to one side and I was able to see his face.

'Fernão! It's Richard.'

Fernão, who had come with me three months ago to Liquisa, the town of the vampires. I remembered him as large and lolloping, but three weeks in the jungle had reduced him painfully. His face had become bony and his shoulders slumped. I felt them through his shirt, loose and angular, as we embraced.

'They are so happy,' said Fernão, as the Timorese celebrated around us.

'What about you, Fernão? Are you happy?'

'I am happy,' he said. 'At the moment when the UN comes, I am happy. But I have heard today that my father is killed. I don't know where is my brother and my family, and our house is gone. I am happy, but I have lost everything.'

East Timor was full of places like Dare, and the aid workers were impatient to drive out to them, to begin counting the refugees and reckoning their need. But Major-General Cosgrove was stubbornly resistant to hurry. It was a week before Interfet travelled the twenty miles to Liquisa, and almost two weeks before it reached Maliana. The rest of the country remained in the hands of the militias and army, and by the time Interfet reached the enclave of Oecussi, more than a month had passed. In the intervening time, as the major-general was establishing himself in Dili, more massacres and mass burials were taking place.

Even within the capital, the Australian troops were forbidden from stepping outside without their body armour. The handful of British officers with Interfet sneered at the Australians' timidity, but these were political instructions: the government in Canberra was risking much with this deployment and the order was to do everything to avoid casualties. The army press officers in the Turismo were jolly and avuncular, but there was a peevishness about the force as a whole, with its foul commandos, its bristling convoys, and the brusque war-hero manners of Major-General Cosgrove. These were the people who had saved the Timorese, but something about them made it hard to feel grateful.

The creepiest thing about Dili was the presence of the Indonesians. The remaining TNI units were preparing to leave, but before their final pull-out they were carefully burning down their barracks. No one ever caught them doing this. You would notice, idly, that soldiers were loading up trucks in front of a military building; two hours later, you would pass by again to see flames crackling through its roof. One day I passed a grain warehouse and saw Indonesian officers selling stores to the refugees. Crowds of people were lining up with plastic bags and cash in hand – the soldiers were auctioning off the government's rice. People from Unamet arrived; the soldiers smiled, and spread their palms, and courteously drove away.

For the first two days after my return I was numb with anticipation and excitement, but the numbness quickly gave way to the depression which I had struggled against in Darwin. For a start, there were the practical difficulties. The Turismo was a series of intact structures, rather than a hotel, without water, power or service; we were camped out in its shell. I slept on a mat beneath a mosquito net in a room with a broken door. After waking, I collected my water ration from the Australian quartermaster and heated up coffee and tins of beans on lumps of paraffin. Over breakfast, people washed and talked and shared what overnight news there was. Then came the question of what to do with the day.

No one was prepared simply to spend it in the hotel, waiting to be briefed by Interfet. But Dili had been looted, of its people as well as of its cars and motorbikes, and transport and inter-preters were scarcer than ever. Many of the journalists arriving with Interfet were strangers to East Timor and to one another, and I felt a petulant resentment towards the newcomers; there was a cliquishness and competitiveness which I had not felt before and for which I had no heart.

An Australian television correspondent approached me in the Turismo on the evening after the journey to Dare.

'Richard,' he said. 'You're OK?'

'Yes.'

'You didn't get into bother out there, out in Dili today?'

'No, why?'

'It's just that there's some guy, a little Timorese guy at the gate, and he's talking about a tall, blond-haired foreigner, a jour-nalist, who fell off the back of his motorbike, or got shot at or something. Anyway, he's very agitated. About something. It's not you, anyway. Don't worry about it.'

Two minutes later, a second Australian television correspon-dent approached me in the same way. 'It's Richard, isn't it? Yeah, Richard, look – you didn't fall off a motorbike out in Dili this afternoon . . . ?'

Timorese were barred by Interfet from entering the Turismo. The visitor was standing on the far side of the tall metal gate; he was already telling his story for the second or third time. His name was Florindo, and he was much in demand as one of the few people in Dili with a functioning motorbike. That after-noon, he explained, he had dropped one journalist off at the front gate and picked up another – tall, light-haired but, unlike me, a fluent speaker of Indonesian. The man had climbed on the back and asked to go to the suburb of Becora. As they had driven past the church three motorbikes, bearing six uniformed riders, approached them from the opposite direction. The soldiers carried automatic rifles and they were shouting.

'So they were about two hundred metres away and they waved at us to stop,' said Florindo. 'But I didn't want to stop and I started to turn round. As soon as I turned the bike they started shooting. Bullets were flying all around. I told the journalist to hold on tight to me, but then they shot the motorbike, I lost control and fell on the ground.'

The motorbike dragged Florindo for another fifty yards until he extricated himself and stood up; I could see as he spoke that his shirt was torn and his skin was scraped and raw. 'I looked to the ground and saw the journalist lying down, unconscious,' he said. 'He was not moving. I started to run. I heard them shouting, "Kill him, kill him!"'

Florindo hid himself among the huts and jungle around Becora, and worked his way back on foot round towards the Turismo.

A small crowd had assembled to hear the story. The jolly Australian press officers were informed and one of them came out. Florindo told his story once again, through the barred gate; he was still not allowed to step inside the hotel. Major Ron did not seem very interested, although he assured us later on that he had passed on the report to Colonel Wally. What Colonel Wally did with it, I never found out.

The Australians, to be fair to them, had much else on their minds that night. Two others had disappeared: an American photographer named Chip Hires, and Jon Swain of the *Sunday Times*, the reporting legend, the veteran of Cambodia, Vietnam and Kosovo. Florindo's puzzling narrative was quickly forgotten; all evening, and long after the generator had shut down, the journalists sat in the candlelit Turismo piecing together what was known of Swain and Hires. The two had also come to grief in Becora, and at about the same time as Florindo and his passenger. The taxi in which they had been driving had come under fire;

their interpreter had been dragged away, and their driver had been dreadfully beaten with a rifle butt. The two journalists had fled and hid in the jungle; it was half past one in the morning when they were eventually picked up. The driver was found alive, but without one of his eyes; the interpreter was never seen again. Their assailants were uniformed Indonesian soldiers. The battalion commander, a man named Major Jacob Sarosa, had driven past and watched it happen.

Late that night, Gwen Robinson, who worked for the *Financial Times*, said, 'I've been thinking about that story about the blond guy on the motorbike, and you know who it could be? Sander.'

Sander worked as a freelancer for the *FT* and the *Christian Science Monitor*; he had flown in from Jakarta that afternoon and dropped off his luggage at the Turismo before hurrying out. No one had seen him since.

Gwen and I went to see Major Ron, but he wasn't very interested in this information either. Two journalists lost and found was enough for one evening. Any others would have to wait until the morning.

Sander Thoenes's body was found soon after dawn. It was discovered by some local boys who led two of the journalists there; they had just got back to the Turismo when I emerged from my room. The news spread outwards across the hotel. Standing by the gate were friends of Sander who had learned of his death a few seconds before. Gwen was there, weeping. Half a dozen other people were weeping, while a few were making preparations to go and see for themselves. I understood immediately that I would not be going with them, and that I had become afraid once again, with the muddled, exhausted fear that had driven me to flee from the compound.

Sander lay a few hundred yards from the main road, in an area of huts and palm trees. He was face down on the ground with a hand outstretched towards his notebook. A trail of blood led up to the body, as if he had crawled to this place or been dragged. His left ear had been sliced off; so had much of the flesh on his face. It wasn't the ragged work of dogs or rats, according to those who saw the body. It had been done cleanly, with a sharp instrument, by a man.

Cameron Barr of the *Christian Science Monitor* pieced together the whole story a few months later: how Battalion 745, an Indonesian infantry unit, had left its barracks in Los Palos to withdraw to Indonesian West Timor; how it had driven towards Dili, shooting, torturing and burning along the way. At least twenty people were murdered by the soldiers during their last days in the country; as they passed through towns and villages on the way they had fired randomly at passers-by. An old woman had been shot through the chest, a mother and baby through the legs. Major Sarosa himself admitted witnessing the shooting up of Jon Swain's car. A local man described how the soldiers dragged Sander's body away from the road towards the place where it was found.

The post-mortem concluded that he had been killed by a bullet through the back which tore his heart and pierced his throat. 'On all the evidence available thus far,' the Australian coroner wrote in his report, 'it is probable that a member or members of the 745 Battalion . . . shot the deceased.'

Major Sarosa was charged with Sander Thoenes's murder by an East Timorese prosecutor in 2002, but no one expects that he will ever be handed over to face trial. Soon after leaving East Timor, he was promoted to Lieutenant Colonel.

Sander Thoenes was the seventh foreign journalist to have been killed by the Indonesian armed forces in East Timor since the 1975 invasion. It would be absurd to exaggerate the significance of this one tragedy, a single European among the 200,000 or more Timorese who had died over twenty-four years. There were many others much more grief-stricken by his death than I – although I had spent evenings with Sander, he was a close acquaintance rather than an intimate. But he was the only person

I had ever known personally who has been murdered by another human being.

Sander didn't step on a landmine or walk into a gun battle. He was travelling unarmed down a public road when he was fired on by Indonesian soldiers, members of one of Asia's biggest armies, a force armed with foreign weapons, its officers trained in Europe, America and Australia. The point about his death was not that it was unusual, but that it was so commonplace.

It was harder than ever to work after that. Plainly Dili was not safe, but it was unbearable to remain in the hotel. So I continued to go out, to see what there was to see. There were no taxis or motorbikes, and the best that you could do was to walk, and keep walking, and then walk back. It was a long time since I had walked so much.

I sank into a deeper and deeper weariness; I became clumsy and absent-minded. Twice, I accidentally set fire to my mosquito net. Once, I left my knapsack in the street among a crowd of hungry refugees; it disappeared with my camera, all my films and a thousand pounds in cash. The next day, having begged a lift on the back of someone's motorbike, I slipped off the back and scraped the skin off my hands and arms. I felt lonely and inept, and it was no relief to be back, because I did not want to be back: I wanted never to have run away.

I would cling on in Dili for two weeks. Then I would fly back to my home in Japan. Months would pass. Within two years, East Timor would become independent – Xanana would be its president. Indonesia would become a noisy, corrupt democracy, but a democracy nonetheless. In Jakarta, parties and presidents would rise and fall, but in his house in Sandalwood Street, old Suharto would live out his old age, unpunished. In Borneo, there would be another outbreak of headhunting and cannibalism, two years after the last. I would continue to work as a correspondent, covering other countries and new wars. I would spend less and less time in Indonesia and East Timor. The woman I loved would come to Tokyo, and we would live together. And over time, my feelings of shame and numbness would ease.

All around Dili, in the fortnight after my return, there were corpses – not in piles or pits, but in small clusters in unexpected parts of the city. In the grounds of the polytechnic were two rough mounds of stones and loose earth, one of them barely long enough to cover a child; they would have passed unnoticed if not for the sickly-sweet smell in the air around them. The body of an old man lay under the first one; his body had been gnawed like an apple core. Beneath the smaller grave was half a body, the lower half, severed at the belly: no head, no arms, no shoulders or chest. Animals might have caused the mutilations to the old man, but no dog can slice a human body across the middle. There was another grave a few yards away, and six more in the nearby jungle.

In Becora, there was a burned-out truck filled with contorted skeletons. In the gutter which ran beside the street in front of the Hotel Tropicale were two lumpy sacks. They seethed with maggots, and the air around them vibrated with flies. But the worst thing was in the yard of the Hotel Tropicale itself.

It was late September when I saw it, and the refugees were beginning to return from their hiding places in the hills. Two of them were playing in the sunshine in front of the hotel – a boy and a girl in T-shirts and dirty shorts. They were eating mangoes and playing with a yellow tennis ball; the boy grinned as he sucked on the mango and the juice ran down his chin. After a while, he took his little sister by the hand and led her into the Tropicale where I had once come with Basilio to see the laid-out body of the Aitarak man. He led her to the edge of a well where a group of people had gathered, pointing down at something with hands held over their mouths and noses. The girl clutched her face and began to cry.

As I approached I was visited by the conviction that I knew

what was in the well. Not the fact of a corpse, which was obvious from the reactions of those around it, but its exact form and visual configuration, as if I had seen it long ago in a picture or a dream. The stench above the mouth of the well was foul, but indescribably rich, like the cooking smell above a pot of stew. A few feet below the rim, the water was twitching in a froth of grey maggots. They were feeding on a lumpy indistinct shape, which resolved itself gradually into recognisable forms: shoulders, torso, a patch of brown skin, the ragged remains of a decomposing man. And sure enough, they were familiar to me, a part of my oldest memory: a memory of childhood, or even earlier: an image locked into mind during infancy, or in the womb, or some time long before.

ACKNOWLEDGEMENTS

Many of the colleagues and friends who helped me most in Indonesia and East Timor are invisible in this account. They are not forgotten, and I am grateful to all of them.

I owe special thanks to Hery Ahien, Subagio Anam, Dina Pura Antonio, Vinny Zainal Arifin, Cameron Barr, Nurcholis Basyari, Jose Antonio Belo, Carmel Budiardjo, Jone Chang, Kyle Crichton and the *New York Times Magazine*, Mike Denby, Hugh Dowson, Barbie Dutter, Toby Eady, Joaquim Fonseca, Dan Franklin, Matt Frei, Nicole Gaouette, Jonathan Head, Ian Jack and *Granta*, Joyo, the Lloyd Parry family, Andrew Marshall, John Martinkus, the late Andrew McNaughtan, Ed McWilliams, Lisabel and Robert Miles, Nicolaus Mills and *Dissent*, Conor O'Cleary, Maria Pakpahan, Haryo Prasetyo, Alex Spillius and Sarah Strickland, Gedsiri Suhartono, Irwan Tanjaya, *The Times*, Greg Torode and Robert Winder. My greatest debt is to my former employer, the *Independent*, and to several generations of its editors, especially Andy Marshall and Leonard Doyle.

I have drawn on the work of the following authors: Benedict Anderson, Robert Cribb, Dini Djalal, James Dunn, R. E. Elson, Donald Emmerson, John Hughes, Jill Jolliffe, Jozef Korzeniowski, Hamish McDonald, Soemarsaid Moertono, Goenawan Mohamad, Niels Mulder, Kevin O'Rourke, Constancio Pinto, M. C. Ricklefs, Geoffrey Robinson, O. G. Roeder, Adam Schwarz, John G. Taylor and Michael Vatikiotis.